Lernbewegungen inszenieren: Performative Zugänge in der
Sprach-, Literatur- und Kulturdidaktik

Susanne Even / Dragan Miladinović /
Barbara Schmenk (Hg.)

Lernbewegungen inszenieren: Performative Zugänge in der Sprach-, Literatur- und Kulturdidaktik

Festschrift für Manfred Schewe zum 65. Geburtstag

narr \f
ranck
e\atte
mpto

Bibliografische Information der Deutschen Nationalbibliothek
Die Deutsche Nationalbibliothek verzeichnet diese Publikation in der Deutschen
Nationalbibliografie; detaillierte bibliografische Daten sind im Internet über
http://dnb.dnb.de abrufbar.

© 2019 · Narr Francke Attempto Verlag GmbH + Co. KG
Dischingerweg 5 · D-72070 Tübingen

Internet: www.narr.de
eMail: info@narr.de

CPI books GmbH, Leck

ISBN 978-3-8233-8173-0

Inhaltsverzeichnis

Tabula Gratulatoria

Boyd, Stephen, Cork

Breidbach, Stephan, Berlin

Bremer, Christine, Cork

Byrnes, Deirdre, Galway

Crowley, Patrick, Cork

Crutchfield, John, Asheville

Dalziel, Fiona, Padua

Department of Italian, Cork

Donnery, Eucharia, Fujisawa

Durnin, Marina, Cork

Dzhyma, Nataliia, Kiew

Eschenauer, Sandrine, Aix-en-Provence

Even, Susanne, Bloomington

Faistauer, Renate, Wien

Fandrych, Christian, Leipzig

Fischäss, Frank, Ravensburg

Fischer, Joachim, Limerick

Fratini, Nathalie, Luxemburg

German Studies, MIC Limerick

Haack, Adrian, Göttingen

Hallet, Wolfgang, Gießen

Hensel, Alexandra, Göttingen

Höfferer, Dagmar, Wien

Hofmann, Gert, Cork

Holfter, Gisela, Limerick

Jogschies, Bärbel, Hannover

Koch, Gerd, Berlin

Krumm, Hans-Jürgen, Wien

Küppers, Almut, Frankfurt/Istanbul

Legutke, Michael K., Gießen

MagShamhráin, Rachel, Cork

Meyer, Hilbert, Oldenburg

Miladinović, Dragan, Cork

Mortell, Siobhán, Cork

O'Donovan, Patrick, Cork

O'Reilly, Claire, Cork

Piazzoli, Erika, Dublin

Riordan, Emma, Cork

Rösler, Dietmar, Gießen

Ross, Silvia, Cork

Sambanis, Michaela, Berlin

Schädlich, Birgit, Göttingen

Schmenk, Barbara, Waterloo	Surkamp, Carola, Göttingen
Schmitt-Kilb, Christian, Rostock	Thiem, Annegret, Paderborn
Schneider, Gisela, Bonn	Vaßen, Florian, Hannover
Schönfeld, Christiane, Limerick	Walter, Maik, Berlin
Schwerdtfeger, Inge C., Köln/Bochum	Weißer, Dirk, Westerstede
Scott, Trina, Cork	Welke, Tina, Wien
Siller, Barbara, Cork	Williams, Chris, Cork
Stinson, Madonna, Griffith University	Witte, Arnd, Maynooth
Stöver-Blahak, Anke, Hannover	Woodhouse, Fionn, Cork

Grußwort

Gert Hofmann

Es öffnete sich die Tür, und es kam, gut im Saft, an den Seiten üppig gerundet, fußlos mit der ganzen Unterseite sich vorschiebend, der grüne Drache ins Zimmer hinein. Formelle Begrüßung. Ich bat ihn, völlig einzutreten. Er bedauerte dies nicht tun zu können, da er zu lang sei. Die Tür mußte also offen bleiben, was recht peinlich war. Er lächelte halb verlegen, halb tückisch und begann: Durch Deine Sehnsucht herangezogen, schiebe ich mich von weither heran, bin unten schon ganz wundgescheuert. Aber ich tue es gerne. Gerne komme ich, gerne biete ich mich Dir an. (Kafka 1992: 547f.)

Diese kleine Szene aus Kafkas Nachlass benutzte Manfred Schewe gelegentlich und gerne in seinen Ansprachen an unsere Studienanfänger*innen, um einerseits deren Einbildungskraft wachzurütteln und sie andererseits sogleich mit einem schillernden Beispiel literarischen Sprachreichtums zu konfrontieren. Dass seine Wahl gerade auf dieses Beispiel fiel, war freilich wohlüberlegt, denn hier zeigt sich überdeutlich, dass sprachlich literarische Einbildungskraft – wie übrigens in vielen der kurzen Prosatexte Kafkas – sich vor allem im *Performativen* auszuleben vermag. Kafkas kleines Textfragment erzählt die Szene der Ankunft einer phantastischen Wahrheit, und folgerichtig appellierte Manfred sogleich an die Vorstellungsperformanz der Studierenden mit der Frage, wie sie sich denn nun *verhalten* würden, wenn genau diese Szene sich hier und jetzt vor ihren Augen abspielen würde.

Uns kann diese kleine Episode vor Augen führen, wie Manfred auch im Kleinen zu realisieren vermochte, was im Großen und Ganzen seines jahrzehntelangen Wirkens als Hochschullehrer, Pädagoge und Wissenschaftler seine bedeutendste Mission war: im praktischen und wissenschaftlichen Diskurs die Synthese von pädagogischer Arbeit und performativer Kunst sowohl konzeptionell aufzuzeigen als auch im beispielhaften Akt vorzuleben. Lehre als Kunst.

Manfred wird daher von seinen zahlreichen Schüler*innen zu Recht als der *Vater der Dramapädagogik* gesehen. Als Kollege und Mitstreiter im großen Projekt einer Erziehung zu transkulturell humanitärer Bewusstheit erschien er mir freilich öfters gar selbst wie eine Epiphanie jenes grünen Drachens Kafkas, also wie eine Verkörperung des menschlichen Urvertrauens in die Existenz phantastischer Wahrheiten, das Bildung als lebenslangen Prozess der individuellen Menschwerdung allererst möglich macht.

Manfred steht hier auch als Pädagoge in einer langen Tradition deutscher Dramaturgie, welche die öffentliche, gesellschaftliche Praxis theatraler Kunst mit dem großen Aufklärungsprojekt einer Bildung zur Humanität verbindet. Gotthold Ephraim Lessing war der Erste, der die strategische Verbundenheit von theatraler Kunst und Menschheitsbildung zum Programm erhoben hatte. War für Lessing (nach Schulte-Sasse 1972: 55) „der mitleidigste Mensch der beste Mensch", so ergab sich für ihn als Selbstverständlichkeit „daß die ganze Kunst des tragischen Dichtens auf die sichere Erregung und Dauer des einigen Mitleidens" (ibid.) zielen musste. Das Wirkungspotential des Trauerspiels sah er unter genuin pädagogischen Gesichtspunkten:

> [Es] soll unsere Fähigkeit, Mitleid zu fühlen, erweitern. [Es] soll uns nicht blos lehren, gegen diesen oder jenen Unglücklichen Mitleid zu fühlen, sondern [es] soll uns so weit fühlbar machen, daß uns der Unglückliche zu allen Zeiten, und unter allen Gestalten, rühren und für sich einnehmen muß. (ibid.)

Friedrich Schillers Spielästhetik radikalisiert den Ansatz Lessings unter dem Eindruck von Immanuel Kants Vernunftkritik und Freiheitsethik. „Denn, um es endlich einmal herauszusagen, der Mensch spielt nur, wo er in voller Bedeutung des Wortes Mensch ist, und er ist nur da ganz Mensch, wo er spielt." (Schiller nach Fricke & Göpfert 1980: 618) Das ist Schillers philosophisches Vermächtnis, wobei die Schönheit spielerischen Handelns einerseits die eigentliche Modalität der Kunst bezeichnet, andererseits aber auch als die Idee der ‚Freiheit in der Erscheinung' verstanden werden kann. Es ist daher vor allem das rein spielerische Geschehen des Theaters, das den Menschen, sei es als Zuschauenden oder Mitspielenden, die Einübung in die praktische Freiheit moralischen Handelns ermöglicht.

Die pädagogische Weisheit, die in dieser Aufklärungstradition deutscher Philosophie, Literatur und Dramaturgie enthalten ist, hat Manfreds Arbeit in all ihren vielfältigen Facetten inspiriert:

> The idea of life as a play as well as the idea of understanding life better through play, has existed for quite some time in the history of European culture [...]. Dramatic art has raised fundamental questions about both the limits and possibilities of human existence [and should therefore play a role] in the field of education. (Schewe 2013: 6)

War vor allem die Fremdsprachenpädagogik Manfreds ursprüngliches Betätigungsfeld, so entwickelte sich sein dramapädagogischer Ansatz als Grundsatzprogramm für pädagogisches Handeln weit über die Grenzen dieser Disziplin hinaus. Manfred verfolgt, ganz im Einklang mit einem modernen Aufklärungsdiskurs, vor allem das Ziel, performative, spielerische Praktiken im Unterricht nicht nur als didaktische Werkzeuge zur Steigerung der objektiven Lernleistung einzusetzen, sondern, im Dienste einer ganzheitlichen Pädagogik, auf diesem Wege Einzelne zu einem gesteigerten und reflektierten Bewusstsein ihres gesellschaftlichen und Welthandelns in allen seinen Aspekten zu erziehen. Das Ziel pädagogischen Handelns kann niemals nur fachliche Bildung sein, sondern zielt vor allem und zuletzt auf Erziehung zum Menschsein ab. Dass Erziehung in diesem Sinne immer auch politische Implikationen hat und zur Kritik an gesellschaftlichen Gewalt- und Repressionsstrukturen befähigt, versteht sich von selbst. Für Manfred ist daher Brechts episches Theater immer auch ein heute noch gültiges Beispiel für die fundamentale Verbundenheit von gesellschaftlicher Pädagogik und performativer Kunst.

Über all dem erscheint aber auch heute noch die große alte Idee eines harmonischen Zusammenlebens von Individuum, Gesellschaft und Natur, wie sie Goethe in seinem Wilhelm Meister entworfen hat – eine Idee, die allerdings, damals wie heute, des Theaters bedarf, um in der Wirklichkeit menschlichen Lebens erfahrbar zu werden:

> Du siehst wohl, daß das alles für mich nur auf dem Theater zu finden ist und daß ich mich in diesem einzigen Elemente nach Wunsch rühren und ausbilden kann. (Goethe 2015: 243)

Literatur

Goethe, Johann Wolfgang von (2015): *Wilhelm Meisters Lehrjahre. Die Goethe Edition.* Altenmünster: Jazzybee.

Schewe, Manfred (2013): Taking Stock and Looking Ahead: Drama Pedagogy as a Gateway to a Performative Teaching and Leanring Culture. In: *Scenario* VII/1, 5-23.

Schillemeit, Jost (Hg.) (1992): *Franz Kafka. Nachgelassene Schriften und Fragmente II.* Frankfurt a. M.: S. Fischer.

Schiller, Friedrich (1980): Briefe über die ästhetische Erziehung des Menschen. In: Gerhard Fricke & Herbert G. Göpfert (Hg.): *Friedrich Schiller. Sämtliche Werke.* Bd. 5. München: Hanser.

Schulte-Sasse, Jochen (Hg.) (1972): *Gotthold Ephraim Lessing, Moses Mendelssohn, Friedrich Nicolai: Briefwechsel über das Trauerspiel.* München: Winkler.

Vorhang auf!

Susanne Even, Dragan Miladinović, Barbara Schmenk

Johannes Comenius zufolge liegt das primäre Ziel von Didaktik darin „die Unterrichtsweise aufzuspüren und zu erkunden, bei welcher die Lehrer weniger zu lehren brauchen, die Schüler dennoch mehr lernen; in den Schulen weniger Lärm, Überdruss und unnütze Mühe herrsche, dafür mehr Freiheit, Vergnügen und wahrhafter Fortschritt" (Große Didaktik 1657). Rund 400 Jahre später ist die Welt anders – beispielsweise wurde das Streben nach der einzigen idealen Unterrichtsweise inzwischen verworfen – und trotzdem behält der Ruf nach mehr Freiheit, Vergnügen und wahrhaftem Fortschritt seine Aktualität.

Wir feiern mit diesem Band 65 Jahre Manfred Schewe, dem – wenn es sie gäbe – ein besonderer Platz in der Hall of Fame der Fremdsprachendidaktik sicher wäre. Manfred ist es immer darum gegangen didaktische Räume zu schaffen, in denen Lehrende und Lernende ihren eigenen Impulsen, Erfahrungen und Ideen nachgehen können, in denen Lehren und Lernen nicht von Mühe, sondern von Neugier, Spannung und Vertrauen in die eigene Imagination gekennzeichnet ist, und wo Fortschritt darin besteht, sich im performativen Handeln gemeinsam Bedeutungen zu erschließen. ‚Fortschritt' ist insofern nicht unbedingt als linear-zielgerichtet zu sehen, sondern als Bewegung, die auch Schritte zurück oder das Betreten alternativer Seitenpfade beinhalten kann.

Manfred hat die performative Wende für das Fremdsprachenlehren und -lernen eingeläutet, sei es mit seiner Forderung nach „Lernen mit Kopf, Herz, Hand und Fuß", über die Notwendigkeit eines Lehrhandelns, das von Aufmerksamkeit und Improvisation geprägt ist, bis hin zur SCENARIO-Initiative, die weltweit neue Foren für Menschen, die performativ lehren, lernen und forschen, geschaffen hat.

Manfreds Wirken umfasst bekanntermaßen nicht nur seine jahrzehntelange wissenschaftliche Arbeit und all die Publikationen, mit denen er die Dramapädagogik weit über die Grenzen des deutschsprachigen Raums und der DaF-Didaktik bekannt gemacht hat. Auch und insbesondere seine vielen Workshops und Fortbildungsveranstaltungen mit Lehrenden und Lernenden in aller Welt sind hier zu nennen. Denn eines ist sicher: Performativität macht nicht nur den inhaltlichen Schwerpunkt seines wissenschaftlichen Wirkens aus, sondern charakterisiert auch seine Aktivitäten als Hochschullehrer, Fortbildner und Vortragender, als Gesprächspartner, Kollege und Freund. Wir haben die relativ traditionelle Form der Festschrift gewählt, um ihn zu feiern, wissen aber, dass diese Form performativ hinter dem zurückbleibt, was Manfreds Wirken verdient hätte. Daher hoffen wir, dass die vorliegende Schrift Leserinnen und Leser zu imaginativ-performativem Weiterdenken und -handeln inspiriert und auf diese Weise lebendig wird.

Wir gratulieren herzlich zum Geburtstag! May the roads rise to meet you, Manfred, and may the wind be always in your back.

Susanne, Dragan und Barbara
Bloomington, USA
Cork, Irland
Waterloo, Kanada

Prinzipien eines performativen Fremdsprachenunterrichts

Eine Bestandsaufnahme

Dragan Miladinović

Ein persönlicher Einstieg

Wenn Sie etwas über Dramapädagogik lernen möchten, dann müssen Sie zu Manfred Schewe. An diesen Satz, der in meinem Masterstudium Deutsch als Fremd- und Zweitsprache in der Methodiklehrveranstaltung an der Universität Wien fiel, erinnere ich mich noch gut. Manfred Schewe? Wer soll denn das sein, dachte ich damals. Ich notierte den Namen und das dazu genannte Schlagwort Dramapädagogik in meinen Collegeblock und entdeckte die Notiz drei Jahre später im Jahr 2015, als ich mich auf das Lektorat des Österreichischen Austauschdienstes in Cork vorbereitete und meine Unterlagen nach Wichtigem durchsuchte. Ich hatte also den Lektoratsstandort sicher, an dem ich bei Manfred Schewe, der seit 1994 am University College Cork tätig ist, etwas über diese Dramapädagogik lernen konnte – was Dramapädagogik bedeutete, inwiefern sie mit einer performativen Fremdsprachendidaktik zusammenhängt und wie mich das noch prägen sollte, war mir zu diesem Zeitpunkt noch nicht bewusst. Auch nicht, dass ich, aufgrund von Manfred Schewes Überzeugungsarbeit, bereits knapp zwei Jahre später in der Organisation der zweiten internationalen SCENARIO Forum Konferenz involviert werden und spätestens damit in die Welt des Performativen eintauchen sollte. Aus diesem anfänglich noch zögerlichen und vorsichtigen Eintauchen ins kalte Wasser der Dramapädagogik und des Performativen wurde ein langes und intensives Forschungstauchen, das zu dem aktuell laufenden Dissertationsprojekt im Bereich der performativen Fremdsprachendidaktik unter der Betreuung von Manfred Schewe führte. Dieser Beitrag setzt an der Methoden- und Kompetenzdiskussion in der Fremdsprachendidaktik an und versucht vor dem Hintergrund von Manfred Schewes Überlegungen zu einer performativen Fremdsprachendidaktik zu reflektieren, welche Prinzipien für einen performativen Fremdsprachenunterricht in Frage kommen.

Methoden, Kompetenzen – quo vadis?

Die Frage(n) nach der einen richtigen Methode, wie Sprachen unterrichtet werden sollen, ist in den letzten Jahr(zehnt)en immer leiser geworden. Seit der kommunikativen Wende und dem damit einhergehenden kommunikativen Ansatz herrscht, zumindest mehr oder weniger, Einigkeit darüber, dass FSU kommunikativ[1], lernenden- und handlungsorientiert ausgerichtet werden und nicht stur einer einzigen als ‚besten' vermarkteten Methode folgen sollte (vgl. Rösler in diesem Band). Eine postmethodische Ära wurde ausgerufen, die nicht nach einer (neuen) alternativen Methode, sondern nach Alternativen zu Methoden als solchen suche (vgl. Kumaravadivelu 2006). Als Hauptziele des modernen FSU wird seit den 80er Jahren die Entwicklung der kommunikativen Kompetenz bzw. später die der interkulturellen Kompetenz sowie einer allgemeinen Kompetenz gesehen (vgl. Harsch 2017: 167, Schmenk 2017: 163, Nieweler 2017: 227). Kompetenzen sind spätestens seit der Formulierung von Bildungsstandards und der Fertigstellung des Gemeinsamen Europäischen Referenzrahmens für Sprachen (GERS) in aller Munde, da sie demonstrieren, was individuelle Lernende können sollten. Es handelt sich um einen Versuch, einen Rahmen für u. a. die Lernzielbestimmung und Lernzielüberprüfung zu geben. Hinsichtlich der Sprachkompetenz werden im GERS Kann-Deskriptoren verwendet, um zu beschreiben, wie es um das fremdsprachliche Niveau eines Individuums steht. Problematisch am GERS ist u. a., dass Bereiche wie interkulturelles Lernen oder literarisch-ästhetische Bildung außen vor gelassen werden; es stellt sich als schwierig heraus, diese Bereiche mithilfe von Kann-Deskriptoren oder anderen Skalen zu messen oder im Sinne von Lernergebnissen zu definieren (vgl. Schmenk 2015: 42). Die häufig zitierten Lernergebnisse bzw. *learning out-comes* an sich sind zu kritisieren, da sie nicht selten als planbare und schnell zu erreichende Ziele von FSU abgesteckt werden, sodass Sprachlernende, unter dem Deckmantel der vermeintlichen Handlungsorientierung und Ganzheitlichkeit, die auch dem GERS zugrunde liegen sollen (vgl. Schwerdtfeger 2001), „zu einem nach ausgeklügelten betriebswirtschaftlichen Prinzipien akkurat planbaren und kontrollierbaren und damit dehumanisierten Elementchen eines weltumspannenden Kapitalismus" (ibid. 439f.) werden. Diese Problematik führt weiters dazu, dass Bereiche im Unterricht unter den Tisch fallen, die anhand von Prüfungen nicht evaluiert werden können (vgl. Schmenk 2015: 42f.), was das häufig kritisierte *teaching to the test* formfokussierter Elemente begünstigt. Wie Küster (2015: 17) aber verdeutlicht, würden die Effekte vieler schulischer

---

1   Für eine kritische Auseinandersetzung mit dem „Kommunikativen" im kommunikativen FSU siehe Schmenk (2007).

Lernprozesse – und dies gilt sicherlich auch für außerschulische – „erst mit deutlicher Verzögerung im Rahmen eines lebenslangen Lernens" ersichtlich und könnten nicht mit kurzfristigen Prüfungen ermittelt werden. Und gerade dies verleihe insbesondere dem Nicht-Normierbaren und mit der Standardorientierung Nicht-Kompatiblem einen Gültigkeitsanspruch. Dass vor allem ästhetisch-künstlerische Bereiche dem Kürzungstrend zum Opfer fallen, kritisiert auch Manfred Schewe und spricht sich daher seit einigen Jahren für eine durch die Dramapädagogik inspirierte, an den (performativen) Künsten orientierte Fremdsprachendidaktik aus, aber auch für eine dementsprechende Lehrausbildung (vgl. u. a. Schewe 2011, 2015). Diese sollte Lehrende „eher zu fachlich versierten ‚KünstlerInnen der Vermittlung und Unterrichtsgestaltung'[...] als vorwiegend zu WissenschaftlerInnen ihres Faches" (Haack 2010: 49-51) ausbilden. Schewe (2011) sieht im „bewusst verlangsamte[n] oder auch betont körperbezogene[n] Unterrichtsprozess" die Möglichkeit, dem Trend von „kurz-schnell-viel" (ibid. 21) und der „Durchökonomisierung und Standardisierung von Schule, Hochschule und anderen Lebensbereichen" (ibid. 20) entgegenzuwirken. Die Bedeutung von ästhetischem Lernen wird insbesondere dann ersichtlich, wenn beobachtet wird, „dass das rein kognitive Bildungssystem nicht mehr mit den Herausforderungen einer globalisierten, sich ständig wandelnden Welt in Einklang zu bringen ist" (Bernstein & Lerchner 2014: V). Dafür werde ein Lernverständnis benötigt, dass die Ganzheitlichkeit berücksichtige und dieses Verständnis liege dem ästhetischen Lernen zugrunde (vgl. ibid).

Ein Kompetenzbegriff, der von Wolfgang Hallet (2010, vgl. auch in diesem Band) in die Bildungs- und Kompetenzdiskussion eingeführt wurde und der das Potential hätte, die Mission nach Mehr an ästhetischem Lernen zu unterstützen, ist jener der *Performativen Kompetenz* (pK). Sie ist zu verstehen als „Bündel von Fähigkeiten des Individuums, die Inszeniertheit allen sozialen Handelns zu verstehen, selbst soziale Interaktionssituationen zu initiieren, diese selbstbestimmt mitzugestalten und die eigene Rolle darin kritisch zu reflektieren" (Hallet 2010: 5). Ausgangspunkt für diese Überlegung ist die Annahme, dass „Alltagshandlungen prinzipiell als theatral und performativ gelten können" (ibid. 10), und Unterricht als besondere Form der Inszenierung verstanden wird (vgl. ibid.). Der Begriff der Inszenierung sei besonders in Hinblick auf die digitale Welt durch spezifische und neue Formen erweitert worden: Visuelle und elektronische Medien dominieren den Alltag und stellen lebensweltliche Inszenierungsformen dar (vgl. ibid. 12), was die Bedeutung der pK weiter hervorhebt. Nur mit einer ausgeprägten pK könnten diese Inszenierungsformen verstanden, reflektiert, kritisch hinterfragt sowie selbst produziert werden. Hallet (ibid. 15) erweitert die Definition des Begriffs um einige weitere Punkte, hier seien vor allem die folgenden in den Vordergrund geholt: Es handle sich bei der pK

– im Kontext von FSU – um die „Fähigkeit zur fremdsprachigen aktiven, ver-
antwortungsvollen, partnerschaftlichen Partizipation an sozialen Interaktionen
und Aushandlungen" und die Fähigkeit zur fremdsprachigen „situationsadäqua-
ten *performance* in verschiedenen Kontexten, auch im Unterricht" (ibid., Herv.
i. O.). Darüber hinaus befähige sie Individuen, kritisch über ihre eigene soziale
‚Rolle', aber auch über unterschiedliche Inszenierungen anderer zu reflektieren
und existierende Interaktionsrollen zu identifizieren und zu bestimmen (ibid.
15 f.). Ein solcher Kompetenzbegriff lässt sich aktuell weder in standardisierten
Skalen oder in den Bildungsstandards finden, noch gibt es ausreichende wissenschaftliche Auseinandersetzungen, wie diese Kompetenz überprüft, getestet
und bewertet werden könnte.[2] Von Relevanz kann diese neudefinierte Kompetenz allerdings auf zweierlei Ebenen werden: Zum einen könnte sie, wenn sie
in den GERS und in die Bildungsstandards aufgenommen würde, dem Trend
entgegenwirken, dass ästhetisches Lernen im Unterricht als nicht-überprüfbare
Kompetenz wegfällt,[3] zum anderen könnte sie dazu führen, dass die Dramapädagogik als wichtige Förderin der pK noch stärker ins Unterrichtsgeschehen
einbezogen wird. Damit könnte der Weg, dessen Ebnungsprozess bereits be-
gonnen hat, weiterbearbeitet und -entwickelt werden, damit die Reise einer
performative Fremdsprachendidaktik fortgesetzt werden kann (vgl. Schmenk
2015, Schewe 2015).

Von der Dramapädagogik zu einer performativen
Fremdsprachendidaktik

Dramapädagogik ist der Begriff, der in der deutschsprachigen Fremdsprachendidaktik für das aus Großbritannien stammende *Drama in Education* verwendet
wird und durch Manfred Schewes *Fremdsprache inszenieren* (1993) erstmals für
den FSU abgesteckt wurde. Darunter wird Unterricht verstanden, der sich an
den dramatischen bzw. performativen Künsten orientiert und sowohl ästhetisch
als auch ganzheitlich abläuft (vgl. Schewe 2017: 48) und dessen wichtige Elemente aus u. a. Inszenierung und szenischem Spiel bestehen (vgl. Schmenk 2015:
37). Dramapädagogik fördert einerseits die Lernenden- und Handlungsorientierung, andererseits auch formorientiertes Lernen (vgl. Even 2003), interkulturelles Lernen (vgl. dazu Küppers et al. 2011, Crutchfield & Schewe 2017) und

---

2   Verwiesen sei hier auf Bosenius (2017), die einen Entwurf eines Bewertungsblatts für
    performative Kompetenzen vorlegt.
3   Die Etablierung von Prüfungs- und Evaluierungskriterien einer solchen Kompetenz ist
    durchaus problematisch zu sehen (vgl. Küster 2015) und es ist fraglich, ob der Zweck in
    diesem Fall alle Mittel heiligt.

bietet sich ebenso für den Literaturunterricht an (vgl. Hallet & Surkamp 2015). Dramapädagogische Ansätze haben spezielle ganzheitliche Bildungsansprüche, die weit über jene des herkömmlichen – nicht-dramapädagogischen – Fremdsprachenunterrichts hinausgehen (vgl. Schmenk 2015: 37). Als ganzheitlich ist zu verstehen, dass Lernende als ‚ganze' Menschen wahrgenommen werden, und daher wird im dramapädagogischen Unterricht „mit Kopf, Herz, Hand und Fuß gelernt und gelehrt" (Schewe 1993: 8). Schewe (2011: 22) sieht in der Dramapädagogik „eine Weiterführung der kommunikativen Didaktik", die allerdings den Einsatz von Körper stärker akzentuiert und sich nicht als „in sich geschlossenes methodisches und theoretisch begründetes System mit eigenen Sprach- und Lernbegriffen" (Müller 2017: 61) versteht, sondern offen ist für neue Impulse – und gerade hier liegt das große Potential dieses Ansatzes. Die Lehrperson gebe zu einem gewissen Maß die Kontrolle ab, womit eine Spontaneität im Unterricht einhergehe, was wiederum Situationen entstehen ließe, in denen sowohl Lehrende als auch Lernende überrascht und einen freieren und dementsprechend emanzipierteren Unterricht erleben würden. Dramapädagogischer Unterricht schaffe es, durch das Erproben unterschiedlicher Rollen in ‚Als-Ob-Situationen' überraschende und ungeplante Lern-, Spiel- und Reflexionsprozesse zu initiieren (vgl. Schmenk 2015: 40). Es gelinge der Dramapädagogik außerdem, die oft starren Grenzen zwischen Wissenschaft und Kunst, Theorie und Praxis aufzuweichen (vgl. Schewe 2012: 82), indem Unterrichtende zu Forschenden werden und ihr pädagogisches Handeln stark reflektieren und diese Erkenntnisse wieder in die Praxis mitnehmen (vgl. dazu auch die Forschungsarbeit von Haack 2018). Allerdings macht Schmenk (2015: 38) hinsichtlich der Theorie und Praxis der Dramapädagogik darauf aufmerksam, dass zwar viele Arbeiten zur praktischen Anwendung vorliegen, jedoch eine Lücke in der empirischen Forschung existiere, die es für die Etablierung der Dramapädagogik zu schließen gelte. Auch deshalb sieht sie im Konzept der performativen Kompetenz einen wichtigen Anschlusspunkt für die weitere Forschung.

Die Dramapädagogik ebne im Kontext des FSU den Weg für eine noch weiterzuentwickelnde *performative*[4] *Fremdsprachendidaktik*, die sich stark an den Künsten orientiert und „die sich nicht nur als Wissenschaft, sondern ebenso als Kunst begreift." (Schewe 2015: 31) *Performativ* wird von Schewe (2015, vgl. auch Even & Schewe 2016b) als Oberbegriff verwendet, um „alle Formen der Fremdsprachenvermittlung zu kennzeichnen, die sich aus den Künsten bzw. den mit diesen assoziierten (kulturspezifischen) Formen drama-/theaterpädagogischer

---

4   Aus Platzgründen sei hier lediglich am Rande vermerkt, dass der Begriff performativ intradisziplinäre Verwendung findet und eine lange Tradition hat. Für einen Überblick vgl. Fleming (2016), Hudelist (2017) und Even & Schewe (2016b).

Praxis ableiten lassen." (Schewe 2015: 33) Hudelist & Krammer (2017: 5) sehen im Performativen kein neues Phänomen, sondern viel mehr „eine andere Art und Weise, bekannte Phänomene zu betrachten, zu begreifen, zu reflektieren." Dies erscheint besonders dann eine lohnenswerte Perspektive, wenn die vielen Paradigmenwechsel in der Fremdsprachendidaktik betrachtet werden, die häufig alte Erkenntnisse verwerfen oder schlichtweg vergessen, um die eigene Innovation hervorzuheben (vgl. Rösler 2019, auch in diesem Band). Eine performative Fremdsprachendidaktik stelle dem ästhetischen Lernen und der Körperlichkeit Räume frei, verstehe sich als handlungs- und sprachhandlungsorientiert und verschiebe den Fokus, im Sinne des *performative turn* (Bachmann-Medick 2006), vom Produkt zum Prozess. Wer performativ unterrichte, befinde sich als Lehrperson „an einem bestimmten Punkt auf einem Kontinuum, das jederzeit neue Bewegung und damit Entwicklungsmöglichkeiten zulässt" (Even & Schewe 2016b: 12). Gerade diese Offenheit hat ein großes Potential: Eine performative Fremdsprachendidaktik lässt Lehrenden/Lernenden genügend Freiräume und gleichzeitig gibt sie ihnen ein Gerüst, an dem sie sich orientieren können. Performatives Lehren bedient sich der Prinzipien von handlungsorientiertem, lernendenzentriertem und kommunikativem Unterricht – auch hier wird ersichtlich, dass es sich um keine völlig unbekannte Herangehensweise handelt – und erweitert diese mit körperlichen und ästhetischen Lehr- und Lernprozessen. Insofern erscheint es kaum verwunderlich, dass von der „Art of Teaching" (Crutchfield 2015: 103), also der Kunst des Unterrichtens, gesprochen wird und Dunn & Stinson auf die Bedeutung einer „teacher artistry" (Dunn & Stinson 2011: 630), also einer Lehrendenkunst, verweisen, die es bildungstheoretisch noch weiter zu begründen gelte (vgl. Schewe 2015: 32).

Schewe (2011) bezieht sich auf seiner Auffassung nach wichtige Elemente für die performative Fremdsprachendidaktik, darunter auch auf die Schriften der Theaterwissenschaftlerin Fischer-Lichte (2004). Dort betont er die Elemente Körper, Stimme, Präsenz und Raum sowie „das konzeptuelle Grundgerüst einer Ästhetik des Performativen" (ibid. 318), die sich in Ereignis, Inszenierung und ästhetischer Erfahrung widerspiegeln. Inszenierungen – Schewe (2015: 27 f.) versteht darunter performative Klein- und Großformen – spielen bei der performativen Unterrichtsgestaltung eine große Rolle. In diesem Beitrag werden die performativen Kleinformen besonders hervorgehoben, da sie „im Rahmen einer Unterrichtsstunde bzw. -einheit realisierbar sind" (Schewe 2015: 28). Darunter fallen beispielsweise pantomimische Darstellungen oder Standbilder, bei denen Lehrende und Lernende abwechselnd in die Rolle von Zusehenden und Mitwirkenden, und zwar auf unterschiedlichen Ebenen, schlüpfen. Aber im Hinblick auf Hallets (2010) Verständnis der Inszeniertheit des Alltäglichen lassen sich diese performativen Kleinformen erweitern durch ‚klassischere' Modelle von

Fremdsprachenunterricht: Beispielsweise stellt auch das Verfassen von Texten mit bestimmten Absichten und mit fiktiven/realen Adressat*innen eine inszenierte Situation dar (vgl. Krammer 2017: 32), die performative Charakteristiken aufweist. Mit diesem Verständnis bietet sich ein breites Bild der performativen Fremdsprachendidaktik, die zum einen, in Anlehnung an Hallet (2010), jegliches Handeln als performativen Akt und damit als Inszenierung versteht, zum anderen, in Anlehnung an Schewe (u.a. 2013, 2015), ihre Inspiration für die Gestaltung des Unterrichts aus den Künsten einholt.

Performative Fremdsprachendidaktik als postmethodischer Ansatz

Susanne Even (2011) zeigt, dass ihr dramagrammatischer Ansatz Parametern einer postmethodischen Didaktik (vgl. Kumaravadivelu 2003, 2006) folgt. Kumaravadivelu (2006: 171-176) unterscheidet drei Arten dieser Parameter. Zunächst definiert er den *parameter of particularity* als wichtigsten Parameter, da er die lokalen Besonderheiten einer Lehrsituation in Betracht zieht. Die postmethodische Didiaktik müsse berücksichtigen, dass es sich um „a particular group of teachers teaching a particular group of learners pursuing a particular set of goals within a particular institutional context embedded in a particular sociocultural milieu" (Kumaravadivelu 2001: 538) handle. Lehrende müssten daher selbstreflexiv beobachten, evaluieren und Probleme identifizieren, sodass sie für die lokalen Gegebenheiten adäquate Lösungen finden können (Kumaravadivelu 2006: 172), anstatt vorgefertigte Konzepte und Methoden aus anderen Sphären krampfhaft auf die eigene zu übertragen versuchen. Dies steht eng im Zusammenhang mit dem *parameter of practicality*, jenem Parameter, der den Zusammenhang zwischen Theorie und Praxis herstellt, indem das Lehrhandeln und dessen Erfolg beobachtet und reflektiert werden. Hier lassen sich Parallelen zu Schewes (2012) Idee einer performativen Fremdsprachendidaktik erkennen, die das Verschwimmen von Grenzen zwischen Theorie und Praxis begünstige. Kumaravadivelu formuliert eine Aufforderung, Lehrenden zu ermöglichen, „to theorize from their practice and practice what they theorize" (Kumaravadivelu 2006: 173). Es reiche dafür allerdings nicht nur, diese Möglichkeit anzubieten, sondern man müsse an Hilfestellungen arbeiten – hier müsste konkret überlegt werden, wie diese in Bezug auf die performative Fremdsprachendidaktik aussehen könnten –, die es ermöglichen, das Wissen, die Fähigkeit, die Einstellung sowie die Autonomie zu dieser *theory of practice* zu entwickeln. Der letzte Parameter, den Kumaravadivelu *parameter of possibility* (ibid. 174f.) nennt, bezieht sich auf Erfahrungen, die Lehrende und Lernende in den Unterricht mitnehmen. Die Teilnehmenden im FSU bringen nicht nur Erfahrungen aus anderen Sprachlernsituationen mit, sondern auch darüber hinausgehende, die es im Unterricht zu berücksichtigen gilt, um ihnen eine kritische Reflexion auf ihre soziale und kulturelle Situation zu ermöglichen. Es geht dabei auch um die Weiterentwicklung der eigenen Identität und darum, auf individuelle Art und Weise mit der Sprache zu arbeiten und diese zur eigenen zu machen.

Folgt man Even (2011), kann festgestellt werden, dass nicht nur der dramgrammatische Ansatz, sondern auch die performative Fremdsprachendidaktik, wie von Manfred Schewe konzipiert, diesen Parametern gerecht wird: Sie ist offen ausgelegt, dass sie immer wieder aufs Neue auf die Zielgruppe und die lokalen Gegebenheiten angepasst werden kann. Sie regt Lehrende dazu an, den eigenen Unterricht zu analysieren und mit den Ergebnissen Schlussfolgerungen für den Unterricht zu ziehen, und darüber hinaus gibt sie Lernenden *und* Lehrenden die Möglichkeit, individuelle und ästhetische Lernprozesse zu initiieren und stößt Reflexionsprozesse an. Insofern kann davon ausgegangen werden, dass eine performative Fremdsprachendidaktik prinzipiell postmethodisch ausgelegt ist.

Prinzipien eines Sprachunterrichts

Wenn sich FSU an flexiblen Ansätzen orientiert, stellt sich die Frage, woran sich Lehrende bei der Unterrichtsplanung konkret halten können. Unterrichtsprinzipien spielen dabei eine wichtige Rolle; als dominanteste sind hier Lernenden-, Sach- und Handlungsorientierung, vor allem aber die bereits angesprochene Kompetenzorientierung zu nennen. Prinzipien sind als Unterrichtsgrundsätze zu verstehen, die auf empirischer und/oder theoretischer Forschung basieren (vgl. Klippel 2016: 316 f.). Von Dörnyei (2013) werden beispielsweise sieben Prinzipien für einen weiterzuentwickelnden, prinzipienorientierten kommunikativen Ansatz („Principled Communicative Approach") vorgeschlagen, die als Leitlinien für Sprachunterricht dienen. Wie der Name verrät, handelt es sich dabei um eine Weiterentwicklung des kommunikativen Ansatzes, der aufgrund fehlender autoritativer Vorgaben – z.T. darauf zurückzuführen, dass zwar Einigkeit zu den Zielen des FSU, jedoch Unsicherheiten zur Art und Weise der Vermittlung herrsche – kritisiert wurde (vgl. Arnold et al. 2015: 5). Im Vordergrund steht eine Rückbesinnung auf das explizite Lehren und Lernen, ohne dabei den kommunikativen Aspekt zu gefährden. Pointiert ließe sich Dörnyeis (2013) Ansatz wie folgt zusammenfassen: Maximiert werden soll die Kooperation zwischen explizitem und implizitem Lehren und Lernen in den Bereichen der Formfokussierung, der Flüssigkeit und Automatisierung und der formelhaften Sprache (vgl. ibid. 165-168). Fritz & Faistauer (2008) gruppieren ihrerseits Prinzipien in didaktische (u.a. Autonomie), methodische (u.a. Ausgewogenheit der Fertigkeiten) und spracherwerbsorientierte (basierend auf Ellis 2005,

u. a. Aneignung von formelhaften Ausdrücken und regelbasiertem Wissen). Kumaravadivelu (2006: 201) schlägt insgesamt zehn allgemein gehaltene „macrostrategies" vor, die er auf den Erkenntnissen aktueller theoretischer und didaktischer Fremdsprachenlehr- und -lernforschung sowie auf den Parametern postmethodischer Didaktik aufbaut. Wichtig ist hier darauf zu verweisen, dass weder eine hohe noch eine niedrige Anzahl an Unterrichtsprinzipien ein Qualitätsmerkmal bzw. Erfolgsmerkmal von Unterricht sind. Im Gegenteil: Gerade eine große Anzahl an Prinzipien erhöhe die Wahrscheinlichkeit, dass diese in Konflikt zueinander stünden, weswegen es wichtig sei, sie nach Kontext und Lehr- und Lernziel zu gewichten und priorisieren. Auch vor der Annahme sei gewarnt, dass es die ‚besten' Prinzipien gebe (vgl. Klippel 2016: 319 f.). An dieser Stelle wird nun exemplarisch auf einige gängige (spracherwerbsorientierte) Prinzipien in der Fremdsprachendidaktik eingegangen.

Ein wichtiges Prinzip im FSU ist sicherlich jenes, das sich auf die Inhalts- und Bedeutungsebene und auf die Relevanz für Lernende bezieht (vgl. erstes Prinzip bei Dörnyei 2013: 168). Kumaravadivelu (2006: 202) sieht in einer seiner Makrostrategien ebenfalls die Bedeutung von „meaningful learner-learner, learner-teacher interaction in class where the learners have the freedom and flexibility to initiate and navigate talk, not just react and respond to it". Wichtig sei es, so Kumaravadivelu weiter, dass eine Interaktion stattfinde, die die Lernenden aktiv involviere, und zwar auf einer zwischenmenschlichen und ideellen Ebene. Fritz & Faistauer (2008: 129) heben hervor, dass Unterricht verständnisbezogen aufgebaut werden müsse und die Aktivitäten im Unterricht Lernende dazu bringen sollten, „Bedeutungen zu verstehen und [sie dazu motivieren sollten,] sie auch in an reale Kommunikation angelehnte Situationen anzuwenden."

Ein weiteres Prinzip sieht vor, dass kontrollierte Übungen die Automatisierung befördern sollten (vgl. Dörnyei 2013: 169), die für eine flüssige Sprachverwendung unabdingbar ist. Dörnyei (ibid.) bezieht sich dabei auf skill-learning-Theorien, die einen deklarativen Initialinput vorsehen, der durch Automatisierung zu implizitem Lernen führe.

Dörnyei (ibid.) arbeitet außerdem die Bedeutung eines optimalen Gleichgewichts zwischen implizitem und explizitem Lernen unter Berücksichtigung eines auf die Bedeutung abzielenden Unterrichts heraus. Er schlägt eine Mischung bedeutungsbasierter und formorientierter Aktivitäten vor. Während Dörnyei eher für eine ausgewogene Verteilung zwischen implizitem und explizitem Lernen vorschlägt, unterstreichen Fritz & Faistauer vor allem die Wichtigkeit von implizitem Lernen. Sie sehen erfolgreichen Unterricht darin, dass er sich einerseits auf die sprachliche Form bezieht, andererseits aber auch „vor allem implizites Wissen entwickeln helfen [soll], ohne dabei ganz auf explizites Wissen zu verzichten" (Fritz & Faistauer 2006: 130). Auch Kumaravadivelu (2006:

204 f.) schlägt sprichwörtlich in dieselbe Kerbe und hebt implizites Lernen hervor, für das Lernende mit genügend Textmaterial versorgt werden müssten, um bestimmte Regeln ableiten zu können. Gleichzeitig sei es aber wichtig, die Aufmerksamkeit der Lernenden auf die formalen Eigenschaften von Sprache hinzuweisen, um damit den Grad des Expliziten zu erhöhen.

Dörnyei (2013: 169) und Fritz & Faistauer (2016: 129) schaffen Raum für das Erlernen von formelhaften Ausdrücken, die Lernende anwenden sollen, „ohne dass sie die Regelhaftigkeiten, die hinter diesen Ausdrücken stehen, erlernen müssen" (ibid.). Die Alltagssprache beherberge eine Fülle dieser formelhaften Ausdrücke und diese seien daher für den Sprachunterricht unabdingbar.

Das Prinzip der *language exposure* (Dörnyei 2013: 169) sieht vor, dass Lernende der Zielsprache stark ausgesetzt werden müssten, sodass ihr implizites Lernen ‚gefüttert' werde. Auch Fritz & Faistauer (2006: 131) fordern einen intensiven Input, sowohl durch ein Angebot an Texten als auch durch die extensive Sprachanwendung durch die Lehrperson bzw. die anderen Lernenden.

Das *focused interaction principle* (Dörnyei 2013: 169) beschreibt die Lernangebote. Es geht darum, Lernenden genügend Möglichkeiten zu geben, um in authentische (d. h. reale bzw. lebensechte) Interaktion zu treten. Diese Gelegenheiten, Output zu produzieren sind wichtig (vgl. Fritz & Faistauer 2006: 131), damit Lernende in einem sicheren Umfeld ihr Sprachkönnen ausprobieren und mit der Sprache in realen Kommunikationssituationen handeln können. Lehrende müssten daher möglichst viele Lerngelegenheiten schaffen und dazu bereit sein, gegebenenfalls ihre Planung dem Unterrichtsverlauf anzupassen (vgl. Kumaravadivelu 2006: 202, vgl. Even in diesem Band). Interaktion im Unterricht soll Lernenden die Möglichkeit geben, sowohl rezeptiv als auch produktiv zu arbeiten und den Schritt über ihre aktuellen Kenntnisse hinauszuwagen.

Prinzipien für performativen Fremdsprachenunterricht

Um Prinzipien für einen performativen FSU (PFSU) erarbeiten zu können, muss über die Relevanz der eben gelisteten Prinzipien reflektiert werden. Darüber hinaus ist es sinnvoll, zu überlegen, inwiefern sie in einem PFSU umgesetzt werden können. Schließlich muss es auch darum gehen, zu identifizieren, welche blinden Flecken es gibt, die potentiell mit einem PFSU abgedeckt werden könnten.

Zunächst lässt sich feststellen, dass die oben erwähnten Prinzipien aus spracherwerbstheoretischer Sicht für den PFSU, der sich als Weiterentwicklung des kommunikativen Ansatzes versteht, relevant sein müssten. Je nach Ziel der Unterrichtseinheit müsste abgewogen werden, welche davon im Fokus stehen, um das angestrebte Lernziel zu erreichen. Es lässt sich jedoch eine große Lücke identifizieren: Die diskutierten Prinzipien berücksichtigen nicht, zumindest nicht explizit, das ästhetische oder körper(sprach)liche Lernen. Diese Problematik ist an sich kein neues Phänomen und deckt sich mit der Kritik der Kompetenzorientierung und des GERS (vgl. Rösler 2012: 269, Küster 2015), beide geben in der Unterrichtsgestaltung jedoch maßgeblich den Ton an. Weiters fehlt auch eine Berücksichtigung des zugegeben relativ neuen Konzepts einer performativen Kompetenz. Diese Lücke vermag die Dramapädagogik, die in einem PFSU grundlegend ist, zu schließen. Sie bezieht einerseits körper(sprach)liches Arbeiten aktiv in das Unterrichtsgeschehen mit ein und gibt dem ästhetischen Lernen und Lehren einen besonderen Stellenwert. Wenn nun Prinzipien für den PFSU formuliert werden, so müssen diese gewährleisten, dass sowohl spracherwerbsorientierte als auch ästhetisch-künstlerische bzw. körper(sprach)liche Elemente zum Tragen kommen. Das soll im Folgenden versucht werden. Die Auflistung von Prinzipien für den PFSU ist dabei weder als vollständig, noch als ausgrenzend zu verstehen – Letzteres wäre auch mit Manfred Schewes Verständnis einer performativen Fremdsprachendidaktik nicht zu vereinbaren. Es ist auch nicht Ziel, einen Paradigmenwechsel oder eine neue Methode zu etablieren (vgl. Rösler 2019, auch in diesem Band). Vielmehr geht es darum, bekannte Konzepte weiterzudenken und aus performativer Sicht neu zu betrachten. Die konkrete Umsetzung und Gewichtung dieser Prinzipien ist immer auch vom jeweiligen Unterrichtskontext und -ziel abhängig. Sie überlappen in vielen Bereichen und ergänzen einander in vielerlei Hinsicht.

PFSU ist postmethodisch.

PFSU erhebt nicht den Anspruch, die ,einzig richtige' Methode zu sein. Wichtig ist hier hervorzuheben, dass PFSU den Parametern Kumaravadivelus (2006) folgt und insofern offen und veränderbar zu gestalten ist. D.h. PFSU kann an neue Zielgruppen angepasst werden und stellt die Lernenden und ihre Individualität in den Mittelpunkt. PFSU initiiert Reflexionsprozesse bei Lernenden, die sich persönlich und individuell weiterentwickeln können, und dies besonders durch ästhetisch und körperlich orientierte Erfahrungen. Im Sinne der Postmethodik wird Lehrenden ermöglicht, ihren eigenen Unterricht zu erforschen, darüber und über ihre eigene Rolle zu reflektieren und gemäß der Schlussfolgerungen zu handeln. Die Dramapädagogik als Trägerin des PFSU versteht sich als offener Ansatz, der all diese Möglichkeiten durch die Vielzahl der Adaptionsmöglichkeiten bietet.

PFSU ist inhalts- und bedeutungsbezogen und schafft Raum für lebensechte Interaktion.

PFSU gibt allen Beteiligten die Gelegenheit, sich in fiktiven Als-Ob-Situationen einerseits in einem realen, bedeutungsvollen und inhaltsbezogenen Kontext zu bewegen, dies aber andererseits im geschützten Raum des Unterrichts auszuprobieren und zu erkunden sowie über die Handlung zu reflektieren.

PFSU bezieht aktiv und bewusst körper(sprach)liches und ästhetisches Lehren und Lernen in den Unterricht ein.

Im PFSU nehmen Körper(sprache) und Ästhetik einen besonderen Platz ein: Sie sind nicht nur Themen, zu denen man sprachlich Stellung bezieht, und die in Form von literarischen oder ästhetischen Schmankerln als Belohnung oder zusätzliche Fleißaufgabe präsentiert werden. Sie sind vielmehr aktiv integrierte und wichtige Bestandteile des Unterrichts, die eine tiefgehende Auseinandersetzung erfordern (mehr dazu weiter unten). Durch die Akzentuierung von körper(sprach)lichem Handeln können Lernende außerdem ein Bewusstsein für ihren eigenen Körper und die der anderen entwickeln, beispielsweise über die Positionierung im Raum, die stimmliche Betonung oder den Körpereinsatz zur Unterstützung von Kommunikationsabsichten.

PFSU braucht intensiven sprachlichen, aber auch ästhetischen und körper(sprach)lichen Input.

Intensiver sprachlicher Input ist in vielen spracherwerbsorientierten Prinzipien verankert. PFSU erweitert dieses Prinzip mit Fokus auf ästhetischem und körpersprachlichem Material, beispielsweise literarischen Texten, Liedern, Filmen oder Bildern. Diese werden nicht auf ihre grammatischen oder lexikalischen Elemente reduziert, sondern als sprachlich-ästhetische Kunstobjekte, die in ihrer komplexen Gesamtheit verstanden werden, gesehen. Diese tiefgehende Auseinandersetzung erfordert ein intensives und häufig wiederholtes Rezipieren des Inputmaterials, was für den folgenden Output elementar ist.

PFSU bietet genügend Gelegenheiten für sprachlichen, aber auch ästhetischen und körper(sprach)lichen Output.

Aufgrund des bewussten Umgangs mit körpersprachlichen und ästhetischen Aspekten und des intensiven Inputs im Unterricht, bieten sich vielerlei Möglichkeiten für Output. Einerseits können sprachliche Äußerungen zu beispielsweise literarischen Texten oder anderen Kunstobjekten getätigt werden. Andererseits wird Lernenden Raum geboten, sich körper(sprach)lich und ästhetisch mit dem Input auseinanderzusetzen, indem beispielsweise Standbilder oder kreative (Parallel)Texte zu literarischen Texten oder Bildimpulsen erstellt werden. Die Produktion eigenen Outputs intensiviert dabei auch die bewusste sprachliche und ästhetische Auseinandersetzung mit dem Ausgangsmedium.

PFSU bietet Gelegenheit, sowohl rezeptiv als auch produktiv an sprachlichen, körper(sprach)lichen und ästhetischen Unterrichtssituationen teilzunehmen und darin zu handeln.

Anknüpfend an die eben genannten Prinzipien wird PFSU so ausgerichtet, dass er Lernenden möglichst viele Gelegenheiten bietet, sich am Unterricht zu beteiligen, und zwar sowohl rezeptiv als auch produktiv. Bei Lernenden, die beispielsweise nicht an dramapädagogische Lernumgebungen gewöhnt sind oder die eher zögerlich aktiv daran teilnehmen, kann das rezeptive Wahrnehmen und Reflektieren eine erste Annäherung an später aktivere Partizipation darstellen. Darüber hinaus wird neben der produktiven Teilnahme dem Reflektieren und Rezipieren ein besonderer Stellenwert zugestanden, auch um die performative Kompetenz zu fördern.

PFSU fördert die Ausbildung einer performativen Kompetenz.

Wenn die Inszeniertheit jeglichen Handelns (vgl. Hallet 2010) als Grundverständnis vorliegt, dann muss PFSU performative Kompetenzen fördern und fordern. Dafür stellt PFSU Raum zur Verfügung, um diese Inszeniertheit wahrzunehmen, darüber zu reflektieren und selbst produktiv daran teilzunehmen. Dies lässt sich einerseits durch dramapädagogische Verfahren umsetzen, indem im Als-Ob-Raum ganzheitlich gehandelt, wahrgenommen und reflektiert werden kann. Andererseits auch dadurch, dass alltägliche Handlungen, wie beispielsweise das Verfassen von E-Mails, als inszeniert bzw. performativ betrachtet und dementsprechend im Unterricht geübt werden.

PFSU stellt sich der Standardisierung und Vereinheitlichung von Lehr- und Lernprozessen entgegen.

PFSU bietet dem Standardisierungsdrang und der Kompetenzorientierung die Stirn. Fundamental von den Künsten inspiriert, ebnet PFSU den Weg zu einem neuen Verständnis von Lernprozessen, in denen nicht die eindeutige Messbarkeit einheitlicher Lernergebnisse, sondern die persönliche und lebenslange Entwicklung der Individuen im Vordergrund steht.

Die hier vorgestellten Prinzipien sind exemplarisch zu verstehen und sie bedürfen noch weiterer Konkretisierung und Fortführung. Sie zeigen dennoch überblicksartig, wofür Manfred Schewe seit Jahrzehnten einsteht. Insofern ist performativer Fremdsprachenunterricht immer auch ein bisschen Manfred Schewe.

Literatur

Arnold, Jane; Dörnyei, Zoltán & Pugliese, Chaze (2015): *The Principled Communicative Approach: Seven criteria for success*. London: Helbling.

Bachmann-Medick, Doris (2006): *Cultural Turns. Neuorientierungen in den Kulturwissenschaften*. Reinbek bei Hamburg: Rowohlt.

Bernstein, Nils & Lerchner, Charlotte (2014): Vorwort. In Nils Bernstein & Charlotte Lerchner (Hg.): *Ästhetisches Lernen im DaF-/DaZ-Unterricht. Literatur – Theater – Bildende Kunst – Musik – Film*. Göttingen: Universitätsverlag Göttingen, V-VIII.

Bosenius, Petra (2017): Assessing performative competence in German ELF-classrooms – The task of teachers and learners. In *Scenario* XI/2, 51-66.

Crutchfield, John (2015): Fear and trembling. The role of „negative" emotions in a performative pedagogy. In *Scenario* IX/2, 101-114.

Crutchfield, John & Schewe, Manfred (Hg.) (2017): *Going Performative in Intercultural Education: International Contexts, Theoretical Perspectives and Models of Practice*. Bristol: Multilingual Matters.

Dörnyei, Zoltán (2013): Communicative Language Teaching in the twenty-first century: The 'Principled Communicative Approach'. In Jane Arnold & Tim Murphey (Hg.): *Meaningful action. Earl Stevick's influence on language teaching*. Cambridge: Cambridge University Press, 161-171.

Ellis, Rod (2005): Principles of instructed language learning. In *System* 33/2, 209-224.

Even, Susanne (2003): *Drama Grammatik. Dramapädagogische Ansätze für den Grammatikunterricht Deutsch als Fremdsprache*. München: iudicium.

Even, Susanne (2011): Drama grammar: towards a performative postmethod pedagogy. In *The Language Learning Journal* 39/3, 299-312.

Even, Susanne & Schewe, Manfred (2016a) (Hg.): *Performatives Lehren, Lernen, Forschen. Performative Teaching, Learning, Research*. Berlin et al.: Schibri.

Even, Susanne & Schewe, Manfred (2016b): Einleitende Gedankensammlung zum performativen Lehren, Lernen und Forschen. In Susanne Even et al. (Hg.), 10-26.

Fischer-Lichte, Erika (2004): *Ästhetik des Performativen*. Frankfurt: Suhrkamp.

Fleming, Mike (2016): Exploring the Concept of Performative Teaching and Learning. In Susanne Even et al. (Hg.), 27-46.

Fritz, Thomas & Faistauer, Renate (2008): Prinzipien eines Sprachunterrichts. In Elisabeth Bogenreiter-Feigl (Hg.): *Paradigmenwechsel? Sprachenlernen im 21. Jahr-*

hundert: Szenarios-Anforderungen-Profile-Ausbildung. Wien: VÖV-Edition Sprachen 2, 125-133.

Haack, Adrian (2010): ‚KünstlerInnen der improvisierten Aufführung'. Performative Fremdsprachendidaktik als Teil des Lehramtsstudiums. In *Scenario* IV/1, 35-53.

Haack, Adrian (2018): *Dramapädagogik, Selbstkompetenz und Professionalisierung. Performative Identitätsarbeit im Lehramtsstudium Englisch.* Wiesbaden: J. B. Metzler/ Springer.

Hallet, Wolfgang & Surkamp, Carola (2015) (Hg.): *Dramendidaktik und Dramapädagogik im Fremdsprachenunterricht.* Trier: WVT.

Hallet, Wolfgang (2010): Performative Kompetenz und Fremdsprachenunterricht. In *Scenario* IV/1, 5-18.

Harsch, Claudia (2017): Kompetenz. In Carola Surkamp (Hg.), 166-169.

Hudelist, Andreas (2017): Performanz, Performativität und Performance. Eine unvollständige Rekonstruktion. In *ide* 3/2017, 9-17.

Hudelist, Andreas & Krammer, Stefan (2017): Sprechen und Handeln im Deutschunterricht. In *ide* 3/2017, 5-8.

Klippel, Friederike (2016): Didaktische und methodische Prinzipien der Vermittlung. In Eva Burwitz-Melzer, Grit Mehlhorn, Claudia Riemer, Karl-Richard Bausch & Hans-Jürgen Krumm (Hg.): *Handbuch Fremdsprachenunterricht.* 6., v. ü. und erw. Aufl. Tübingen: A. Francke, 315-320.

Kumaravadivelu, Balasubramanian (2001): Toward a Postmethod Pedagogy. In *TESOL Quarterly* 35/4, 537-560.

Kumaravadivelu, Balasubramanian (2003): A postmethod perspective on English language teaching. In *World Englishes* 22/4, 539-550.

Kumaravadivelu, Balasubramanian (2006): *Understanding Language Teaching. From Method to Postmethod.* Mahwah: Lawrence Erlbaum Associates.

Kumaravadivelu, Balasubramanian (2012): *Language Teacher Education for a Global Society. A Modular Model for Knowing, Analyzing, Recognizing, Doing, and Seeing.* New York/London: Routledge.

Küppers, Almut; Schmidt, Torben & Walter, Maik (Hg.) (2011): *Inszenierungen im Fremdsprachenunterricht. Grundlagen, Formen, Perspektiven.* Braunschweig: Schroedel/Diesterweg/Klinkhardt.

Küster, Lutz (2015): Warum ästhetisch-literarisches Lernen im Fremdsprachenunterricht? Ausgewählte theoretische Fundierungen. In Lutz Küster, Christiane Lütge & Katharina Wieland (Hg.): *Literarisch-ästhetisches Lernen im Fremdsprachenunterricht. Theorie – Empirie – Unterrichtsperspektiven.* Frankfurt a. M.: Peter Lang, 15-32.

Müller, Thomas (2017): *Sprachliche Kognitivierung im dramapädagogischen Deutsch-als-Fremdsprache-Unterricht. Eine Bestandsaufnahme und empirische Expertenbefragung.* München: Iudicium.

Nieweler, Andreas (2017): Lernziel. In Carola Surkamp (Hg.), 226-227.

Rösler, Dietmar (2012): *Deutsch als Fremdsprache. Eine Einführung.* Weimar: J. B. Metzler

Rösler, Dietmar (2019): The only turn worth watching in the 20th century is Tina Turner's. How the sloganization of foreign language research can impede the furthering of knowledge and make life difficult for practitioners. In Barbara Schmenk, Stephan Breidbach & Lutz Küster (Hg.): *Sloganization in Language Education Discourse. Conceptual Thinking in the Age of Academic Marketization.* Bristol: Multilingual Matters, 42-56.

Schewe, Manfred (1993): *Fremdsprache inszenieren. Zur Fundierung einer dramapädagogischen Lehr- und Lernpraxis.* Oldenburg: Pädagogisches Zentrum.

Schewe, Manfred (2000): DaF-Stunden dramapädagogisch gestalten – wie mache ich das? In Gerald Schlemminger, Thomas Brysch & Manfred Schewe (Hg.): *Pädagogische Konzepte für einen ganzheitlichen DaF-Unterricht.* Berlin: Cornelsen, 72-105.

Schewe, Manfred (2011): Die Welt auch im fremdsprachlichen Unterricht immer wieder neu verzaubern – Plädoyer für eine performative Lehr- und Lernkultur. In Almut Küppers et al. (Hg.), 20-31.

Schewe, Manfred (2012): Auf dem Wege zu einer Performativen Fremd- und Zweitsprachendidaktik. In İnci Dirim, Hans-Jürgen Krumm, Paul R. Portmann-Tselikas & Sabine Schmölzer-Eibinger (Hg.): *Theorie und Praxis. Jahrbuch für Deutsch als Fremd- und Zweitsprache 1/2012. Schwerpunkt: Körper, Klang, Rhythmus.* Graz: Praesens Verlag, 79-94.

Schewe, Manfred (2013): Taking stock and looking ahead: Drama pedagogy as a gateway to a performative teaching and learning culture. In *Scenario* VII/1, 5-23.

Schewe, Manfred (2015): Fokus Fachgeschichte: Die Dramapädagogik als Wegbereiterin einer performativen Fremdsprachendidaktik. In Wolfgang Hallet et al. (Hg.), 20-36.

Schewe, Manfred (2017): Dramapädagogik. In Carola Surkamp (Hg.), 48-51.

Schmenk, Barbara (2007): Kommunikation ist alles. Oder? Wider die Trivialisierung des Kommunikativen im kommunikativen Fremdsprachenunterricht. In *Deutsch als Fremdsprache* 3/2007, 131-139.

Schmenk, Barbara (2015): Dramapädagogik im Spiegel von Bildungsstandards, GeRS und Kompetenzdiskussionen. In Wolfgang Hallet et al. (Hg.), 37-50.

Schwerdtfeger, Inge C. (2001): Ganzheitliches Lernen und Leiblichkeit im Fremdsprachenunterricht – Zwei Seiten einer Medaille. In *Info DaF* 28/5, 431-442.

Surkamp, Carola & Hallet, Wolfgang (2015): Dramendidaktik und Dramapädagogik im Fremdsprachenunterricht. Zur Einleitung. In Wolfgang Hallet et al. (Hg.), 1-18.

Surkamp, Carola (2017) (Hg.): *Metzler Lexikon Fremdsprachendidaktik.* 2. erw. Aufl. Stuttgart: J. B. Metzler.

Taking the cloth off the telescope

Reflections on a paradigm shift in language education

Erika Piazzoli

Introduction

The Drama/Foreign Language Summer School 2017 was held in Padua, Italy. Manfred Schewe gave the opening keynote speech titled *The State of the Art* and started the address with an examination of the actual phrase *The State of the Art*. The expression originally comes from engineering, dating back to 1910, when it was first recorded in the Oxford English Dictionary. It was quickly endorsed by the marketing industry and by the mid-80s had already become overused – with a connotation of false praise to it. By 1994, using *State of the Art* was considered a cliché to be avoided in advertising (Zweig 1994).

To steer clear of this cliché, Schewe proposed a modification of the title of his talk, namely *The State of the Art(s)*, with the sub-title: *Going Performative in (Foreign) Language Education* and spoke on the foundations of performative language teaching, learning and research. It was a particularly inspirational address, so much so that in this paper I will quote from it in some detail, using it as a spring board to reflect on the implications of changing the paradigm in language education, moving towards a performative epistemology of practice.

"When teachers themselves are taught to learn"

Introducing the topic of innovation in education, Schewe quoted the following lines from Brecht's *Life of Galileo* (1939):

> In the year sixteen hundred and nine
> Science's light began to shine.
> At Padua City, in a modest house
> Galileo Galilei set out to prove
> The sun is still, the earth is on the move
> (Scene 1)

This was followed by another quote:

> The world of teachers[1] takes a crazy turn
> when teachers themselves are taught to learn
> (Scene 6)

The quotes had been chosen well: By referencing this play in particular, Schewe showed awareness of the local context: *Life of Galileo*'s first scene is set in Padua and so was the 2017 Summer School. The connection is not just geographical, but also historical: Galileo Galilei actually held a professorship in mathematics at the University of Padua between 1564 and 1642, and the University still preserves the lectern where he taught in the *Aula Magna* (Great Hall).

Furthermore, the quotes were very much aligned with the audience of the Summer School: Schewe was addressing a group of teachers with an interest in theatre and drama who were there to deepen their own knowledge of the art form and examine its applicability to language education. This community of teachers had congregated in Padua from different parts of the world with the intention to be "taught to learn". By drawing on Brecht's *Life of Galileo*, and speaking at the University of Padua, Schewe's choice was astute. But then, in a surprising twist, Schewe presented us with his own variation:

> In the year two thousand and seventeen
> The leading light of the Arts was seen
> At Padua City, in a summer school
> The participants set out to prove
> Education will go performative, is all ready now to move.
> (Schewe 2017)

This playful adaptation suggested that the time was ripe for education to go performative. Referring to Eisner (1985; 2003), Schewe advocated a change of paradigm that places the arts at the centre of a performative curriculum.

Schewe's gesture held a 'performative' intention, in Austin's (1962) original sense. For Austin, "performatives" are those utterances that are not just describing, but actually doing, or performing an action: "The uttering of the words is, indeed, usually a, or even the, leading incident in the performance of the act" (ibid. 8). To appreciate Schewe's performative intention in the creative appropriation of this particular play, let us go back, once again, to Brecht's figure of Galileo. In discussing the consequences of a paradigm shift, Kuhn (1962), the well-known contemporary epistemologist, reflects on the innovation

---

1   I am using Manfred Schewe's translation here as he used it in his presentation. For all other references, I used John Willett's translation (2012).

in Galileo's work. Galileo was interpreting his reality from a different paradigm, leaving behind the Aristotelian conception, chartering towards unexplored territories. Questioning the Ptolemaic system and the centrality of God was an inconvenient truth, which not many authorities were ready to concede. Kuhn's philosophical investigation brings forth the concept of a *revolution*, implicit in any change of paradigm. Schewe obviously made this connection too, as after introducing the opening of the play, he reflected that, just like the earth being on the move was a revolutionary concept at the time, calling for a performative move in the language curriculum was also revolutionary – and that is what brought him to the play.

Schewe's re-interpretation of the opening of *Life of Galileo*, in the context of a Drama/Language Summer School opening keynote, was a performative hint to make us question the epistemology of practice. It was also, in itself, a an illustration of the essence of performative teaching: choosing aesthetic material that resonates with the teacher (it is no secret that Schewe is fond of Brecht's work); demonstrating attention to the local context (a play set in Padua); hinting at the current state of affairs in education, and at the potential consequences of a paradigm shift ("the world ... takes a crazy turn"); highlighting the importance of reflective practice ("when teachers themselves are taught to learn"); denoting a playful attitude and, importantly, exercising agency by re-arranging the opening of the play to advance a potent metaphor that suited the here-and-now of the context. Schewe remarked that learning is an endeavour that never ends for a teacher – highlighting the importance of flexibility for teachers to be open to new things. Such openness to flexibility, he added, is what characterises teachers working in a performative way.

In closing, Schewe advocated for teachers to develop teacher/artist identities that allow for the emergence of aesthetic spaces in the curriculum. This raises several questions: in light of such a paradigm shift, what does a teacher/artist identity mean in (foreign) language teacher education? What do aesthetic spaces look like in the language classroom? And what would be learners' perceptions of such a change? Inspired by Schewe's points above, I will reflect on these issues and contemplate some possibilities in the areas of teacher education and teacher identity.

Identity formation and the teacher/artist

In a research project on a teacher/artist initiative in Ireland, six primary teachers and six artists formed teacher-artist partnership as a model for Continuing Professional Development (CPD). The partnerships extended over a year, with the aim of creating arts projects in the schools where the teachers were working. The study looked at the creation of a partnership, its development, challenges and benefits (Kenny & Morrissey 2016). Inevitably, the boundaries between the teachers' identities and the artists' identities were re-negotiated as the partnerships progressed. While all teachers were experienced in one or more art forms, and had self-selected for the study, only one of the six teachers initially identified herself as an artist. At the end of the project, each pair in the partnership recognised that there was a sense of mutual ownership and a sense of co-teaching.

However, something very interesting emerged: the artists' cohort reported to have learnt a lot about teaching, while the teachers' cohort tended to down-play their own expertise. In the researchers' words: "While the artists in this initiative clearly identified a role for themselves in 'teaching' the teachers, the teachers neither recognized, nor acknowledged that they might, in turn, 'teach' the artists" (2016: 58). Why would the teachers be less confident than the artists about their impact on the partnership? Are artists more wired for flexibility, for soaking up those skills they have been exposed to?

This may be especially true, as Anderson and Jefferson (2016) argue, when teachers abide to the false expectation that they are not creative and have not been gifted by the Muses' creative juices, as if still subscribing to the Socratic paradigm of creativity as a godly gift of Divine Madness.

My response to these findings is to suggest a different perspective, looking not so much at teacher/artist partnerships, but at the construct of identity formation in the teacher *as* artist, and the artist *as* teacher. Identity can be defined as a fluctuating, contradictory construct involving not one, but multiple sub-identities (Akkerman & Meijer 2011). This view moves beyond a tradition that focuses on the acquisition of 'assets' (knowledge, competencies, and beliefs) as the basis for professional development. On the contrary, professional development and identity are interconnected, as professional development can be part of a teacher's identity. This aligns with a view in which teachers are *active agents* in the creation of their own professional development. In a dialogical self theory framework (Hermans 1996), teacher identity can be described, "as *both* unitary and multiple; *both* continuous and discontinuous and *both* individual and social" (Akkerman & Meijer 2011: 309). Identity formation in teacher education thus emerges as a multifaceted and non-linear, with several sub-identities, sometimes conflicting or disagreeing with each other, in an ongoing process of negotiation of multiple I-positions.

Looking through these lenses at identity formation in the teacher/artist, we have one individual, engaged in an ever-morphing identity balancing act, drawing on sometimes aligned, sometimes conflicting, sub-identities. In his key-note, Schewe (2017) alluded to the issue of identity construction in the teacher as artist, and artist as teacher, proposing an identity continuum encompassing the teacher and the artist (see Fig. 1).

Figure 1: Teacher/Artist Continuum. Schewe (2017)

Within the paradigm of teaching as an art, it is fascinating to delve deeper into the blurred identity boundaries of those of us who identify both as teachers and as artists (Eisner 1985; Lutzker 2007; Crutchfield 2015). As Even and Schewe (2016) argue: "Teachers are – in terms of their professional biography, always at a certain point on a continuum that allows constant movement and new opportunities for growth" (ibid. 175). Where are we presently, on our teacher/ artist biographical continuum? And what are the forces that push us in either direction, at different times of our lives? This continuum is flexible and open to constant renegotiation. Several factors influence where we are in our biography. We may be shifting across the continuum at different points in our lives, starting as teachers, and gradually being drawn into the arts – learning about the arts as we teach. Or vice versa, we may be starting as artists and then gravitate towards the teaching profession. Schewe made the point that both teachers and artists can learn from each other as they fluctuate across the teacher/artist continuum.

Creative doing

In his keynote, Schewe argued that 'going performative' means to put *creative doing* at the centre of education. He de-mystified the notion of the artist as the gifted genius, a myth perpetuated throughout history from Plato onward. And it is still in great need of being debunked as seen in the Irish teacher/artist partnership project discussed above.

For Schewe, *creative doing* is as at the core of performative practices. Sound, voice, image, movement, space and embodied action all facilitate aesthetic learning processes (see Fig. 2).

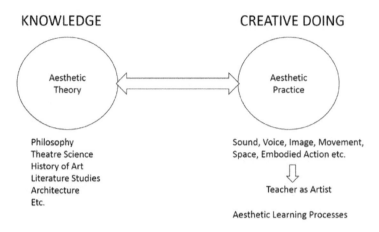

Figure 2: Knowledge and Creative Doing. Schewe (2017)

As Schewe's diagram shows, he sees creative doing related to aesthetic theory, with theory and practice being interconnected. Yet, how can these aesthetic processes be facilitated in sedentary grammar-oriented language classrooms, particularly in a test-oriented culture? Contemporary instructed Second Language Acquisition (SLA) approaches, including task-based, content-based, concept-based (Loewen & Sato 2017), all focus, in their own ways, on teaching language in meaningful social contexts. Similarly, performative language teaching, an action-oriented approach (Even & Schewe 2016), focusses on teaching language in a meaningful, co-created context. What the performative approach adds to the spectrum is the practice of meaning-making through story, metaphor, symbol, imagination – involving movement, voice and the body.

This does not mean, however, that a focus on performative pedagogy precludes the teaching of grammar as it is sometimes erroneously believed. Even's (2011) *drama grammar* and Lapaire's (2014) concept of grammar in motion are two illustrations of the use of drama to facilitate language learning, focussing on grammar. Other practitioners have researched drama and the acquisition of vocabulary (Kalogirou, Beauchamp & Whyte 2017), fluency (Galante & Thomson 2016, Ni Rian 2014) and intercultural competence (Rothwell 2017), just to name a few. The key element that all these studies have in common is a performative stance to second language education.

Schewe (2017) encouraged teachers to allow for performative processes to emerge in the foreign language curriculum. It is not the first time that Schewe has issued such a call; this *Festschrift* is, in its own way, a manifestation of it. In 2003, Schewe called for a performative paradigm shift in foreign language education (Schewe 2003). Ten years earlier, in 1993, he published a book on drama in the language classroom: *Fremdsprache inszenieren: Zur Fundierung einer dramapädagogischen Lehr- und Lernpraxis*. The book was never translated into English. More than twenty years later, due to popular demand, he wrote an English commentary to it, published in 2016 by the Goethe Institute. The 2016 article *Teaching and Learning with the Head, Heart, Hands and Feet* echoes the 1993 German publication. In it Schewe argues:

> Let us imagine that more and more teachers in the next few decades design their classes and seminars with their heads, hearts, hands and feet, trusting in their spontaneity and creative potential and thereby ensuring that (foreign) worlds are created time and time again on the simple boards of seminar rooms and classrooms, generating endless fascination. (Schewe 2016: n.p.)

This quote encapsulates well the potential of performative approach to the language curriculum. Trust in one's spontaneity and creative potential, as Schewe put it, are required by teachers to generate 'endless fascination'.

Learners' experiences and perceptions

In 2014, I worked with a group of international students, aged 20 to 30, investigating their experiences in learning Italian as a second language through a performative approach. On one occasion, I was asked to cover for a colleague in a 12-hour intensive language course. I was bound by a prescribed lesson plan, which I did not choose nor could change, as it was set by the institution. I interpreted the lesson plan through a performative lens, engaging the class in 12 hours of drama – focussing on the main points, but embodying, rather than delivering, the lesson plan. I sought ethical permission to interview five male and female students, who volunteered to take part in interviews – from Mexico, Russia, New Zealand and Germany.

I was struck by Lisa (pseudonym), the New Zealander student, when she talked about her language learning experience in the school: "I don't have *the gift of learning languages* [embarrassed laughter], so I guess, the grammar part of it, and the pronunciation... I find it very difficult". While most her classmates spoke more than one language, this was Lisa's first experience as a foreign language learner, and she had studied Italian for five weeks only. Her comment reveals a system of beliefs, according to which learning language is a *gift*, one she was convinced, at the time of the interview, she was not bestowed with. Commenting on the drama-based experience, she stated: "That was a lot easier for me, because there was a group of us, we were working together, and someone'd know this word, someone'd know that word, so we could piece it together and make a story". She thus identified a key aspect of learning through drama. She reported enjoying the performative approach, feeling social, feeling relaxed, having agency to play and generate laughter, and getting to know her classmates, "rather than asking odd questions".

However, when asked how she rated the usefulness of drama for her language learning, she stated it was neutral, adding: "I wouldn't say I got a huge amount out of it, just because of where I am I'm lower than most people in the class". In other words, her paradigm about language learning (language learning as a *gift* or *talent*) influenced not only her self-esteem as a learner, but also her evaluation of the usefulness of performative approaches. Here is where a shift in paradigm, one advocated by Schewe, can be beneficial for our learners. One may be tempted to encourage Lisa to reconsider her reference point: learning through play, feeling relaxed in the classroom, engaging in a social, dialogic process, getting to know her fellow peers on a more authentic level. All these aspects she identified would also impact on the quality of her language learning experience.

Yet, just as when not everyone was willing to look through Galileo's telescope, an educator cannot force a learner to change their viewpoint. Affording the experience and engaging in meta-reflection on what learning a language is about can be an insightful tool for learners, one through which they can interpret an experience, but it is an individual choice. The role of the educator, then, may be to make the telescope available to the learner, so to speak, but it is up to her to take the cloth off it.

Conclusion

In his *State of the Art(s)* keynote, Schewe (2017) playfully appropriated Brecht's opening of *Life of Galileo* recalling that "the light of the Arts was seen" and positing that "Education will go performative; is all ready now to move." Schewe's offering is more than just a play on words; he is advancing a metaphor for the teacher/artist operating in contemporary society, a reference to Galileo's struggle and crisis. As Kuhn (1962) argues, changes in paradigm have generated periods of crisis. In Brecht's play, Galileo explains to Andrea, his faithful pupil: "For two thousand years people have believed that the sun and all the stars of heaven rotate around mankind." He adds: "But now we are breaking out of it, Andrea, at full speed. Because the old days are over and this is a new time" (Brecht 1939: 6). From a Kuhnian perspective, "breaking out" of something necessarily brings forth a crisis and, history tells us, that was necessary to yield a scientific revolution.

As Kuhn reflects in the preface of his treaty, he gained the insights that brought him to conceive his theories while having to teach physics to non-physicists. He writes about being "greatly surprised" (1962: 7) having to approach his own field from a different angle – and how that threw him into a "crisis" (ibid.) as to his own viewpoint. Having to de-centre, to view his own field from the point of view of the non-specialist, was a catalyst for Kuhn to come to his own theory of epistemology and change. To evoke a paradigm shift, one that places the arts at the centre of the curriculum, we need to be prepared to undergo a time of crisis. That applies to both teachers and learners, as we negotiate expectations related to identity, artistry and education. In drawing on Galileo to call for a performative paradigm, I interpret Schewe's call as urging us to view instances of crisis as a catalyst for change.

The challenge for us, then, as teacher/artists, is to make ourselves vulnerable for moments of crisis, but to not let that deflate our passion. In contemporary times this is no easy task, with sedentary classes in test-oriented culture being the norm, and the arts struggling to keep its place in the curriculum globally. Just as Galileo provoked a crisis, the legacy of which continues far beyond his existence, we can only hope that a change of paradigm alters future educational and political choices. As Brecht's (1939: 81) Galileo urged: "Take the cloth off the telescope and point it at the sun!" In doing that, let us not destroy the retina of our passion eye. Let us, instead, use the two lenses[2] of teacher artistry and creative doing to focus our sight towards a sharp vision.

References

Anderson, Michael & Jefferson, Miranda (2016): Teaching creativity: unlocking educational opportunity. In Peter O'Connor (ed.): *The Possibilities of Creativity*. Cambridge: Cambridge Scholar, 151-170.

Akkerman, Sanne F. & Meijer, Paulien C. (2011): A dialogical approach to conceptualizing teacher identity. In *Teaching and Teacher Education* 27, 308-319.

Austin, John L. (1962): *How To Do Things with Words*. Oxford: Clarendon Press.

Barone, Tom & Eisner, Elliot (2011): *Arts Based Research*. Los Angeles: Sage.

Brecht, Bertolt (2012): *The Life of Galileo*, transl. by John Willett. London: Bloomsbury.

Crutchfield, John (2015): Fear and trembling: The role of negative emotions in a performative pedagogy. In *Scenario* IX/2, 101-114.

Eisner, Elliot (1985): *The Educational Imagination*. New York: Macmillan.

Eisner, Elliot (2003): The arts and the creation of mind. In *Language Arts 80/5: Imagination and the Arts*, 340-344.

Even, Susanne (2011): Drama grammar: Towards a performative postmethod pedagogy. In *Language Learning Journal* 39/3, 299-312.

---

2   Telescopes work by using two lenses to focus the light.

Even, Susanne & Schewe, Manfred (eds.) (2016): *Performative Teaching, Learning, Research – Performatives Lehren, Lernen, Forschen*. Berlin et al.: Schibri.

Galante, Angelica & Thomson, Ron I. (2017): The effectiveness of drama as an instructional approach for the development of second language oral fluency, comprehensibility, and accentedness. *TESOL Quarterly* 51/1, 115-142.

Hermans, Hubert J. M. (1996): Voicing the self: From information processing to dialogical interchange. In *Psychological Bulletin* 119/1, 31-50.

Kalogirou, Konstantina; Beauchamp, Gary & Whyte, Shona (2017): Vocabulary acquisition via drama: Welsh as a second language in the primary school setting. In *The Language Learning Journal*, 1-12.

Kenny, Ailbhe & Morrissey, Dorothy (2016): *Exploring Teacher-Artist Partnership as a Model of CPD for Supporting and Enhancing Arts Education in Ireland: A Research Report*. Dublin: Department of Education and Skills and the Department of Arts, Heritage and the Gaeltacht/Department of Arts, Heritage, Regional, Rural and Gaeltacht Affairs.

Kuhn, Thomas (1962): *La Struttura delle Rivoluzioni Scientifiche*. Torino: Einaudi.

Lapaire, Jean-Remi (2014): *À corps perdu ou le mystère de la désincarnation des langues*. Paper presented at the Langues en mouvement: didactique des langues et pratiques artistiques / Languages in Motion, Université de Nantes, France.

Loewen, Shawn, & Masatoshi, Sato M. (eds.). (2017): *The Routledge Handbook of Instructed Second Language Acquisition*. New York/London: Routledge.

Lutzker, Peter (2007): *The Art of Foreign Language Teaching: Improvisation and Drama in Teacher Development and Language Learning*. Tübingen: Francke Verlag.

Ní Riain, Isobel (2014): Drama in the Language Lab – Goffman to the Rescue. In *Scenario* VIII/1, 99-107.

Platone (250 B.C. / 1994): Fedro. In Giovanni Fornero (ed.): *Filosofi e Filosofie nella Storia: I Testi* (Vol. 1). Torino: Paravia.

Rothwell, Julia (2017): Using process drama to engage beginner learners in intercultural language learning. In John Crutchfield & Manfred Schewe (eds.): *Going Performative in Intercultural Education: International Contexts, Theoretical Perspectives and Models of Practice*. Bristol: Multilingual Matters, 147-171.

Schewe, Manfred (1993): *Fremdsprache Inszenieren: Zur Fundierung einer Dramapädagogisken Lehr- und Lernpraxis*. Oldenburg: Pädagogisches Zentrum.

Schewe, Manfred (2013): Taking stock and looking ahead: Drama pedagogy as a gateway to a performative teaching and learning culture. In *Scenario* VIII/1, 5-23.

Schewe, Manfred (2016): *Drama in Foreign Language Classes: Teaching and Learning with the Head, Heart, Hands and Feet*. Goethe Institut, https://www.goethe.de/en/spr/mag/20866409.html, last accessed: 03/01/2018.

Schewe, Manfred (2017): *The State of the Art(s). Going Performative in (Foreign Language) Education*. Università degli Studi di Padova: Drama/Language Summer School, August 28-Sept 1, 2017.

Zweig, Mark (1994): Better Writing. In Mark Zweig: *Management from A to Zweig: The Complete Works of Mark Zweig*. Fayetteville: ZweigWhite, 115.

The Teaching Lab: An Immodest Proposal

John Crutchfield

Doing It The Hard Way: Teaching as Craft

As prelude to my immodest proposal, I'd like to make an embarrassing confession: for over twenty years now I've been doing something professionally that I was never taught how to do. I was never taught how to teach. Well, not *really* how to teach. As part of my 'funding package' for graduate school in English Literature, I was given a teaching assistantship, which required me to teach classes in Composition and Rhetoric to first-year college students. The summer before I began, there was a sort of workshop taught by members of the Composition faculty, which introduced us novices to the standard textbook and instructed us in the proper way to design and grade student writing assignments. These instructions were supplemented by a list of readings in something called Composition Theory – which, however, appeared to impugn the very idea of objective standards of quality in writing. I admit I found this somewhat confusing. Nevertheless, two things seemed clear to me: 1) the primary medium of communication between my students and me would be writing, and 2) what they wrote and what I wrote back need not necessarily have anything to do with each other. To the degree that I thought about it at all, I probably assumed that what happened minute-by-minute in the actual classroom would somehow just take care of itself. Maybe I would write some sentences on the blackboard.

And thus I walked into my first class on the first day of the semester with not the faintest phosphorescent glimmer of an idea of what I was doing. This is equivalent to a being handed a brick and getting thrown into a raging, ice-cold river as a first swimming lesson. (The brick in the analogy is the textbook, by the way.)

This is a rather brutal, though hardly unprecedented, way of teaching someone how to do something. I suppose it has the advantage of encouraging a kind of self-reliance. One might even call it 'experiential'. And since all of us novices were essentially in the same situation, it also encouraged a degree of collegiality, albeit predicated on shared anxiety, frustration and despair. In retrospect, however, it occurs to me that if I applied to my own teaching the principles by which I was taught how to teach, I would long ago have been sued for incompetence, or worse. And unfortunately, twenty years of casual observation since then have not convinced me that my experience as a teacher-in-training was an anomaly. Far from it.

So I offer you a rhetorical question: shouldn't the teaching of teachers exemplify the best teaching of all? (The answer is yes.) Then how are we to explain the general fact of its failure to do so? It's as if teacher education were conceived on an entirely different basis from other forms of education, where the essential idea is to lead students out of themselves and into a skillful engagement with a specific social and professional reality. But future teachers are often being taught in ways that, it seems to me, have little to do with the reality of teaching.

Let's consider that reality for a moment, the reality of the classroom. It unfolds in real time, it involves real human beings who are embodied and co-present, and it traces instantaneous, autopoietic feedback loops of astonishing complexity, in which intuitive, unconscious, hereditary, somatic, environmental and aleatory factors play as large if not a larger role than any intentional rule or procedure (Fischer-Lichte 2004). In short, it is a *performative* situation, which makes teaching a *performative art*, i.e. an art that aims at entering such feedback loops and shaping them for conscious purposes.[1] Where those conscious purposes involve learning a foreign language, performance becomes not only the means, but also the end. A performative foreign language teacher training, such as Manfred Schewe has been calling for since the publication of his ground-breaking study *Fremdsprache inszenieren* (Schewe 1993), makes sense not only because teaching itself is performative and because performative pedagogies have been shown to work, but because learning a foreign language in particular means learning a new mode of performance (Schewe 2011, Hallet 2010). This becomes especially clear when one considers the intercultural dimension (Crutchfield & Schewe 2017). I can memorize the Duden cover to cover, but if I can't perform effectively in the live, embodied, intercultural communicative situation of speaking with a flesh-and-blood German, I've probably wasted my time.

Enough. The idea that teaching is an art, and a performative art at that, is, I trust, nothing new in this company. I would like to be clear about one thing, however: by using the word *art*, I do not mean to invoke vague, post-Romantic notions of original Genius, prophetic visions, opioid swoonings, caves of ice, monotonous ravens croaking "Nevermore...," etc. On the contrary, I mean art

---

1 This is different from controlling the feedback loop, much less constituting it or determining its trajectory. The feedback loop of performance is self-constituting (autopoietic) and far too complex to be controlled completely. The teacher's job as performative artist is to enter it fully, negotiate it intelligently and empathically and guide it skillfully toward pedagogical ends – knowing of course that its complexity requires an openness to the unexpected and hence a robust ability to improvise.

in the sense of that species of activity that embodies both creative intuition and practical knowledge, and in which standards of quality actually matter. In the English-speaking world, this is more properly called *craft*. Anyone who approaches an activity in this way, be it teaching, playing the violin, diagnosing illness, framing houses, directing plays, managing an office, programming computers or conducting lab experiments, could be called a *craftsman* or *craftsperson*. Their achievements we would call *craftsmanship*. In German, we might say, *Sie kennt ihr Handwerk*, she knows her craft. The concept of craft should interest us here, because it resolves in a compelling way the apparent dialectic between the *scientific* or rational and the *artistic* or intuitive aspects of teaching. In other words, one way to acknowledge that teaching is both a creative art and a rational science is to call it a craft. But calling it a craft has certain consequences, especially for how teaching is taught. More on this in a moment.

Let's first take some time to unpack the concept of craft. Most importantly, craft means *praxis*: interacting with some sort of concrete reality or material. The German equivalent, *Handwerk* turns out to be a useful heuristic: it suggests that this praxis is primarily physical or manual in form, involving the actual hand or hands. It would be tempting at first to dismiss this as folksy or anachronistic. After all, what of the poet's craft, or the philosopher's? What of the doctor's craft, or the software engineer's? Surely the practice of their craft is not dependent on the skill of their hands the same way a carpenter's or violinist's is? But if we take the hand in *Handwerk* as metonym for the body as a whole, or rather, for embodiment, then we begin to see the truth in it. The poet's craft, for instance, depends not only upon a radicalization of the senses, and particularly the sense of *hearing language*, but also on developing bodily habits conducive to composition, such as the ability to sit still for long periods of time in solitude – or even to create an inner sense of solitude where external solitude is impossible.[2] That is not easy. The philosopher's craft depends on similar skills: habituating the body to practices that make it possible to think, practices which may or may not come easily or naturally or conduce to physical health. In this sense, doing and thinking are deeply interrelated. The carpenter too is thinking and listening, albeit differently than the poet or philosopher. He must be able to

---

2   In some poetic traditions, e.g. the surrealist tradition going back to Arthur Rimbaud, the poetic praxis involves a certain violence toward the body: "Il s'agit d'arriver à l'inconnu par le dérèglement de tous les sens," (Rimbaud 1871). ("The idea is to reach the unknown by the derangement of all the senses.") Though on the surface very different from the poet who sits for long hours in a bare room at a writer's retreat, the basic idea is the same: the practice of poetry depends on training the body to experience reality in unconventional or even 'unnatural' ways, freed from ossified habits and clichés of perception. In other contexts this would be called asceticism.

imagine vividly the material project before him as both temporal/spacial process and product. He must not only know which tool to use for what task, he must also be able to sense the correct amount of force to be applied given the material he's working on. The cheap yellow pine used in construction framing resists differently than does oak, birch, poplar, hickory or walnut. The carpenter's craft, no less than the poet's, involves an interplay of knowledge, rational analysis, experience, intuition, sense perception, and imagination.

But this suggests that craftsmanship consists merely or primarily in skills, or 'competencies' as they're sometimes called. Translated to the realm of teaching, we might think of the skills of classroom management, of planning a lesson, unit, or entire course, of negotiating conflict and handling disruptive behavior, of giving constructive feedback and fair assessment, as well as such 'actorly' skills as speaking clearly, standing and moving confidently, gesturing expressively etc. All of which can be learned, probably in a lot less time than the proverbial ten thousand hours of practice required to master a musical instrument. But this would only be the surface. Here I'm going to draw upon some observations by the American pragmatist philosopher Richard Sennett. Craftsmanship as praxis, according to Sennett, rests on a certain approach to ambiguity, to the resistance inherent in materials and to the dialectic of problem solving and problem finding. These point toward an ethical dimension to craftsmanship, which Sennett calls "the desire to do a job well for its own sake" (Sennett 2008: 9), an expression which should remind us of Plato's definition of virtue, ἀρετή. For the craftsman, the reason for doing good work is not exterior to the work itself, in the form of some personal benefit – money, recognition etc. Of course such rewards *ought to* accrue to good work, but they do not always, or even usually, and thus cannot be relied on as the *motivation* or *cause* for good work. What can be relied on is the intrinsic pleasure and satisfaction – one might say pride – in *the doing of good work*. The craftsman's basic attitude in fact is that good work is the only kind worth doing.

But as Sennet is quick to point out, craftsmanship also depends upon what we might call tradition. The skills involved in craftsmanship, the ethical attitude at the root of those skills, no less than the standard of what is to be considered 'good' are collective and cumulative, and hence dependent on communication. And now we reach the crux of the problem: how does craftsmanship – in terms both of skills and ethics – get communicated, 'passed on' from one generation to the next?

Well, through some form of teaching, obviously. But what if teaching itself is the craft that is to be passed on? Then, as I hinted earlier, the *content* to be communicated (the skills, practical knowledge, ethical attitude, etc.) and the *form* of its communication are inextricably interwoven. In a very concrete way, the teacher of teachers must teach by example, and what is being exemplified must be made explicit and transparent. In other words, teacher education must embody what Sennett calls "sociable expertise" (ibid. 249). And yet, too often the practical knowledge and skills of good teaching remain implicit and private; they do not get passed on and thus die out like garden annuals, which have to be re-seeded every year. The failure to communicate expertise results in what Sennett calls the "Stradivari Syndrome": believing his expertise to be ineffable, the great luthier neglected to communicate it explicitly to the apprentices and assistants in his workshop (ibid. 248). When he died, his expertise died with him. And despite several hundred years and much expense of money and effort, it has never been rediscovered. No one knows how he made the Davidoff cello.

But this sort of knowledge-hoarding has another danger: by wrapping expertise in the shroud of ineffability – which we inadvertently do whenever we call it 'talent,' 'intuition,' 'artistry' or 'genius' – we also insulate it from criticism. In Sennett's words, the point of transparency is that "the standards of good work must be clear to people who are not themselves experts", and that "the effort to devise such a language jolts experts into working better and more honestly" (ibid. 249). The danger is thus not only that craftsmanship won't be passed on to the next generation, but that it will stagnate in itself. Teaching is in this sense the life-line of craft: it forces the craftsman to remain in constant dialogue with the social reality that is the context of their work, a context that, personified in their apprentices or students over the years, never ceases to change.

The antidote – Sennett's sociable expertise – I would prefer to call *mentoring*. I like this term better than 'expertise' because to me the latter suggests an endpoint, and there is in fact no such thing in craftsmanship. One passes a series of thresholds, perhaps, but that series is infinite and convergent. Perfection continually recedes, albeit in smaller and smaller increments as skill increases. Thus the mentor is not gazing back from some final destination or resting place, but merely from somewhere farther along the path. Moreover, the relationship with the mentee is a mutually transformative one: the mentee is initiated into the journey of craftsmanship, and the mentor is kept honest by the challenge of communicating his or her knowledge and of continually reexamining and revising it. In fact, this sense of being forever on the journey of craftsmanship is the basis of the mentor's authenticity and hence of their authority. After all, authenticity means 'doing it oneself' (Gk: *autos + hentes*).

A View With a Room: Teaching Spaces

The mention of Stradivari and his Cremona workshop brings us to the question I've been slowly working my way around to: what sort of *institutional space* would enable authentic mentoring in teacher education? Clearly a workshop like Stradivari's, in which the apprentices ate, slept, worked and prayed together for years on end is neither feasible nor desirable. But the modern classrooms and lecture halls where teachers are usually educated today seem equally problematic, not least because they enforce through their architecture a physical passivity that is antithetical to the very idea of *Handwerk*. One does not learn how to teach by talking about it while sitting in a chair, much less by listening to someone else talk about it, even if that person is standing at a lectern and flanked by the empyrean gods of Powerpoint. Imagine an acting school in which the actors did nothing but read books on acting and discuss them in class. Reading and discussion may indeed be an important supplement to learning a craft, but as we have seen, the essence of craft is practical and embodied: it consists in the 'bedding in' of skills within the body itself, and this only happens through practice. Lots of practice.

The medieval workshop does provide a useful model, however, in its emphasis on collaborative, hands-on experience. The apprentices work directly with the master, and they are learning their craft by actually practicing it. Through practice, their bodies are habituating the gestures that conduce to excellence while their minds are learning to judge quality, to discriminate, to engage productively with ambiguity, with the resistance inherent in materials, and with the dialectic of problem-solving and problem-finding. But the workshop has its limitations. For one thing, its hierarchical structure can easily tip into despotism or guruism, in which the master's expertise is beyond question and the apprentices are forced to compete for favor. All too often, this leads to the abuse of power. Then it doesn't really matter what particular 'contents' are taught and learned: the real lesson is one of humiliation.

A corrective appears in the mentoring relationships I alluded to earlier, which are associated with traditional *rites of passage*: mentor and mentee meet in a ritualized zone of *liminal space*, a "betwixt and between" where normative modes of social interaction are temporarily suspended, and where the transformation from *initiand* to *initiate* takes place (Van Gennep 1904, Turner 1964). Within liminal space, gestures and words carry a special significance. They are "sacred" or archetypal as opposed to "profane" and personal (Eliade 1958). The mentor's sole responsibility is to guide the young person in her care through the initiation and into full adult citizenship in the tribe. The survival of the tribe depends upon her success, and consequently, she is never alone: the tribal elders are deeply involved in making sure the initiation proceeds correctly. For a mentor to set herself up as infallible or otherwise abuse her power would be a clear dereliction of sacred duty and a defilement of sacred space.

The difficulty with this model is obvious: it depends upon an essentially religious world view, structured by the fundamental distinction sacred/profane. Few of us in the West today live in societies where this is the case. Victor Turner's substitution of the concept *liminal space* for Mircea Eliade's earlier *sacred space* reflects an attempt to locate a more general, sociological phenomenon free from theological overtones. But the sorts of initiations we find in such de-sacralized liminal spaces of modern life tend to be either structurally incomplete or pathological: gang initiations, fraternity 'hell week', military and paramilitary hazing etc.

Besides, even if mentoring and liminal space are useful concepts for thinking about teacher education (and I believe they are), they still fall short of ensuring that craft is communicated explicitly in language as well as implicitly through archetypical actions observed and imitated. For this we need something like the actor's studio as a reference point: a space in which craft is explicitly broken down into its component skills, embodied in specific exercises, so that aspiring craftspeople are made aware of exactly what they are learning and why. Moreover, they are given opportunities to assay these skills in an environment in which they receive explicit, critical, constructive feedback not merely from the expert or mentor, but from their peers too. The craft of acting, we should also note, is not a monolith but an evolving corpus, one that must be constantly reexamined, revised and renewed in dialogue with a social reality that is itself constantly in flux. As Harry Dawe has noted, the same is true of teaching (Dawe 1984). But unlike an acting teacher, who need not be a great actor herself, an education teacher must be a great educator, since in this case, *the teaching of the craft is an example of the craft.* There's just no way around it: in teacher education, the medium and the message are the same.

The proposal I'd now like to make is immodest in the sense that it places exorbitant demands on an institutional system and a dominant culture that are ill prepared to realize it, or even to see the need for it. And yet it is necessary. Our education systems as they stand are coming under tremendous pressure from a variety of mutually exacerbating factors: increased global migration, resurgent nationalism and xenophobia, fake news and fear-mongering, terrorism, climate change, economic inequality, the general erosion of human and civil rights, and the double-edged sword of digital technology. Of course education alone cannot solve these problems; but nor can the problems be solved without education. The need for better teaching – in all fields and at all levels – is obvious.

As a society, we must re-imagine our forms of education – our entire "Lehr- und Lernkultur", as Manfred Schewe would have it –, and this means first and foremost re-imagining our education of teachers. Instead of lecture halls, we need institutional structures that combine the collaborative, hands-on ethos of the medieval workshop with the mentoring relationships as found in the liminal spaces of traditional rites of passage as well as the explicit, skills-oriented, experimental and experiential format of an acting studio. I'd like to call this new form a Teaching Lab. What would it look like in practice?

"Git 'er done": The Teaching Lab

First, let's briefly consider the curriculum. The basic idea is that, throughout the course of their degree programs, education students from all fields would come together in the Teaching Lab to receive a significant part of their training. (Subject-knowledge would continue to be taught in the separate academic departments.) This course of study would be arranged not serially by topic but in parallel: from the very beginning, the three primary practical aspects of the craft of teaching would be addressed – performative skills, interpersonal skills and ethical orientation. Each succeeding iteration (or course) would deepen and intensify these skills through mentored practice, reflection and critique. The Teaching Lab would also be responsible for integrating this praxis with education theory. Everything the students learn about theory and methodology would be tested in the performative situation of the classroom. This idea of testing or assaying through performance would be bolstered by training in empirical research methods, and in particular, in action research.

Thus in conjunction with learning the complex history and theory of their profession, education students would be thoroughly trained in the 'actorly' skills of expressive use of voice, gesture, face and body, as well as improvisation and spontaneity, all of which are essential to the craft of teaching. Closely related would be the strengthening of individual creativity and the capacity for rigorous self-reflection and self-critique. Likewise, students would be trained in such essential interpersonal skills as cognitive and emotional empathy, listening, precise observation of social dynamics, mediation of conflict, and fairness. This in turn would open up the ethical dimension of teaching for critical exploration. One can imagine also a 'through-line' of professional ethics: above all, training in collegiality and collaboration, but also in self-care: stress management and emotional health as well as physical wellness.

Training in the Teaching Lab would be holistic and multi-sensory: kinaesthetic, auditory, visual, olfactory, haptic, imaginative, with an emphasis on performance: drama as well as music and dance. Emotions and sensations would be taken seriously. Fun would be taken seriously and cultivated. Technology would be used only as an enhancement of, never as a replacement for, embodied action in real time. Video and audio recordings, for example, might effectively be used for the fine-grained analysis of individual performances. The curriculum as a whole would emphasize collaborative learning between mentors and mentees. There would be continuous critical reflection on all activities: group feedback and group critiques in addition to one-on-one coaching from the mentor, with a constant orientation toward craftsmanship: the pursuit of excellence for its own sake. The concept of excellence in teaching would be made transparent and communicable. A vocabulary and dialogic style would be developed for talking openly and precisely about teaching with one's future peers in the profession. Assessment too would be collaborative: the trainees' own self-evaluations – perhaps in the 'long form' of journals – would constitute a significant part of their grade, and the grade itself would be marked as one reference point among many in charting one's progress on the path of craftsmanship. Like apprenticeships in medieval times, the training would culminate in a *chef d'oeuvre* demonstrating the trainee's successful embodiment of the skills, knowledge and values of the craft of teaching. This work would have two parts, corresponding to the two aspects of teaching as art and as science: a public performance and an accompanying scholarly paper or critical essay.

What might such a Teaching Lab look like in concrete institutional terms? First of all, given the essential place of embodiment in the curriculum, it must be an actual physical place. Not a chat room, not a webinar, not a discussion thread or blog, not an online course,[3] but an actual brick and mortar space or collection of diverse spaces in which actual people meet in real time to work on their craft. Architecturally, it might look more like a theatre rehearsal studio than a traditional classroom: a multi-use space that could be rendered completely bare of furniture for movement-based exercises, but which could be filled with chairs and desks for classroom simulations or 'rehearsals' as well as for public performances or for days when discussion is on the agenda. It would be difficult to overemphasize the importance of this essential emptiness, with its endless possibilities of filling, configuring and reconfiguring.[4] By this means, teachers-in-training can learn how to make the classroom their own, transforming it into what the philosopher

---

3   See Cook-Sather 2006 on an interesting, and in my view highly problematic, email-based mentoring project within a teacher training program. Cook-Sather rightly sees teacher-training as a version of Victor Turner's famous "betwixt and between" phase of initiation, but she neglects the crucial importance of embodiment in the craft of teaching, and in teaching and learning in general. Nevertheless, in her analysis, email offers other advantages that might render it serviceable as a technological support to teacher training as I discuss it here.

4   The point here is the possibility of creating a variety of experimental spaces, including 'terrible classrooms' of the kind practicing teachers all too often find themselves forced to teach in (see below). Teachers-in-training could thus be given a chance to 'rehearse' working in such spaces, and to explore ways to resist, reshape and render them more conducive to learning.

Gaston Bachelard calls *felicitous space*: space "that may be grasped, that may be defended against adverse forces, the space we love." (Bachelard 1969: xxxv)

By way of contrast, consider for a moment the worst classrooms you've ever taught in. In my experience these rooms are typically windowless, poorly ventilated, denuded of sensory stimuli and yet over-full of immobilized stuff: desks and chairs bolted to the floor in a geometric pattern. Such spaces resist being made one's own, and they are virtually impossible to love. There's hardly room to move, and while the students sit inertly at their desks, the teacher is forced to pace back and forth in the narrow lane in front of the chalkboard or projection screen, or to stand like a minister at the lectern. These classrooms embody and enforce a particular theory of education: teacher as pontificator, student as passive recipient. The addition, at huge expense, of wireless internet, ipads, SmartBoards etc. does little to change this fundamental dynamic, but in fact only further disrupts the possibility of actual human interaction. In the end we have something akin to the architect Rem Koolhaas's idea of *junkspace*: "overripe and undernourishing at the same time." (Koolhaas 2002: 176)[5]

The spaces I envision would not, however, be devoid of *techné*: they would have various musical instruments on hand for voice and rhythm exercises, perhaps drawing and sculpting materials as well, and a few hand props and set pieces for improvisation exercises. There would be yoga mats and bolsters. There would be red clowns' noses and costumes, masks and juggling balls. But the most important things it would contain would be the heads, hands and hearts of the students themselves and of the mentor or mentors whose job it is to fully communicate the best of what they know about teaching. And perhaps of equal, if somewhat paradoxical, importance: the space would contain time, lots of time: the slow time of craftsmanship.

The biggest challenge to realizing this immodest proposal, however, is not time, space or even money, but personnel. Where will these exceptional mentors be found? Where will we find the teachers of the teachers, the master craftspeople of teaching? Perhaps for the time being, the problem will have to be solved through what it in theatre is called 'multiple casting': a team of experts – in performance, in interpersonal relations, in professional ethics and wellness, and

---

5   An exercise I often like to do on the first day of a new course is one I call 'Archeologists From the Future': we all exit the classroom, and I have the students imagine that we are a team of archeologists from the year 3100. I tell them we have stumbled upon an extraordinary archeological site: an ancient structure from the early 21st Century, fully intact, whose purpose we do not know. Then I open the classroom door and together we enter, taking note of everything we see. We discuss our observations and propose theories as to what the room was used for and by whom. The theories have been remarkably consistent over the years: whether the students think the room was used for religious rites of some kind (human sacrifice?) or political indoctrination, the theme of authority is always clear.

in education research. But however immodest the proposal, the hope is real that one day we may have mentors leading our Teaching Labs who fully embody the craft of teaching in all of its aspects, since this is ultimately what each individual teacher must strive to do.

References

Bachelard, Gaston (1969): *The Poetics of Space*, trans. Maria Jolas. Boston: Beacon Press.

Cook-Sather, Alison (2006): Newly Betwixt and Between: Revising Liminality in the Context of a Teacher Preparation Program. In *Anthropology & Education Quarterly* 37/2, 110-127.

Crutchfield, John & Schewe, Manfred (eds.) (2017): *Going Performative in Intercultural Education: International Contexts, Theoretical Perspectives and Models of Practice*. Bristol: Multilingual Matters.

Dawe, Harry (1984): Teaching: A Performing Art. In *The Phi Delta Kappan* 65/8, 548-552.

Eliade, Mircea (1958): *Rites and Symbols of Initiation: The Mysteries of Birth and Rebirth*, trans. Willard Trask. New York: Harper.

Fischer-Lichte, Erika (2004): *Ästhetik des Performativen*. Frankfurt a. M.: Suhrkamp Verlag.

Hallet, Wolfgang (2010): Performative Kompetenz und Fremdsprachenunterricht. In *Scenario* IV/1, 5-14.

Koolhaas, Rem (2002): Junkspace, *October* 100, 175-190.

Rimbaud, Arthur (1871): *Lettre à Georges Izambard du 13 Mai 1871*, www.abardel.free.fr, last accessed: 02/05/2017.

Schewe, Manfred (1993): *Fremdsprache inszenieren: Zur Fundierung einer Dramapädagogischen Lehr- und Lernpraxis*. Oldenburg: Pädagogisches Zentrum.

Schewe, Manfred (2011): Die Welt auch im fremdsprachlichen Unterricht immer wieder neu verzaubern – Plädoyer für eine performative Lehr- und Lernkultur! In Almut Küppers, Torben Schmidt & Maik Walter (eds.): *Inszenierungen im Fremdsprachenunterricht: Grundlagen, Formen, Perspektiven*. Braunschweig: Schroedel/Diesterweg/Klinkhardt, 20-31.

Sennett, Richard (2008): *The Craftsman*. London: Penguin Books.

Turner, Victor (1987): Betwixt and Between: The Liminal Period in Rites of Passage. In Louise CarusMahdi, Steven Foster & Meredith Little (eds.): *Betwixt and Between: Patterns of Masculine and Feminine Initiation*. La Salle: Open Court, 3-19.

van Gennep, Arnold (1909/2004): *The Rites of Passage*, trans. Monika Vizedom and Gabrielle Caffee. London: Routledge.

Performative Fremdsprachendidaktik als Leitprinzip des Fremdsprachenlernens?

Dietmar Rösler

Zu den Merkmalen, die dem wissenschaftlichen Diskurs im deutschsprachigen Raum zugeschrieben werden[1], gehört, dass er eristisch sei (vgl. Ehlich 1993). Man soll sich streiten. Zu den Konventionen einer Festschrift scheint zu gehören, dass man sich mit dem zu feiernden Jubilar nicht streitet, zumindest nicht allzu sehr. Was tun? Man kann ohnehin nicht bestreiten, dass mit Schewe (1993) ein Text die fremdsprachendidaktische Bühne betreten hat, der als inzwischen kanonischer Text die Diskussion um das Fremdsprachenlernen nicht nur für das Fach Deutsch als Fremdsprache bereichert hat. Auf dieser Ebene kann es im Folgenden also keinen Beitrag zur deutschen Streitkultur geben.

Womit man sich aber schon kritisch auseinandersetzen kann, ist das, was ein Vierteljahrhundert nach Schewe (1993) in Fortbildungen und akademischen Publikationen so alles unter Dramapädagogik verstanden wird. So wird sich der erste Teil dieses Beitrags mit der Frage befassen, wie sinnvoll es ist, wenn Dramapädagogik auf dem wissenschaftlichen Markt als (neue) Methode angepriesen wird. Der zweite Teil wird diese generelle Frage nach der Dramapädagogik als den gesamten Lernprozess umfassende Methode dann im Hinblick auf einen Teilaspekt, auf die Lernenden als Handelnde konkretisieren, eingeleitet mit der flapsig formulierten Frage ‚Wer bin ich als Lerner und wie viele?'.

---

1   Die amüsanteste Beschreibung von ‚kulturgeprägten' Wissenschaftstraditionen findet sich immer noch in Galtung (1985). Der teutonische Stil wird dort als sehr stark in der Theoriebildung und stark in der Paradigmenanalyse charakterisiert, der sachsonische in diesen beiden Bereichen hingegen als schwach. Dieser fördere jedoch Debatte und Diskurs (vgl. ibid. 157), während sich beim teutonischen Stil niemand von seinem Wege abbringen lasse oder unnötige Höflichkeit walten ließe (vgl. ibid. 158). Diese klaren Zuordnungen bringen mich in eine Zwickmühle: Wie schreibt jemand, der im Teutonenland akademisch sozialisiert wurde, aber einen nicht unbeträchtlichen Teil seiner akademischen Berufstätigkeit in Irland und England verbracht hat, einen Festschriftbeitrag für jemanden, der in Deutschland schon eine höchst ‚unteutonische' Dissertation verfasst hatte und seine Zeit als Hochschullehrer dann in einem Land des sachsonischen Stils verbracht hat? Und natürlich eigentlich noch tiefergehend stellt sich bei mir die Frage: Darf man als Ostfriesenkind überhaupt zu einem Jubelband für jemanden beitragen, der in Oldenburg promoviert hat?

Dramapädagogik im Alltag: eine (alternative) Methode?

Dramapädagogik ist eine Methode. Zumindest wenn man einem der freien Formate der IDT 2017 in Fribourg folgt: „Neue Impulse für den Fremdsprachenunterricht – Niederschwellige Zugänge zur dramapädagogischen Methode" ist das freie Format 3 überschrieben und im Ankündigungstext liest man „gerade für literaturdidaktische und interkulturelle Themen, aber auch z. B. für Grammatik bietet diese Methode großes Potenzial".

Im Vorwort zu Tselikas 1999 – Paratexte sind als Quelle für die einem Text zugrunde liegenden Intentionen zumeist besonders ergiebig – findet man den Satz: „[...] möchte ich [.] danken, der sich, als ich *diesen Ansatz und die Methode* zu entwickeln begann [...]" (Tselikas 1999: 12 f., Herv. D.R.). Zum einen wird hier die Dramapädagogik also dem Bereich Ansätze und Methoden zugeordnet, zum anderen müsste man die koordinierende Konjunktion *und* wohl so interpretieren, dass hier jemand einen Ansatz UND eine Methode entwickelt hat. Das ist für das Jahr 1999 erstaunlich[2], denn seit den 1970er Jahren hatte sich ja in der allgemeinen Methodendiskussion der Terminus *Ansatz* als Referenz auf ein kommunikativ oder interkulturell geprägtes Vorgehen etabliert, als Gegenbegriff zu den als weniger offen gesehenen audiolingualen, direkten oder grammatikorientierten Vorgehensweisen der Vorgängeransätze, die als Methoden bezeichnet wurden.

Indikatoren dafür, dass man diese Dramapädagogik in den Topf mit alternativen Methoden werfen könnte[3], sind in diesem Buch programmatische Sätze wie:

---

2 Erstaunlich ist auch, dass hier ein Buch mit dem Erscheinungsjahr 1999 die Entwicklung eines Ansatzes für sich reklamiert, ohne in der Arbeit, die ja ein Literaturverzeichnis und Endnoten mit Literaturangaben enthält und zumindest behauptet, dass im ersten Kapitel theoretische Hintergründe behandelt werden (vgl. ibid. 14), die für den deutschsprachigen Raum grundlegende Aufarbeitung der dramapädagogischen Tradition und Fundierung eines dramapädagogischen Herangehens an den Fremdsprachenunterricht von Schewe (1993) zu erwähnen.

3 Es gibt also durchaus gute Gründe dafür, Spielarten der Dramapädagogik zu den alternativen Methoden zu rechnen, und je nach Differenziertheit der eigenen Argumentation auch gute Gründe, diese Zuordnung zurückzuweisen: „Während dramapädagogische Konzepte in manchen Veröffentlichungen (z. B. Ortner 1998) den 'alternativen Methoden' zugeordnet werden, wird ihnen in dem Sammelband *Pädagogische Konzepte für einen ganzheitlichen DaF-Unterricht* (Schlemminger, Brysch & Schewe 2000) ein klarer Platz als eigenständige Konzepte innerhalb des sprachdidaktischen Fachdiskurses eingeräumt" (Schewe 2007: 148). Even (2003: 52) hält die Zuordnung der Dramapädagogik zu den alternativen Methoden durch Ortner nicht für zutreffend, da diese auf „Methodenvorschläge abzielt, die sich in Abgrenzung zu konventionellen Ansätzen konstituieren, was bei der „expliziten kommunikativen Verankerung" (ibid.) der Dramapädagogik nicht gegeben sei.

„Das vorliegende Buch schlägt neue Wege im Bereich der Sprachvermittlung ein. Es begreift das Sprachlernen als einen umfassenden und mehrdimensionalen Lernprozess, der im Rahmen eines bestimmten sozialen und kulturellen Milieus stattfindet." (ibid. 15)

Dass Sprachenlernen sozial und kulturell kontextualisiert ist und ein komplexes Phänomen[4] darstellt, gehört zum Hintergrundwissen jeder wissenschaftlichen Herangehensweise an das Fremdsprachenlernen. Postuliert man dieses als eigenen neuen Beitrag, führt man eine für alternative Methoden typische Operation durch: Ein manchmal vernachlässigter, oft sehr wichtiger Aspekt des Fremdsprachenlernens wird (wieder) entdeckt und zum Ausgangspunkt einer eigenen Methode gemacht, die nun wiederum die Komplexität des Lernprozesses, und, aufgrund des Drangs, sich als Innovation darzustellen, auch vorhandene Erkenntnisse ignoriert.

Die häufig wiederkehrende Betonung der Bedeutung der Dramapädagogik für den gesamten Lernprozess ist verständlich, wenn man sich vor Augen führt, wie man sie missverstanden hat als Auflockerung des Unterrichts nach getaner harter Spracharbeit[5], wie sie sich von den Rollenspielen des frühen kommunikativen Ansatzes abgrenzen[6] oder als Basis der Kritik an den klassischen *conversation classes* der englischen und irischen Universitäten dienen musste[7] und, wie man auch immer wieder feststellen musste, dass Dramapädagogik etwas anderes ist als die Aufführung eines Schultheaterstücks, so sinnvoll und interessant diese auch sein kann.

---

4   Die Komplexität des Fremdsprachenlernens als Herausforderung für die Forschung gehört ja seit den 1970er Jahren zu den ‚Gründungsmythen' der sich in Abgrenzung zu Linguistik und Psychologie konstituierenden Sprachlehrforschung (vgl. Koordinierungsgremium im DFG-Projekt Sprachlehrforschung 1977).

5   In meinem schulischen Englischunterricht in den frühen 1960er Jahren ‚durften' wir – freiwillig und außerhalb des normalen Stundenplans – ab und an einmal den Einführungstext einer Lektion aufführen, aber natürlich erst, nachdem im ‚ordentlichen' Unterricht der Wortschatz und die grammatischen Phänomene, die in der Lektion eingeführt wurden, abgearbeitet waren.

6   „Fortgeschrittene DaF-Lerner an Universitäten fühlen sich von solchen reinen sprachfunktionalen Rollenspielen in der Regel unterfordert. Für sie müssen m.E. anspruchsvollere szenische Verfahren entwickelt werden, die mehr Raum lassen für individuelle und gemeinsame kreative Ausgestaltung" (Schewe 1988: 431).

7   „Abgesehen von einzelnen Sternstunden gerät er [der Konversationsunterricht – DR] in der Regel zum künstlichen Sprechduell, wobei der Lektor als Sekundant fungiert, indem er in Form fotokopierter Blätter argumentative Munition vom Kaliber landeskundlicher und literarischer Inhalt nachschiebt. Die meisten Konversationsstunden kranken daran, daß die Studenten sich persönlich nicht betroffen fühlen. Es mangelt an bedeutungsvoller Interaktion im entsinnlichten Unterrichtsraum" (Schewe 1988: 430).

Diese Marginalisierung zu kritisieren und herauszuarbeiten, für welche Lerngegenstände, Zielgruppen usw. dramapädagogische Herangehensweisen produktiv sind, ist aber etwas anderes, als einfach als Gegenposition zu postulieren, der gesamte Fremdsprachenunterricht müsse dramapädagogisch gestaltet sein. Und dies ist wiederum etwas anderes als ein Anerkennen der Tatsache, dass Menschen in ihren sozialen Interaktionen sich permanent inszenieren. Dies ist richtig, es gilt aber unabhängig davon, ob Interaktionen im Klassenzimmer dramapädagogisch ausgerichtet sind oder nicht.

Die Methodenfrage in den Arbeiten von Even und Schewe

Schaut man sich die Arbeiten der Schlüsselautoren Susanne Even und Manfred Schewe selbst an, stellt man im Hinblick auf die Methodenfrage unterschiedliche Nuancen fest. In Even (2003), dem gelungenen Versuch, Dramapädagogik mit dem fremdsprachendidaktischen Kernthema Grammatikvermittlung, also einem im kommunikativen Ansatz nicht unproblematischen Gegenstand, zu verbinden, ist die Rede von einem „ganzheitlich, dramapädagogisch *orientierten* Grammatikunterricht" (ibid. 51, Herv. D.R.), aber auch von einem „dramapädagogische[n] Lehr- und Lernansatz" (ibid. 53). Even (2011) stellt zunächst einmal fest, dass die Entwicklung der Dramapädagogik zu einer Zeit erfolgte, als der Methodendiskussion „eigentlich schon der Garaus gemacht worden war" (ibid. 39). Für den von ihr vorgestellten performativen Grammatikunterricht gelte deshalb, dass es kein methodisches *one size fits all* geben dürfe, stattdessen „setzen Lehrende dramagrammatische Unterrichtsentwürfe unter Berücksichtigung der jeweiligen Unterrichtsbedingungen vor Ort ein" (ibid. 40).

Mit Bezug auf sein Sternemodell spricht Schewe (1993) von „einem dramapädagogischen Fremdsprachenunterricht, in dem Lernsituationen geschaffen werden mit Methoden, die sich aus der Dramapädagogik ableiten lassen" (Schewe 1993: 3), und eine Seite später von "Methoden, sie [sic!] sich aus dramatischen Kunstformen ableiten lassen" (ibid. 4). Hier ist also nicht von der Methode Dramapädagogik die Rede, sondern von Methoden im Sinne von auf konkrete Situationen bezogenen methodischen Vorgehensweisen, die sich aus dem Konzept eines dramapädagogischen Fremdsprachenunterrichts entwickeln lassen.

Gut 20 Jahre später[8] ist die Wortwahl weniger eindeutig. In einem Artikel, der auf Fischer-Lichtes (2004) *Ästhetik des Performativen* aufbaut, ist die Rede von

---

8   Wie stark die Dramapädagogik inzwischen vom ‚Mainstream' integriert wurde, ist
    schwer zu sagen. Man könne immerhin, so Küppers, Schmidt & Walter (2011), feststellen,
    „dass ausgewählte Übungsformen aus dem Bereich der Bühne und des Theaters, z. B. das
    Standbild oder der bekannte *Hot Seat*, das Methodenspektrum des traditionellen Fremd-

einer zu entwickelnden performativen Fremdsprachendidaktik (Schewe 2011: 22), einem Begriff, parallel gebildet zu kommunikativer Fremdsprachendidaktik, also einem Begriff aus der Diskussion um globale Ansätze mit ihren Ansprüchen, das Fremdsprachenlernen insgesamt zu umfassen. Einen umfassenden Zugriff kann man auch aus diesem Artikel herauslesen:

> Inwiefern ist es möglich, Fremdsprachenunterricht so zu gestalten, dass er [...] ‚ereignishaft' wird und Faktoren wie Körperlichkeit, Lautlichkeit, Atmosphäre, Zirkulation von Energie, Erzeugung von Bedeutung stark akzentuiert? Denn es ist wohl davon auszugehen, dass fremdsprachlicher Unterricht vielerorts nach wie vor stark werkbezogen aufläuft, in dem die Lehrperson darauf fixiert ist, im Laufe des Unterrichts einem literarischen Werk bzw. einem Lehrwerk gerecht zu werden. Was würde sich aber im Unterricht ereignen können, wenn er weniger ‚werkgetreu' abliefe und mehr imaginativen Spielraum ließe? Was wäre gar, wenn temporär keine Lehrwerke oder sonstige Materialien zur Verfügung ständen, sondern im Fremdsprachenunterricht *ausschließlich* mittels der Imagination und der durch sie ausgelösten Tätigkeiten sprachliche und nicht sprachliche Bedeutung erzeugt würde? (Schewe 2011: 28 f., Herv. D.R.).

Stärker ist diese Tendenz zum umfassenden Zugriff, der m. E. auch durch den terminologischen Wandel von *Dramapädagogik* zu *performativer Fremdsprachendidaktik* signalisiert wird, noch in Schewe 2015. Dort ist zwar zunächst davon die Rede, dass die Dramapädagogik in den letzten zwei bis drei Jahrzehnten „zu einer wichtigen Bezugsdisziplin für die Fremdsprachendidaktik avanciert" (ibid. 31) ist, einige Absätze später heißt es jedoch:

> Einer performativen Fremdsprachendidaktik geht es um eine *neue* Lehr- und Lernkultur, in der Formen ästhetischen Ausdrucks ein *zentraler* Stellenwert eingeräumt wird (ibid., Herv. D.R.).

Man kann natürlich sagen, es sei doch egal, ob hier von Methoden oder Ansätzen oder Konzepten die Rede sei. Wichtig sei doch, was an Bereicherung für die Praxis des Fremdsprachenlernens entstanden ist. Letzteres ist zweifelsohne richtig, doch sollte man die hegemoniale Kraft, die in der Festlegung einer bestimmten Vorgehensweise als globale Methode/Ansatz mit umfassendem Anspruch liegt, nicht unterschätzen (vgl. Rösler 2012a: 65-67). Die Diskussion um die globalen Methoden, egal ob direkt, audiolingual, kommunikativ oder interkulturell, enthält nicht nur eine Dimension des Alleinvertretungsanspruchs

---

sprachenunterrichts mittlerweile erweitert haben und sogar als einzelne Aufgabenvorschläge in einigen Textbüchern der neuesten Lehrwerkgeneration zu finden sind" (ibid. 8).

und eine meist damit einhergehende Überschätzung der Reichweite der in der jeweiligen Methode propagierten Aktivitäten, sie führt auch in die Versuchung, bestimmte Fragen nicht mehr zuzulassen und alternative Konzepte als nicht dem eigenen Lager zugehörig zu ignorieren. Es wäre schade, wenn auch die performative Fremdsprachendidaktik Teil der Sloganisierung fremdsprachendidaktischer Konzepte würde (vgl. Rösler 2019b) und es wäre noch ‚schader‘, wenn die Wirkmächtigkeit des wunderschönen Konzepts der Inszenierung den Blick auf die Vielfalt des Fremdsprachenlernens und des Repertoires von im Unterricht zur Verfügung stehenden Interventionsmöglichkeiten zur Unterstützung des Fremdsprachenerwerbs trüben würde.

Wer bin ich als Lerner und wie viele?

Gegen das dramatische Defizit der Übungsformen in Lehrwerken hatte Schewe (1993) das Postulat der bewussten Inszenierung fremdsprachlicher Lernprozesse gesetzt, gegen die unvorbereiteten szenischen Improvisationen von in Lehrwerken nur oberflächlich angelegten Rollenspielen die vorbereitete szenische Improvisation. Mit der Unterscheidung von außerschulischer Alltagsrealität und der Realität der dramatischen Inszenierung im Klassenzimmer[9] unterscheidet sich die Dramapädagogik von einer anderen, auch über einfache Rollenspiele hinausgehende und den Fremdsprachenlernenden komplexere kommunikative Situationen anbietende, sich ebenfalls der Ganzheitlichkeit verpflichtet fühlenden Vorgehensweise, der besonders in der Didaktik der romanischen Sprachen beheimateten globalen Simulation (vgl. Sippel 2003), wo angenommen wird, dass fiktive Identitäten konstruiert werden können, „die es den Mitspielenden jeweils erlauben, während des Spiels in eine neue Haut zu schlüpfen" (ibid. 27)[10].

Auf diese kann hier[11] nicht weiter eingegangen werden, es lohnt sich jedoch, die bei diesen beiden Vorgehensweisen unterschiedlich angelegten, leitenden

---

9 „In der Schule wie auf der Theaterbühne dient die Inszenierung dazu, Themen, Inhalte, Konflikte oder Sachverhalte aus dem ursprünglichen (Lebens-)Kontext herauszulösen, mitunter durch Kunstgriffe zu akzentuieren und zu verdichten, um sie einer bewussten Reflexion zugänglich zu machen" (Bonnet & Küppers 2011: 34).

10 Die dabei entstehende ‚doppelte Identität‘ erlaube es den Lernenden, zitiert Sippel (2003: 27) die französischen Autoren Alonso und Roig, „die Fixierung auf die eigene soziale Rolle zu überwinden und sich selbst als Sprecher und Einheimischer einer anderen Kultur zu erfahren".

11 „Die globale Simulation hat also im Gegensatz zu den klassischen Rollenspielen einen weitergehenden Anspruch an die Lernenden im Hinblick auf ihr Selbst-Bewusstsein. So interessant an diesem Ansatz das kommunikativ-spielerische Element ist, so problematisch ist die, verglichen mit dramapädagogischen Vorgehensweisen der Inszenierung, doch recht naive Vorstellung, ich sei eine andere Person, wenn ich diese in einem fremd-

Vorstellungen von der ‚Identität' der Lernenden im Klassenzimmer und deren Repräsentation im Lehrmaterial zu diskutieren im Hinblick auf die Frage, wie sie deren unterschiedliche Dimensionen aufnehmen. In Rösler 2012b und 2013 bin ich ausführlich auf die unterschiedlichen Vorkommensweisen von ‚ich' in Unterricht und Lehrmaterial eingegangen. Grob zusammengefasst kann man prototypisch unterscheiden zwischen:

- Trotz eines ‚Ich' in einer Übung ist jedem Beteiligten klar, dass die Lernenden nicht als sie selbst angesprochen werden. Das geschieht z.b. in eindeutig formfokussierten, weitgehend kontextfreien Übungen.
- Der Lernende spricht oder schreibt eindeutig als eine andere Person. Das kann bei der formfokussierten Übung auch auf der Niveaustufe A bereits durch den Einsatz von einfachen Inquit-Formeln erreicht werden, prominenter in der Diskussion sind in der handlungs- und produktionsorientierten Literaturdidaktik[12] beschriebene Aktivitäten zum Perspektivenwechsel von stärker fortgeschrittenen Lernenden.
- Der Lernende spricht als er selbst. Das geschieht beim selbstinitiierten Reden über das eigene Lernen oder über Glück und Probleme außerhalb des Klassenzimmers. Das geschieht auch innerhalb der Szenariendidaktik, wenn ein eingeführtes Thema eines ist, zu dem der Lernende eine starke ethisch oder politisch motivierte Position vertritt und aus dem spielerischen Vertreten einer Position das engagierte Plädoyer wird.

Das ‚Ich' im kontextlosen Üben hat es seit der kommunikativen Wende schwer, von Fremdsprachendidaktikern überhaupt noch ernst genommen zu werden[13]. Die beiden anderen ‚Ichs' bestimmen die Diskussion: Je stärker [a] es die Lernenden schaffen, etwas zu sagen, was sie mitteilen möchten, und [b] nicht lediglich etwas aussprechen, was das Lehrwerk ihnen vorschreibt, desto besser ist dies sowohl für ihre Lernmotivation als auch für den Erwerb der verwendeten sprachlichen Phänomene. Die klare Trennung zwischen den beiden letztgenannten ‚Ichs' ist auf der Ebene der Prototypik sinnvoll, obwohl Überschneidungen stattfinden. Wenn z.b. in einer Aufgabe eine fiktionale Person schreiben

---

sprachlichen Klassenzimmer oder einem extra für die Simulation gebauten Ort spiele (Rösler 2012b: 104).

12 Dass die Ich-Perspektive in fiktionalisierter Form sich auch sehr gut im Bereich der Grammatikvermittlung einsetzen lässt, zeigt z.b. Schmenk (2011) am Beispiel der Vermittlung von Passivkonstruktionen: Einem traditionell beschreibenden Text über einen Koch, der einen Fisch gekauft hat und ihn zubereitet, wird ein Text aus der Perspektive des Fisches entgegengesetzt.

13 Dass dies nicht nur ein Fortschritt ist, habe ich in Rösler (2019a) zu zeigen versucht.

soll, wird das real schreibende Individuum trotzdem durch die getroffene Auswahl, durch Positionen, die verstärkt oder abgeschwächt werden, usw. sichtbar.
Dramapädagogisch wird durch die Trennung von Aktivitäten in der ästhetischen Realität im Klassenzimmer und der Welt draußen gewährleistet, dass
das Mitteilen im So-tun-als-ob bleibt, die Schutzfunktion des Klassenzimmers
bleibt erhalten. Die Transzendenz des Klassenzimmers fördernde Aktivitäten
versuchen hingegen, das beim Fremdsprachenlernen in Bildungsinstitutionen
nicht hintergehbare So-tun-als-ob so weitgehend wie möglich zugunsten einer
‚authentischen' Kommunikation zurückzudrängen[14]. Dies kann zu unerwünsch-
ten Nebenwirkungen führen:

> Ein auf Mitteilungen aus seiner Perspektive verpflichteter Lernender möchte der
> Gruppe [...] bestimmte Dinge über sich vielleicht gar nicht mitteilen, aber aufgrund
> des Sprachnotstandes [...] gelingt es ihm nicht, sich kommunikativ angemessen ‚her-
> auszureden', sodass er mehr über sich preisgibt, als er es in einer vergleichbaren Situ-
> ation in seiner Erstsprache getan hätte. Es könnte auch sein, dass das, was er mitteilen
> möchte, mit einer derart emotionalen Intensität behaftet ist, dass das Reden darüber
> den relativ unverbindlichen interpersonellen Rahmen des Klassenzimmers sprengen
> würde. [...] Hier besteht also die Gefahr, dass der kommunikative Zwang, über sich
> selbst reden zu müssen, dazu führt, dass Lernende lieber schweigen und auch nicht
> den Ausweg wählen, einfach eine Biografie zu erfinden, weil ihnen das Thema zu ernst
> ist. Je stärker also im Fremdsprachenunterricht versucht wird, Lernende als sich selbst
> reden zu lassen, desto wichtiger ist es, dass Sätze der Art ‚Darüber möchte ich nichts
> sagen' den Lernenden früh als sprachliche Elemente zur Verfügung stehen und dass
> vor allen Dingen auch tatsächlich respektiert wird, dass sie sich zu einer bestimmten
> Thematik nicht äußern möchten (Rösler 2012b: 102 f.).

Dramapädagogik und die Maximierung echter Kommunikation

Aufgabenorientierung, Projektdidaktik und Dramapädagogik sind innerhalb des
großen Rahmens der kommunikativen Orientierung die wichtigsten Versuche,
die Fremdsprachenlernenden dazu zu bringen, so früh, so intensiv und so selbstbestimmt wie möglich zu kommunizieren. Sie sind die Herangehensweisen,
die am stärksten versuchen, das im Klassenzimmer unvermeidliche So-tun-
als-ob ‚echter' Kommunikation anzunähern, die einen dadurch, dass sie über
das Klassenzimmer hinausgehen wollen, die anderen dadurch, dass sie einen
ästhetischen Rahmen schaffen, in dem nicht-triviale Kommunikation auch bei

---

14 Zur Einschätzung der und Kritik am Status von Authentizität in der kommunikativen
    Didaktik vgl. Rösler (2012a: 37-40).

nicht-fortgeschrittenen Lernenden möglich wird und in dem selbst den in der kommunikativen Didaktik ‚ungeliebten Kindern' Grammatikvermittlung[15] und der Ausspracheschulung[16] originelle Erwerbssituationen geboten werden. Durch die Digitalisierung und die damit einhergehende Gamifizierung besteht im 21. Jahrhundert die Möglichkeit, sowohl die inszenierenden Aspekte des Fremdsprachenlernens als auch eine noch weitergehende Annäherung der klassenzimmerorientierten Kommunikation an ‚echte' Kommunikation voranzutreiben (vgl. Rösler 2000, Schmidt 2011). Diskutiert wird darüber hinaus, inwieweit die Dominanz des Klassenzimmers aufgebrochen werden kann durch eine Umorientierung, die das Klassenzimmer als Ort institutioneller Unterstützung beim Umgang mit medial lebensweltlich gemachten Spracherfahrungen und Sprachnotständen begreift[17]. Eine performative Fremdsprachendidaktik, die in ihrem Selbstverständnis das Gesamt des Fremdsprachenlernens anleitet, stünde einer derartigen Entwicklung eventuell entgegen, weil sie durch ihre Rahmungsvorgaben diese Überschreitungen des So-tun-als-ob nicht fördern oder sogar behindern würde. Eine performative Fremdsprachendidaktik, die sich als eine wichtiger Spielerin im großen Konzert der Möglichkeiten sieht, das Lernen in Bildungsinstitutionen soweit wie möglich durch kreative und inhaltlich selbstbestimmte Äußerungen der Lernenden zu bereichern, wäre eine wichtige Unterstützerin dieser Entwicklung.

---

15 Wie stark die Lernenden engagierend eine dramapädagogische Herangehensweise an eine unter Langeweile-Verdacht stehende Aufgabe wie das Üben von lokalen Präpositionen ist, zeigt die 12minütige Videodokumentation von Baliuk et al (2018).

16 „Indem dramapädagogischer Fremdsprachenunterricht der Arbeit an der Ausdrucksform einen hohen Stellenwert einräumt, kommt der Übung der Aussprache eine größere Wichtigkeit bei als in einer Methodik, die durch ihre Fokussierung auf Alltagssituationen nicht-alltägliche, ästhetische Formen fremdsprachlicher Erfahrung eher ausblendet" (Schewe 1993: 175; Herv. i. O.).

17 „Wenn Menschen unabhängig davon, wie viele Flugstunden sie von einem Ort, an dem die Zielsprache gesprochen wird, entfernt sind, nun viel mehr als früher medial in dieser Sprache kommunizieren können, dann könnten sie auch viel früher und viel intensiver nicht nur Sprachlerner, sondern auch inhaltlich selbstbestimmte Sprachnutzer sein. Und dann ließe sich viel früher und viel intensiver als bisher das Sprachenlernen mit Inhalten, die die konkreten Lernenden tatsächlich interessieren und mit sprachlichen Handlungen, die sie tatsächlich ausführen möchten, verbinden. Es ist also eine Entwicklung des Fremdsprachenlernens vorstellbar, das konsequent von Kommunikationsabsichten und inhaltlichen Lernerinteressen ausgeht" (Rösler 2019a: 118 f.).

Literatur

Baliuk, Natalia; Buda, Filippa; Rösler, Dietmar & Würffel, Nicola (2018): Einführung Dramapädagogik. In DAAD (Hg): *Dhoch3 Studienmodule Deutsch als Fremdsprache.* Online unter: moodle.daad.de, eingesehen am 24.04.18.

Bonnet, Andreas & Küppers, Almut (2011): Wozu taugen kooperatives Lernen und Dramapädagogik? Vergleich zweier populärer Inszenierungsformen. In Almut Küppers et al. (Hg.), 32-52.

Ehlich, Konrad (1993): Deutsch als fremde Wissenschaftssprache. In *Jahrbuch Deutsch als Fremdsprache* 19, 13-42.

Even, Susanne (2003): *Drama Grammatik: dramapädagogische Ansätze für den Grammatikunterricht Deutsch als Fremdsprache.* München: iudicium.

Even, Susanne (2011): Mit Vergnügen und Verstand. Performative Grammatik Deutsch als Fremdsprache. In Barbara Schmenk et al. (Hg.), 37-47.

Fischer-Lichte, Erika (2004): *Ästhetik des Performativen.* Frankfurt: Suhrkamp.

Galtung, Johan (1985): Struktur, Kultur und interkultureller Stil. Ein vergleichender Essay über sachsonische, teutonische, gallische und nipponische Wissenschaft. In Alois Wierlacher (Hg.): *Das Fremde und das Eigene: Prolegomena zu einer interkulturellen Germanistik.* München: Iudicium, 151-196.

Koordinierungsgremium im DFG-Projekt Sprachlehrforschung (1977): *Sprachlehr- und Sprachlernforschung.* Kronberg: Scriptor.

Küppers, Almut; Schmidt, Torben & Walter, Maik (Hg.) (2011): *Inszenierungen im Fremdsprachenunterricht: Grundlagen, Formen, Perspektiven.* Braunschweig: Schroedel/Diesterweg/Klinkhardt.

Ortner, Brigitte (1998): *Alternative Methoden im Fremdsprachenunterricht: lerntheoretischer Hintergrund und praktische Umsetzung.* Ismaning: Hueber.

Rösler, Dietmar (2000): Fremdsprachenlernen außerhalb des zielsprachigen Raums per virtueller Realität. In Gerd Fritz & Andreas Jucker (Hg.): *Kommunikationsformen im Wandel der Zeit.* Tübingen: Narr, 121-135.

Rösler, Dietmar (2012a): *Deutsch als Fremdsprache. Eine Einführung.* Stuttgart: Metzler.

Rösler, Dietmar (2012b): So echt wie möglich und/oder so tun als ob? Aufgaben im Kontext sich verändernder Privatheitskonzepte. In Katrin Biebighäuser, Marja Zibelius & Torben Schmidt (Hg.): *Aufgaben 2.0 – Konzepte, Materialien und Methoden für das Fremdsprachenlehren und -lernen mit digitalen Medien.* Tübingen: Narr, 93-118.

Rösler, Dietmar (2013): Große Fragen, kleine Antwort: „Ich[1]", „Ich[2]" „Ich[3]" und „Ich[4]" in Lehrmaterialien und Methoden. In Eva Burwitz-Melzer, Frank G. Königs, & Claudia Riemer (Hg): *Identität und Fremdsprachenlernen. Anmerkungen zu einer komplexen Beziehung.* Tübingen: Narr, 247-255.

Rösler, Dietmar (2019a): Grammatik, Kommunikation, Inhalt – Freunde, nicht Gegner. In Elisabeth Peyer, Thomas Studer & Ingo Thonhauser (Hg.): *IDT Tagungsband Teil 1: Vorträge/Ko-Vorträge.* Berlin: ESV.

Rösler, Dietmar (2019b): The only turn worth watching in the 20th century is Tina Turner's. How the sloganization of foreign language research can impede the furthering of knowledge and make life difficult for practitioners. In Barbara Schmenk, Stephan Breidbach & Lutz Küster (Hg.): *Sloganization in Language Education Discourse. Conceptual Thinking in the Age of Academic Marketization.* Bristol: Multilingual Matters, 42-56.

Schewe, Manfred (1988): Fokus Lehrpraxis: Für einen integrierten, dramapädagogischen Deutsch als Fremdsprache-Unterricht für Fortgeschrittene. In *Info DaF* 4, 429-441.

Schewe, Manfred (1993): *Fremdsprache inszenieren: zur Fundierung einer dramapädagogischen Lehr- und Lernpraxis.* Oldenburg: Pädagogisches Zentrum.

Schewe, Manfred (2007): Drama und Theater in der Fremd- und Zweitsprachenlehre. Blick zurück nach vorn. In *Scenario* I/1, 142-153.

Schewe, Manfred (2011): Die Welt auch im fremdsprachlichen Unterricht immer neu verzaubern – Plädoyer für eine performative Lehr- und Lernkultur! In Almut Küppers et al. (Hg.), 20-31.

Schewe, Manfred (2015): Fokus Fachgeschichte: Die Dramapädagogik als Wegbereiterin einer performativen Fremdsprachendidaktik. In Wolfgang Hallet & Carola Surkamp (Hg.): *Handbuch Dramendidaktik und Dramapädagogik im Fremdsprachenunterricht.* Trier: WVT, 21-36.

Schmenk, Barbara (2011): Grammatik ganz autonom? Werch ein Illtum. In Barbara Schmenk et al. (Hg.), 97-110.

Schmenk, Barbara & Würffel, Nicola (2011) (Hg.): *Drei Schritte vor und manchmal auch sechs zurück.Internationale Perspektive auf Entwicklungslinien im Bereich Deutsch als Fremdsprache. Festschrift für Dietmar Rösler zum 60. Geburtstag.* Tübingen: Narr.

Schmidt, Torben (2011): ‚So tun als ob' 2.0. – Computergestützte Projektarbeit und die ‚Entkünstlichung' des Fremdsprachenlernens. In Barbara Schmenk et al. (Hg.), 315-324.

Sippel, Vera Alexandra (2003): *Ganzheitliches Lernen im Rahmen der "Simulation globale". Grundlagen – Erfahrungen – Anregungen.* Tübingen: Narr.

Tselikas, Elektra (1999): *Dramapädagogik im Sprachunterricht.* Zürich: Orell Füssli.

Doing a Manfred

Über die willkommene Unvorhersehbarkeit von Lernprozessen

Susanne Even

Performatives Lernen oder: Eine unendliche Geschichte

Die unendliche Geschichte von Michael Ende (1979) ist eine Geschichte in einer Geschichte. Der Protagonist Bastian wird Teil des Buches, das er liest, und seine Fantasie, seine Entscheidungen und sein Handeln beeinflussen, verändern und gestalten den Lauf der Ereignisse mit. Diese Erfahrungen ermöglichen es ihm am Ende, in die eigene Welt zurückzukehren und diese wiederum zu verändern. Fast jedes Kapitel der *Unendlichen Geschichte* enthält die Zeilen „... aber dies ist eine andere Geschichte und soll ein andernmal erzählt werden" – nämlich immer dann, wenn neue Wesen, Gegenden und Ereignisse erfunden werden und damit die Anfänge neuer Geschichten entstehen.

Die Reise in die performative Pädagogik ist auch eine unendliche Geschichte. Und dieses Mal heißt der Protagonist Manfred Schewe, der mit seinem Lebenswerk an der Universität Oldenburg, am University College Cork und als Begründer und Herausgeber der Zeitschrift *SCENARIO* unzählige neue Geschichten inspiriert hat. Einige dieser Geschichten sollen dieses Mal erzählt werden.

Lernen erfahren oder: Das Blockseminar in Oldenburg

Vor langer Zeit studierte ich Deutsch und Englisch auf Gymnasiallehramt an der Carl-von-Ossietzky-Universität Oldenburg. Viele Pädagogikvorlesungen fanden in großen Aulas statt, wo wir alle saßen, den Lehrenden zuhörten, uns Notizen machten, und danach fortgingen. An die Inhalte dieser Vorlesungen kann ich mich nicht mehr erinnern. Auch nicht an die meisten Seminare. Aber eines weiß ich noch; es ging um handlungsorientierten Englischunterricht. Wir lasen Bach und Timm (1989), schrieben uns für Referate ein, hörten den Referaten der Mitstudierenden zu, stellten am Schluss eventuell ein paar Diskussionsfragen und gingen dann wieder unserer Wege. Handlungsorientiert war das nicht wirklich.

Und dann nahm ich von 1993 bis 1994 an dem zweisemestrigen Blockseminar „Dramapädagogik im Fremdsprachenunterricht" teil. Zwanzig Studierende kamen ein Jahr lang einmal pro Woche für vier Stunden zusammen. Anstatt über dramapädagogischen Unterricht lediglich zu lesen und zu diskutieren, erlebten wir ihn am eigenen Leibe. Wir erschufen Inseln und ihre Bewohner*innen, wir trafen uns als Lady Jane, Frieda Kahlo und die Schwester von Shakespeare, wir gingen mit der Titanic unter. Wir handelten als fiktive Figuren und probierten unterschiedliche Kontexte aus, wir lernten Grenzen zu ziehen, und wir lernten dem nachzugehen, was wir spontan vor unseren Augen entstehen ließen. Der Prozess des kollaborativen Erschaffens war in seiner Unvorhersehbarkeit immer wieder faszinierend.

Manfred Schewe, unser Seminarleiter, gab uns weder Gebrauchsanweisungen für angehende Lehramtskandidat*innen, noch versuchte er uns die „richtige Art zu unterrichten" zu verkaufen. Stattdessen hat er uns zum Nachdenken gebracht. Und zum emotionalen Erleben. Mit nachhaltigen Effekten. Und neuen Geschichten.

Mal ganz anders sein können oder: Der Bankbeamte in Dötlingen

Eines Tages sollten wir folgende Situation improvisieren: Ein Angestellter einer Bankfiliale in einem kleinen Dorf hat einen unvorsichtigen Kredit gewährt, der geplatzt ist. Die Filialleiterin zitiert diesen Mitarbeiter nun zu sich. Im Gespräch sollte die Situation improvisiert werden. Ich war die Filialleiterin.

Zu meiner eigenen Überraschung wurde ich plötzlich zu einer rechthaberischen und unfairen Chefin und nahm meinen Angestellten nach Strich und Faden auseinander. Der arme Mensch kam kaum zu Wort; ich unterbrach ihn ständig, überhäufte ihn mit fiesen Vorwürfen, und warf ihn schließlich einfach raus.

Was war geschehen? Ich hatte zum ersten Mal die Erfahrung gemacht, jemand ganz Anderes und richtig bösartig sein zu können. Diese Dynamik war unglaublich. In der ‚richtigen Welt' hätte ich nie so gehandelt – und plötzlich war im Schutz der Fiktion eine Figur entstanden, die ich zwar selbst nicht mochte, aber die genau dahin gehörte, und *ich* hatte sie ins Leben gerufen.

Im Laufe meiner eigenen Unterrichtskarriere mache ich immer wieder ähnliche Erfahrungen: Lernende entwickeln in dramapädagogischen Situationen, in denen sie nicht als sie selbst sprechen und handeln, oft eine erstaunliche Stimme und nehmen einen solchen Moment als bedeutsam wahr; sie haben Einfluss auf den Lauf des Geschehens und erleben sich als Schöpfende von Dingen, die vorher nicht da waren.[1]

---

1   Zur Problematik von ‚Authentizität' in der kommunikativen Didaktik siehe Rösler in diesem Band.

Dinge erfinden oder: Der kleine blaue Vogel mit nur einem Flügel

Solche Erfahrungen entstehen nicht von selbst. Eine mit Dramapädagogik un-
vertraute Lerngruppe wird nicht von heute auf morgen performativ tätig; alle
neuen Herangehensweisen erfordern Zeit und Raum zum Ausprobieren. Da ist
die Lehrperson selbst gefragt. Ihre Bereitschaft, sich ebenfalls auf die Unvorhersehbarkeit performativer Lehr- und Lernsituationen einzulassen, ist gerade zu
Beginn eine zentrale Komponente.

Als ich vor mehreren Jahren das Seminar *Magical Literature* an der Indiana
University-Bloomington (USA) unterrichtete, habe ich erlebt, wie mein eigenes
Agieren eine treibende Kraft für den ganzen Kurs wurde. Wir lasen *Tintenherz*
von Cornelia Funke (2003), und ich wollte den Nebencharakter Darius auf dem
Hotseat haben. Die Studierenden waren mit Standbildern und Einfühlungsfragen bereits vertraut, aber der ‚Heiße Stuhl‘[2] war ihnen neu. Daher übernahm ich
die Figur von Darius selbst und stellte mich *in role* den Fragen der Lernenden.

Wenn Darius aus einem Buch vorliest, kann es sein, dass er Figuren aus dem
jeweiligen Buch in die ‚Realität‘ liest – eine Fähigkeit, die auch andere Charak-
tere in *Tintenherz* besitzen. Allerdings kann er es nicht besonders gut; mit den
Figuren, die er aus Büchern herausliest, stimmt immer etwas nicht: Sie hinken,
können nicht mehr sprechen oder haben seltsame Markierungen auf der Haut.
Als ich – als Darius – gefragt wurde, warum ich meine Kunst nicht mehr ausübte,
sagte ich ohne nachzudenken: „Das Letzte, was ich herbeigelesen habe, war ein
kleiner blauer Vogel, und der hatte nur einen Flügel. Danach habe ich aufgehört.“

Zwei Dinge passierten gleichzeitig. Ich musste wirklich schlucken; der kleine
blaue Vogel mit nur einem Flügel, das war ja so traurig. Zur gleichen Zeit war
da Euphorie: Der war vorher nicht da, den hab ich mir einfach so ausgedacht,
und jetzt existiert er!

Im Unterricht habe ich das nicht thematisiert, aber meine Studierenden haben
diese Dynamik eindeutig wahrgenommen. Als ich ein paar Stunden später fragte, ob jemand den Hotseat übernehmen wolle, gab es einen Andrang an Freiwil-
ligen, und *Hotseating* wurde zu einer der Lieblingsaktivitäten der Lerngruppe.

Perspektiven erkunden oder: Wollen Hänsel und Gretel wirklich nach Hause?

Im Herbstsemester 2017 unterrichtete ich den englischsprachigen Märchenkurs
Fairy Tales from Grimms to Today mit 60 Teilnehmenden und einem Doktoran-

---

2   Für *Standbilder, Einfühlungsfragen* und *Hotseating* siehe auch Even (2008, 2011a).

den als Co-Seminarleiter, der im Jahr davor an meinem Pädagogikkurs teilge-
nommen hatte und daher mit performativen Herangehensweisen ansatzweise
vertraut war.

Wir begannen mit *Hänsel und Gretel*.[3] Schnell stellte sich heraus, dass niemand das Original kannte, in dem Hänsel und Gretel in den Wald geführt werden mit der Absicht, sie dort loszuwerden. Alle waren mit der Variante groß
geworden, dass die Kinder sich im Wald verlaufen und dass die Moral darin
besteht, eben nicht fortzulaufen und brav bei den Eltern zu bleiben. Die Handlungen der Eltern im Original gaben Rätsel auf – wer macht denn sowas?

Um die Studierenden an eine tiefere Auseinandersetzung mit dem Märchen
durch Erfinden und Ausgestaltung von Details heranzuführen, ging mein Kollege Finn[4] spontan als die Hexe auf den Hotseat. Finn hatte im vorangegangenen
Jahr diese Technik im Pädagogikseminar kennengelernt, den Hotseat aber nie
selbst eingenommen. Die Studierenden waren von der Hexe hingerissen, die
gekrümmt und kurzsichtig (Finn hatte seine Brille abgenommen) vor ihnen saß
und, von ihren Fragen geleitet, die Kindheit einer Hexe entwarf, die als kleines
Mädchen merkte, dass es anders war, aus seinem Dorf verstoßen wurde und
schließlich auf eine Gemeinschaft von Kinderfresserhexen stieß.

Finn beschreibt diese Erfahrung folgendermaßen:[5]

I originally decided to slouch like an old hag and take off my glasses in order to better
assume my role as 'witch' and provide a light-hearted gesture that would cue the
students (and myself) to the fact that a break, something new, was about to happen.
It was only after the fact, however, that I realized how symbolically appropriate the
removal of my glasses was in terms of what takes place during hotseating. The students and I had become quite familiar with the tale by this point, yet this now blurry
mass of sixty-or-so faces and their impending questions felt like something distinctly
*un*familiar. Our individual observations, curiosities, and outrages with respect to the
tale had not been staked out explicitly. They were circling just below the surface
where neither I nor any other student could see them. It was out of this initial moment
that questions were thrown out, one by one: "When did you first get your taste for
human flesh?" – "Why did you decide to fatten up Hansel and not Gretel?" – "Are
you actually the wicked stepmother in disguise?" What followed was nothing short
of a cooperative dance. A failure to come up with a convincing answer was redeemed
by their persistence and creativity. Their moments of sarcasm bumped against my
cheeriness. The responsibility for what unfolded stretched across everyone present.

---

3   http://www.pitt.edu/~dash/grimm015.html, letzter Zugriff: 24.07.2018.
4   Name geändert.
5   Mein Dank geht an Finn, der diesen Text unabhängig verfasst und mir ihn als ‚Innen-
     perspektive' für diesen Beitrag zur Verfügung gestellt hat.

Through this process of asking and fielding questions we began to redraw the intersections of what is relevant, interesting, and arbitrary, defining an altogether new flavor and trajectory for the story.

Der „kooperative Tanz" wurde im *multiple hotseating*[6] fortgesetzt, in dem Studierende sich als Figuren aus dem Märchen den Fragen der anderen Teilnehmenden stellten. So entstand der Vater als gefühlvoller, aber willensschwacher Mensch, der sich seiner Frau gegenüber nicht durchsetzen kann und es nun bitter bereut, seine Kinder im Wald zurückgelassen zu haben. Er schiebt diese Entscheidung seiner Frau in die Schuhe, versucht aber gleichzeitig, diese mit dem Hinweis auf die wirtschaftliche Not zu verteidigen. Hänsel und Gretel kehren trotz allem nach Hause zurück – wohin sollten sie sonst? – und eine resolute Gretel behauptet mit Zuversicht, mit der Stiefmutter schon irgendwie klarzukommen; schließlich habe sie sich auch gegen die Hexe durchgesetzt. Bei der Stiefmutter wurde die Idee, die aus dem Hotseating mit der Hexe hervorgegangen war, in der Klassendiskussion weitergesponnen: Vielleicht *war* die Stiefmutter (die ja vor der Rückkehr der Kinder mirakulöserweise gestorben war) die Hexe, die den Mann nur genommen hatte, um an die Kinder zu kommen?

In diesem Hotseating haben die Studierenden Entscheidungen getroffen, die auf Charakteristika von Märchen aufbauen und im Folgenden immer wieder zum Thema wurden: die genretypische Auseinandersetzung von Gut und Böse sowie die Abwesenheit von heute nicht immer direkt nachvollziehbaren Sinnzusammenhängen. Die Reue des Vaters holt ihn wieder in das Lager der ‚Guten'; die Gleichsetzung von Stiefmutter und Hexe liefert einen klareren Grund für die Kindesaussetzung. Gleichzeitig wird Gretels Initiative genauer herausgearbeitet und spiegelt den Trend heutiger Märchenverfilmungen wider, Frauen und Mädchen unabhängiger und stärker darzustellen.[7]

Andere Ansichten vertreten oder: Die Konferenz der Diebe

Im gleichen Kurs beschäftigten wir uns mit dem Märchen *Der Meisterdieb*.[8] Hier ist der Protagonist ein junger Mann, der als Heranwachsender von seinen Eltern – armen Bauern – weggelaufen ist und nun als wohlhabender Mann zurückkehrt. Nicht ohne Genugtuung berichtet er, ein Dieb geworden zu sein, und zwar ein Meisterdieb. Die Eltern sind schockiert, so auch der Graf, sein Pate. Unter der Bedingung, drei Mal seine Kunst zu beweisen, darf der Meisterdieb

---

6 Für *Multiple Hotseating* siehe Even (2011b).
7 Siehe z. B. die Walt Disney-Verfilmungen *Frozen* (2013) und *Tangled* (2010).
8 https://ebooks.adelaide.edu.au/g/grimm/g86h/chapter193.html, letzter Zugriff: 24.07.2018.

unbehelligt die Gegend verlassen. Die Proben besteht der Meisterdieb natürlich auf das Allerbeste.

Das Märchen ist insofern faszinierend, als dass die Grenzen zwischen ‚Gut' und ‚Böse' nicht klar gezogen werden können – der Held ist moralisch nicht einwandfrei (aber einfallsreich und kreativ), der Graf ist trotz seiner Funktion als Taufpate (und damit mit geistlicher Macht ausgestattet) der Gegenspieler; der Held rettet niemanden und verbessert auch keine Lebensumstände – er reitet fort, nachdem er seine Kunst bewiesen hat, und lässt seine Eltern in Armut zurück.

Die Kursteilnehmenden hatten bislang Märchen gelesen, wo Gut und Böse mühelos zuzuordnen waren. Um sie für die Dynamik des *Meisterdiebs* zu sensibilisieren, wurde die 60-köpfige Gruppe in zehn Kleingruppen eingeteilt, die jeweils einen Dieb – aus Mythologie, Legende, Fiktion, Film und Realität – recherchieren und darstellen sollten. Auf der ‚Konferenz der Diebe' trafen nun ganz verschiedene Figuren aufeinander: Prometheus, Robin Hood, Fagin (aus *Oliver Twist)*, Jesse James, der Gestiefelte Kater, Jacob Reckless (aus *Reckless)*, Bonnie & Clyde, die Räuber aus *Der Teufel mit den drei goldenen Haaren*[9], der „Barefoot Bandit" aus dem 21. Jahrhundert[10] und natürlich der Meisterdieb.

Auf dieser Konferenz trafen diese unterschiedlichen Diebe im Rahmen einer Podiumsdiskussion aufeinander. Die Studierenden erhielten folgende Fragen zur Vorbereitung:

- What things do you usually steal?
- Who do you usually steal from?
- What do you do with the things you steal?
- What is your mode of operation?
- Do you work alone or with others?
- How/why did you become a thief?
- What's your professional philosophy?

Die Podiumsdiskussion entwickelte sich zu einer zwischenzeitlich sehr lebhaften Debatte, weil die Diebe sich gegenseitig übertrumpfen wollten, sei es mit dem Hinweis darauf, dass sie zum Wohl anderer stehlen würden, oder durch die Betonung ihrer Kreativität oder durch schlichten Pragmatismus in Anbetracht widriger gesellschaftlicher Umstände, usw.

Als Abschluss wurde der ‚Dieb des Jahres' gekürt. Die Auszeichnung ging mit überwältigender Mehrheit an Prometheus (Wohltätigkeit mit weitreichenden Folgen), mit dem Meisterdieb auf dem zweiten Platz (Kreativität und Humor).

---

9   https://www.cs.cmu.edu/~spok/grimmtmp/022.txt, letzter Zugriff: 24.07.2018.
10   https://www.seattletimes.com/seattle-news/barefoot-bandit-gets-6-1-2-years-says-re-morse-is-heartfelt/, letzter Zugriff: 24.07.2018.

Die ‚Konferenz der Diebe' erfreute sich großer Beliebtheit, die sich in den Lerntagebüchern der Studierenden widerspiegelte. Eine große Anzahl von Teilnehmenden schrieb aber nicht nur über den Spaß-Effekt der Aktivität; die Vielfalt der unterschiedlichen Diebesmotive führte zu einer Ausdifferenzierung und Relativierung von ‚Gut' und ‚Böse'. In diesem Zusammenhang wurde die Figur des Meisterdiebs auch noch einmal genauer beleuchtet als jemand, der von den Reichen stiehlt, aber alles für sich behält, der eine Berufsehre hat, sich aber gleichzeitig außerhalb der gesellschaftlichen Normen bewegt und diese auch nicht ändern will oder kann. Damit erlebten die Studierenden das Märchen nicht nur als ungewöhnlich, sondern arbeiteten auch soziale Dynamiken einer feudalistischen Gesellschaft heraus.

Ästhetisch handeln oder: Die Goldene Gans

In *Die goldene Gans*[11] wird, wie in manchen anderen Märchen, das dritte Kind benachteiligt. Die Eltern ziehen ihre ersten zwei Söhne klar vor, während der jüngste Bruder als ‚Dummling', der nichts kann, verhöhnt wird. Die Freundlichkeit und Hilfsbereitschaft des Dummlings werden dann aber belohnt: Während seine Brüder sich weigern, ihr Essen mit einem kleinen Männchen im Wald zu teilen, gibt der Dummling bereitwillig davon ab und bekommt dafür eine goldene Gans (und schlussendlich die Königstochter zur Frau).

Mit der Technik des Standbilds[12] bereits vertraut, stellte die Lerngruppe in Eigenregie unterschiedliche Momente des Märchens dar. Im folgenden Standbild erhält der älteste Bruder von der Mutter ein sorgsam gepacktes Lunchpaket, bevor er zum Arbeiten in den Wald geht. Er lehnt die Bitte des hungrigen Männchens mit einer klaren Geste ab. Als er sich daraufhin anschickt einen Baum zu fällen, verletzt er sich prompt den Arm (Abb. 1).

Abbildung 1: Die goldene Gans (Foto: Susanne Even)

---

11 http://www.authorama.com/grimms-fairy-tales-50.html, letzter Zugriff: 24.07.2018.
12 Für eine detaillierte Diskussion von Standbildern und deren Einsatz siehe Schewe & Woodhouse (2018).

Hier haben die Studierenden zwei unterschiedliche Dynamiken herausgearbeitet. Zum einen ziehen Handlungen klare Konsequenzen nach sich: Selbstsucht, Geiz und fehlendem Mitgefühl folgt die Strafe auf dem Fuße (jedenfalls in Märchen). Das Standbild drückt aber auch noch etwas Anderes aus, was weniger offensichtlich ist, nämlich dass die Erfahrung von Zuwendung nicht notwendigerweise dazu führt, dass man andere auch gut behandelt. Hier zeigten sich im Kurs entwickelte ästhetisch-symbolische Kompetenzen; anstatt lediglich den Text chronologisch in Bildern wiederzugeben, werden Zusammenhänge präsentiert, die als verkörperte Metaphern Bedeutungen non-verbal einfangen.[13]

Performatives Lehren oder: I don't give a damn where Coventry is

Alle diese Geschichten erzählen von performativen Lernsituationen, in denen konkrete Ausgestaltung von Kontexten und Verlauf der Handlung offen bleiben und Wege eröffnet werden zu persönlicher Erfahrung und Auseinandersetzung mit Lerninhalten. Handelnde nehmen unterschiedliche Rollen und Perspektiven ein; sie machen die Erfahrung, als jemand anders handeln zu können, vertreten Meinungen, die nicht unbedingt mit den eigenen übereinstimmen, erfinden Figuren und Zusammenhänge, die vorher nicht existierten; sie stellen Dynamiken körperlich-ästhetisch dar und verkörpern damit ihre Erlebnisse und Entscheidungen. Der Prozess des Lernens wird inszeniert und reflektiert, wobei jede Inszenierung/Reflexion wiederum weitere Lernprozesse anregt.

Als Teilnehmerin am dramapädagogischen Seminar in Oldenburg bewunderte ich immer wieder die Fähigkeit von Manfred Schewe, solche Lernmomente scheinbar mit wenig Vorbereitung spontan ins Leben zu rufen, und nannte dies (etwas despektierlich) „Doing a Manfred". Der Begriff blieb, obwohl der Eindruck falsch war: Was den Teilnehmenden als mühelos erscheinen mag, erfordert Vorbereitung, darüber hinaus aber auch hohe Konzentration und Präsenz auf Seiten der Lehrperson. Erst meine eigenen Erfahrungen als Seminarleiterin brachten mich zu der Erkenntnis, dass sorgfältige Unterrichtsplanung und kreative Impulsideen nicht ausreichen – was in der Planungsphase gradlinig und überschaubar aussieht, entwickelt sich im gemeinsamen Handeln manchmal in ganz andere Richtungen. Es gilt, den Ideen der Lernenden nachzugehen und gemeinsam Reaktionen und Handlungen zu einem Netz von Bedeutungen zusammenzuknüpfen. Und darin, laut Manfred Schewe, liegt das Wesen performativen Unterrichtens:

---

13 Dazu Schewe (1997: 249): „Ästhetische Erfahrung wird ermöglicht durch Lehr-/Lernformen, die Sinnlichkeit, Gefühl und Verstand in Beziehung setzen."

Performative as a larger concept means a complete rethinking of education, and you could apply elements of theater aesthetics. If you look at theater aesthetics, one factor is physicality. We need more of that. We have the factor of emergence, meaning that teachers are open to what is emerging in a lesson. So it's not all pre-packaged, pre-planned. Something happens in the classroom; [let's say you have] a student response … why not build on that and have the competence to improvise, and then teach on the basis of what actually happens in the classroom. Theater means to be present […], the teacher has to be in the space, with full concentration, and has to be able to relate to the students. (Schewe 2014, Interview[14])

Damit tritt Manfred Schewe in die Fußstapfen von Dorothy Heathcote (1926-2011), einer der Hauptakteurinnen der britischen *drama in eduation* Tradition. Es war Heathcotes zeitlebende Überzeugung, mit den Ideen der Lernenden arbeiten zu müssen:

When I meet a group for the first time, I don't go in with definite ideas of what's going to happen, because I think I must use their ideas. And I want them to see their ideas coming into this marvelous action that they bring. (Heathcote 1971: Interview)[15]

Im Dokumentarfilm *Three Looms Waiting* arbeitet Heathcote unter anderem mit einer Gruppe von etwa 9-14 Jahre alten Schülern, die das Thema *prison camp* gewählt haben. Einer der Schüler erklärt sich bereit, einen in das Gefangenenlager eingeschleusten deutschen Spion zu spielen. Heathcote bereitet ihn auf diese Rolle mit Fragen vor – wer er vorgibt zu sein, ob sein Vater noch lebt, und woher seine Familie kommt. „London" antwortet der Junge auf die letzte Frage. „Where in London?" hakt Heathcote nach. – „Coventry". – Heathcote nickt nachdenklich. „That's a good place." – Im folgenden Interview wird gefragt, warum Heathcote an dieser Stelle nicht darauf hingewiesen hat, dass Coventry kein Teil von London ist (es ist eine Stadt in der Mitte von England). Heathcotes Antwort überrascht noch heute:

Because I don't give a damn where Coventry is. At that point, he felt right. He was working on an intensity of feeling – not on facts at all. I said 'you got to convince Englishmen!' and he said 'Yes!' And that's the level we're working on. If he'd said 'the man in the moon' – as long as he'd believed it at that point, it's okay by me. After all, what's a fact? I just happen to know Coventry isn't in London but there's loads of things equally stupid if you're looking at that kind of stupidity. If the other boys of

---

14   https://www.youtube.com/watch?v=3dhpa6Yz5_M&t=184s, letzter Zugriff: 24.07.2018.
15   Teil 2 des Dokumentarfilms *Three Looms Waiting* von Ron Smedley (1971): https://www.youtube.com/watch?v=p6YF35Urz9w, letzter Zugriff: 24.07.2018. Für den gesamten Film siehe Bibliographie.

course had suddenly jeered at him I would have had to defend him. But nobody jeered because it was as right for them 'cause they were feeling it too. (ibid.)

Im Jahr 2009 machte ich mit Heathcote Bekanntschaft und fragte sie unter anderem, welche Anregungen aus ihrer Herangehensweise für den Fremdsprachenunterricht gezogen werden könnten. Sie spreche zwar keine Fremdsprache, so Heathcote, aber „if I were to teach German, I would immediately try to come up with situations where it is necessary to speak German *badly*." – Sofort entstanden Orte im Kopf: ein internationaler Flughafen, ein Heim für Asylsuchende, die Kneipe, von der Udo Jürgens in *Griechischer Wein*[16] singt, usw. Die Idee, Situationen zu kreieren, in denen Deutsch auf unterschiedlichen Kompetenzniveaus an der Tagesordnung ist, ist geradezu ein Musterbeispiel lernerorientierten Lehrens: Die Lernenden sind genau da richtig, wo sie sind, eben *weil* ihr Deutsch nicht perfekt ist, und von dort werden sie abgeholt.

Performatives Lehren lernen oder: Die Unvorhersehbarkeit von Lernprozessen

Als Sprachkoordinatorin im Department of Germanic Studies an der Indiana University bin ich für die Lehrausbildung aller Doktorand*innen zuständig, die die Deutschkurse für die *undergradute students* unterrichten. Ich werde immer mal wieder gefragt, wie ich unsere Doktorand*innen dazu bringe, „mit Drama" zu unterrichten. Und die Antwort lautet immer wieder „gar nicht". Die, die mit performativen Elementen arbeiten, entscheiden das für sich – andere finden andere Wege. Genauso wie Manfred Schewe uns vor einem Vierteljahrhundert keine Vorschriften, sondern Angebote gemacht hat, schreibe ich meinen Doktorand*innen vergleichsweise wenig vor, sondern mache sie mit früheren Methoden, heutigen Ansätzen, performativer Pädagogik und dem Konzept von *post-method*[17] vertraut und unterstütze sie darin, didaktische Entscheidungen auf der Grundlage ihrer jeweiligen Lerngruppe und ihrer eigenen Lehrpersönlichkeit bewusst zu treffen.

Aber wie gestalte ich vor meinem performativen Hintergrund die tägliche Betreuung angesichts voller Lehrpläne und einer Testkultur mit Fokus auf Faktenwissen? Wie kann ich meine Doktorand*innen auf die Unvorhersehbarkeit von Lernprozessen vorbereiten im Sinne einer performativen Lehr- und Lernkultur, die Manfred Schewe u. a. wie folgt umreißt:

---

16 https://www.youtube.com/watch?v=1ePvZ3ZZy2A&index=2&list=RDuc9uTJtAt4s, letzter Zugriff: 24.07.2018.

17 Zum Zusammenhang von performativer Pädagogik und *post-method* siehe Even 2011a sowie Miladinović in diesem Band.

Die Abläufe sind nicht ausschließlich von der Lehrperson kontrolliert; im Gegenteil, die Schüler entscheiden oft den Fortgang der Stunde durch ihren jeweiligen kreativen Input. Sowohl die Lehrperson als auch die Lernenden werden immer wieder vom Unterrichtsgeschehen überrascht [...]. (Schewe 2011: 22)

Eines meiner zentralen Anliegen besteht darin zu vermitteln, dass solche Überraschungen keine Störfaktoren sind, die einen sorgfältig konzipierten Unterrichtsentwurf durcheinanderbringen, sondern integrale und geradezu wünschenswerte Komponenten kollaborativer Lernprozesse.

Gerade für Neulinge ist das zunächst eher irritierend – sie möchten klare, konkrete Angaben und unfallsichere Vorgehensweisen und sind froh, wenn sie sie mit ihren eigenen Unterrichtsstunden einigermaßen planmäßig über die Runden kommen. Je länger sie unterrichten, desto sicherer werden sie, erfahren aber auch, dass manche Stunden trotz detaillierter Vorbereitung gar nicht so laufen wie geplant. Sind sie damit schlechte Lehrer*innen? Verlieren sie die Kontrolle über ihre eigene Show? Mit der Zeit lernen sie, dass ihre Show gar nicht ihnen allein gehört, sondern im Zusammenspiel von Lehrenden und Lernenden immer wieder neu entsteht. Meine Rolle sehe ich darin, den Doktorand*innen in diesem Lernprozess zur Seite zu stehen, sie auf ihren Gratwanderungen zwischen institutionellen Rahmenbedingungen und konkreten Unterrichtsabläufen zu begleiten und Raum für die Entwicklung individueller Lehrpersönlichkeiten bereitzustellen.

Unterrichtsbeobachtungen und -reflexionen finden regelmäßig statt. Neulinge sind normalerweise recht nervös, wenn ich zum ersten Mal in ihren Unterricht komme – nehmen aber in den Nachbesprechungen wahr, dass es nicht darum geht, was sie „alles falsch gemacht" haben, sondern darum, sich mit dem eigenen Unterricht auseinanderzusetzen, und dass der übergreifende Prozess wichtiger ist als das Endprodukt einer einzelnen Unterrichtsstunde. Die Entwicklung individueller Lehrpersönlichkeiten braucht Raum und Zeit, und ich habe über die Jahre gelernt, dass es kontraproduktiv ist, diesen Prozess von außen beschleunigen zu wollen. Damit sind meine Beobachtungen keine Bewertungs- und Kontrollinstrumente, sondern tragen der komplexen, dynamischen Natur von Lehren und Lernen Rechnung.

Dass die besten Unterrichtsstunden nicht unbedingt die sind, die am gründlichsten geplant wurden, ist eine verblüffende Erfahrung, die alle unsere Doktorand*innen irgendwann einmal machen. Selbstverständlich soll hier nicht dafür plädiert werden, Unterricht nicht vorzubereiten. Aber trotzdem: Manchmal laufen gerade bei nicht so richtig ausgearbeiteten Unterrichtsentwürfen die konkreten Stunden (nicht alle, aber doch einige) besonders gut. Warum ist das so? Wenn man – aus unterschiedlichsten Gründen – nicht so perfekt vorbereitet in die Stunde geht, ist Improvisation gefragt; man muss präsent sein, hört den Lernenden besser zu und gestaltet die Stunde auf der Basis dessen, was tatsächlich im Unterricht abläuft. Meine Aufgabe besteht für mich darin, meine Doktorand*innen für solche Dynamiken zu sensibilisieren, sie in Momenten des (individuell erlebten) Ungenügens aufzufangen und sie zu ermutigen, ihre performativen Fähigkeiten wahrzunehmen und auszubauen.

Denn erst wenn Unterrichten als ein grundlegend kollaboratives, performatives Unterfangen gesehen wird, das Lernende *und* Lehrende mit ihrer ganzen Person wahrnimmt, herausfordert und fördert, können weitere unendliche Geschichten entstehen – die ein andernmal erzählt werden sollen.

Literatur

Bach, Gerhard & Timm, Johannes-Peter (1989): *Englischunterricht. Grundlagen und Methoden einer handlungsorientierten Unterrichtspraxis.* Tübingen: A. Francke Verlag.

Ende, Michael (1979): *Die unendliche Geschichte.* Stuttgart: Thienemann.

Even, Susanne (2008): Moving in(to) imaginary worlds: Drama pedagogy for foreign language teaching and learning. In *Unterrichtspraxis Deutsch/Teaching German* 41.2, 161-170.

Even, Susanne (2011a): Drama Grammar: Towards a Performative Postmethod Pedagogy. In *Language Learning Journal*, 299-312.

Even, Susanne (2011b): Multiple Hotseating. In *Scenario* V/2, 112-113.

Funke, Cornelia (2003): *Tintenherz.* Hamburg: Cecilie Dressler Verlag.

Schewe, Manfred & Woodhouse, Fionn (2018): Performative foreign language didactics: About still images and the teacher as 'Formmeister' (form master). In *Scenario* XII/1, 53-69.

Schewe, Manfred (1997): DaF-Lehrer/innen-Ausbildung: Nicht nur als *Wissenschaft*, sondern ebenso als *Kunst!* In Armin Wolff, Gisela Tütken, & Horst Liedtke (Hg.): *Materialien Deutsch als Fremdsprache 26.* Regensburg: Fachverband Deutsch als Fremdsprache, 245-254.

Schewe, Manfred (2011): Die Welt auch im fremdsprachlichen Unterricht immer wieder neu verzaubern: Plädoyer für eine performative Lehr- und Lernkultur! In Almut Küppers, Torben Schmidt & Maik Walter (Hg.): *Inszenierungen im Fremdsprachenunterricht: Grundlagen, Formen, Perspektiven.* Braunschweig: Schroedel/Diesterweg/Klinkhardt, 20-31.

Smedley, Ron (1971): *Three Looms Waiting.* BBC Omnibus Documentary on Dorothy Heathcote. https://www.youtube.com/watch?v=owKiUO99qrw, letzter Zugriff: 28.07.2018.

Hope and drama pedagogy[1]

Helping learners to 'read' and 'write' the world

Madonna Stinson

Introduction

Manfred Schewe and I have been engaging with our passion for drama and language at opposite ends of the world, and our approaches and practices have much in common. My offering to the celebration of Manfred's work is a presentation and discussion of how I go about making pedagogical decisions. I will illustrate my own planning process through sharing the details of my 'Bukit Merah' drama, and illustrate how I attempt to hold both "the artistry of the form and the intended learning in one hand" (Dunn & Stinson 2011: 618) when drama is employed as a medium for language learning.

> Drama does things with words. It introduces language as an essential and authentic method of communication. Drama sustains interactions between students within the target language, creating a world of social roles and relations in which the learner is an active participant. [...] The language that arises is fluent, purposeful and generative because it is embedded in context. (Kao & O'Neill 1998: 4)

The above quote from Kao and O'Neill is enticing in its advocacy for drama as a language learning medium. However, claims such as authentic communication, sustaining interactions, and language being purposeful and generative run the risk of romanticizing the possibilities of drama processes if accepted without thorough questioning of: What sort/s of drama? When might these claims be true? and for whom? Drama is manifested in many forms and contexts. Those of us who choose to use drama as a pedagogy need to ask ourselves whether the choices we make from within our performative and dramatic pedagogical repertoire allow for quality and complex drama/language learning to take place. In essence, we must ask ourselves whether we are providing opportunities for students to experience language as an authentic method of communication, with

---

1   This chapter is a revised version of the keynote presentation given at the SCENARIO Forum Conference, Cork in 2017.

concomitant understandings of power and control that language may exert. Do we create worlds where the learner is an active participant? Do we provide learning opportunities for purposeful and generative language that is carefully and thoughtfully contextualized? Do we support learners in their attempts to read and write the world?

In this chapter I hope to shed some light on my own pedagogical decisions as a drama teaching artist, using the example of the Bukit Merah drama I developed for one particular research project in Singapore (Stinson 2008, 2012; Stinson & Freebody 2006).

Drama pedagogy

While I value and employ improvisation, play building and text interpretation for language teaching, the form I most readily turn to is process drama.

Process dramas (Haseman 1991, O'Neill 1995, O'Toole 1992) are collaboratively co-created texts which draw on the lived experiences of the participants to bring personal meaning to a dramatic text. In process dramas participants are text-creators and not merely text-consumers. Indeed, process drama is a collaborative experience under the control of the entire group, not just the leader, and this allows for student agency within the learning situation. The starting point for most process dramas is a pre-text that establishes possibilities for the dramatic world to be encountered, developed and explored. A pre-text contains a puzzlement or an enticement that challenges the participants to investigate the possibilities it offers. It provides a potential framing of the drama that will emerge as the participants work within the fictional context and suggests possibilities for roles, relationships, situations, and driving tension. However, the drama moves beyond simple re-enactment of the pre-text, instead using it as the impetus to explore larger issues of relevance to the participating group. Learning is experienced actively, in role and through collaborative dramatic enactment. While each process drama structure is carefully pre-planned, the co-creation of the text offers many opportunities for negotiation and input by participants. In essence, each drama is an ephemeral and unrepeatable event, the product of a collaborative meaning-making process through the medium of role. Process dramas do not lead to performances or presentations of the devised material to audiences who have remained outside the drama. One of the reasons that the form of process drama engages me is that I align with Neelands who suggests that process dramas "seek to both unmask and to de-stabilise the comfortable stasis of [the] culture of power" (Neelands 2004: 52). Power, in its manifestations and applications, is also fundamental to language and thus process drama and language learning go hand in hand.

It seems to me that the drama work we engage with needs to be meaningful and connected to the lives of our learner-participants. The work is positive and purposeful when learners are engaged in authentic contexts and when their agency and actions have the potential to produce positive change. Thus, Paolo Freire's pedagogy of hope plays an important part in my teaching philosophy and practice. Freire's work demonstrates that in order to overcome social injustice and oppression the use of the imagination is crucial. To him, any educational intervention must start with "unravelling the why" of a given situation. So rather than a pedagogy of unsubstantiated hope, or optimism alone, Freire proposes *critical* hope by which he means an optimism and a belief that the future can be made; that it can be changed by human action. Freire contends that, by harnessing humankind's curiosity, relentlessness, inventiveness, and ingenuity, the future can be improved, through "unravelling the fabric in which the facts are given, discovering their 'why'" (Freire 1992: 22). It is through dissecting the fabric of circumstances, of power, of relationships, of authority and control we come to recognise the complex interplay of cause and effect. And when we develop a critical understanding of the present we allow glimpses of possibility for change, for hope, for the belief that we, as individuals can contribute to change in the future.

This suggests that our practice must involve explorations of power, of authority, relationships, and consider the driving tensions and perspectives that contribute to cause and effect. Rich, complex and nuanced exploration of these components of human endeavour are the foundations of much of our drama work. And so they should be. I turn to another personally inspirational figure: Maxine Greene, in admiration of her relentless self-questioning and reflexion. She says, "I ask myself what is the meaning of what I have done?" (quoted in Pinar 1998: 1), thus offering an important reminder to consider the moral imperative of educators, i.e. to consider not just what I have done but what is the meaning of what I have done? Greene considers herself to be in a perpetual state of becoming, allowing for alternative selves to emerge. Like her, I see the chances for exploration of self and identity in drama work. Indeed, the drama process may allow alternative "possible selves" to be explored. Possible selves are "conceptions of our selves in the future, including at least to some degree, an experience of being an agent in a future situation" (Erickson 2007: 356).

So, for me, explorations of power, authority, register, self, perspectives, and the interrelationships amongst these are the very essence of drama work. To illustrate how these beliefs can be embedded in drama practice I offer an example of my work, and briefly unpack the decisions underpinning the selection and sequencing of learning experiences.

Unpacking the drama: The Legend of Bukit Merah Drama

This drama is framed by a familiar, traditional tale chosen to engage participants in language learning in a multilingual classroom context in Singapore. The work was developed for Secondary 4 students (16 years old). The drama originally was planned as a series of three one-hour lessons as the final component in a research study into the impact of process drama work on student results in oral English examinations (Stinson 2008, 2012, Stinson & Freebody 2006, 2009).

The sequence of activities discussed below has been carefully designed and scaffolded in episodes, though individual activities may be adapted to suit differing contexts. The drama will work as a single all-day learning experience, or may be divided into shorter episodes to suit specific time requirements. It is important, however, to adhere to the sequence provided. The plan is presented and explained in the hope that it offers a model of practice that is adaptable, transferable and translatable.

Resources required:

- The story of *The Legend of Bukit Merah*[2]. A complete version will be needed, as well as a version with the story divided into sections for small group work (see Episode 2).
- A framed or mounted (at least A4) picture of the main character of the story, the Sultan. This should be light enough to be easily carried about and propped against the wall or back of a chair. An alternative is to use a shadow puppet or a traditional marionette from the region if you have access to resources such as those.
- A large and ornate cushion or throne, or a chair that can be draped with some suitable fabric, e.g. batik.

Episode 1 (Focus – speaking and listening, establishing the dramatic context, introducing power and status)

1. Participants work in pairs. A can tell B to do whatever they want and B must do it. Participants reverse roles and repeat.
2. Participants move about the space staying as far away from each other as possible. The teacher changes the tempo and quality of the movements but giving directions such as:

---

2   http://singaporelegends.tripod.com/bukitmerah.htm, last accessed: 21.08.2018.

- You are hurrying to meet your boss because you will be scolded if you are late.
- Your boss has given you a task that you *really* don't want to do.
- You are heading home to the family after a long, hard day at work.
- You are heading home to the family and your favourite dinner is ready.
- Finally:
  You are the most powerful person in the world.

3. As the teacher counts backwards from 10, the participants gradually change to become the least powerful people in the world.
4. A chair (symbolising a throne – see Resources above) is placed in the centre of the room. A volunteer sits in the chair as the most powerful person in the world.
5. The teacher reads aloud: *Long ago lived a Sultan, the most rich and handsome in the land. No one could compare to him and, as time passed, he grew proud and haughty, always seeking praise. If others around him were praised for cleverness or acts of bravery he would become angry and vindictive. In fact, he would actually kill those who drew attention away from him.*
6. The teacher invites the participants to enter the space one by one, and say, "Your highness, if it please you, I will ..." and offer something that aims to please the Sultan. If the offer pleases the "Sultan", they present/perform the offer, but if not, the "Sultan" clicks his fingers and the student "dies" in a dramatically violent and horrible way. If there is time, other participants invited to take turns to sit in the Sultan's chair.

Activities explained

Episode 1 starts with warm-up activities that emphasize power and status. These offer opportunities for the participants to use the language of "controlling" (Haseman & O'Toole 1990) and related paralinguistic features as they follow instructions and make offers to the Sultan. They begin to use the vocabulary and language register of giving orders. In addition, they are introduced to some of the characters that will be explored, as well as the notion of limitless power. We will see the consequences of the latter as the drama unfolds. Please note: even though the language used in the story signals predominantly male characters, it is important to cast those roles "against type" to allow for implications of gender and personal attributes to be considered in the reflections, which are invaluable to the discussions/reflections at the end of each lesson. Language reflections may include discussion of status and register, as well as related paralinguistic features. The activities described here are individual and playful, designed to be moderate in challenge and fun, so that participants can readily engage in the work to follow.

Episode 2 (Focus – reading and listening, establishing the narrative, introducing tension)

1. Participants are given a copy of the text and the teacher reads or retells the remainder of the story. Participants read the text silently and highlight, on the printed copy, key words or phrases that strike them in some way. The teacher might want to re-read the whole story and ask the participants to join in when it comes to the words they have highlighted. This "chorusing" supports both confident and developing readers. Even though this is a very familiar story in Singapore, the actual narrative may differ from the versions the participants may have heard. This activity ensures that all participants share a common version of the story.

2. The class is divided into small groups. Each group is given a section of the story and asked to create a still image of that section. If these are to be shared with the whole class, the teacher taps in to selected participants in each still image to hear them express thoughts and feelings at that instant in the story.

3. Each group decides on a caption for their still image (and who will speak the caption) and the groups are arranged around the space in the story sequence. The story is then told in images and captions.

Activities explained

Episode 2 introduces the pre-text (Bowell & Heap 2001, O'Neill 1995) of the drama. The foundational elements of drama (Haseman & O'Toole 2017) i.e. human context, and driving tension are also established. The 'chorusing' provides practice in pronunciation and highlights key language important to the story. By speaking in a scaffolded but unrehearsed chorus, participants feel supported in taking the risk to speak aloud. This is both an individual and collective activity. The chorusing often helps in establishing mood, and this provokes discussion about why many participants choose the same words, contributing to language reflection. Still image, sometimes called freeze frame or tableau, is a simple technique that can be effective with even beginning drama learners. The collaboratively created images physically embody the characters and the relationships between them, and provide a clear focus for the dramatic action which may unfold. Speaking aloud captions allow for additional low-risk engagement (Krashen 1981). Many students enjoy negotiating the best selection of vocabulary and phrasing for their captions. Language reflection includes discussion of the vocabulary selected and rejected for captions as well as the sequence of the story.

Episode 3 (Focus – speaking and writing, considering roles and relationships).

1. The teacher explains that some aspects of the story the participants don't know much about are going to be explored, and invites the participants to agree to do this together.
2. The participants are asked to list some "persons of significance" to the Sultan. These people may not be named in the story but would be important to him in his life, e.g. the Captain of the Guard, the First Wife, a child of the Sultan, a Chief Advisor etc.
3. In small groups, participants create a role description for the characters, including attitude toward the event, power to persuade, and attitude toward the Sultan. they add a phrase that the character might commonly use to the role description.

Activities explained

This is where the imaginative work of the drama really begins. Rather than reproducing the existing story, the group imagination is harnessed to explore characters and perspectives that are intrinsic (but not evident) in the traditional tale. Moving outside the given story shows participants that imaginative acts are valued within drama processes. It also intrigues the participants who realise that the stories of each of these characters are, as yet, unknown to them. Role descriptions form the basis for character analysis, and the single phrase each character may speak helps the construction of character and understanding of language register and idiosyncratic language use. While the Sultan is the centre of power within the story, introducing other characters provides opportunities for investigating those who may enable or challenge powerful individuals and consideration of moral concerns with relation to power.

Episode 4 (Focus – speaking and listening, deepening commitment and empathy within the drama)

1. As a large group, participants draw a map of the location of the village and mark in family homes and the location of the palace.

2. In small groups, they choose a home from the map and allocate family roles e.g. parent, grandparent, aunt/uncle. Each family grouping must have one male child.

3. A typical morning in the life of the village is created, with families breakfasting, greeting neighbours, cleaning, preparing for work etc. This can be presented as an occupational mime.

4. An announcement is made that the Sultan is on his way to inspect the village. Participants, in family groups, must pay the proper homage to the Sultan as he moves around the space. The Chief Advisor (as teacher-in-role) directs the homage to the Sultan, emphasizing the importance of pleasing the Sultan, and also that the Advisor is sympathetic to the people in the village. The Sultan may be represented by the cushion from the throne or another suitable symbol.

5. Participants take a break from role and discuss responses to what is going on in the drama so far.

Activities explained

This sequence provides a meditative space. The miming of daily rituals become rhythmic and symbolic. The mapping of the community allows all participants to see how individuals contribute and belong to a collective identity. The group is working concurrently, collaboratively and individually. The male child in each family group will become important later.

Episode 5 (Focus – speaking and listening, increasing the tension, adding a complication).

1. Back in the village, the villagers are going about their daily business while discussing the Sultan and how indebted they are to the boy.[3] Freeze.

2. Teacher narration: *One of the servants from the palace rushed to the village with terrible news: the Sultan had heard the villagers speaking so well of the boy. He is furious because he sees this as a betrayal. He has decided to kill all the young boys in the village as a way of punishing them for their disloyalty.*

3. Out of role, the participants discuss strategies that the villagers might use to save their sons' lives.

---

3   The 'boy' saved the beaches of Singapore from a lethal swordfish. He is central to the story and was established as a character by the reading of the story at the beginning of the lesson sequence.

4. Everyone back in role. The Chief Adviser (teacher-in-role) offers to help them try to reason with the Sultan and offers to set up meetings with significant people who have influence with him.

5. Participants choose 3 or 4 of the people (from the list drawn up earlier – Wife, Captain of the Guard, etc.) who might be able to influence the Sultan. They form new groups – one for each of the chosen roles – and construct and rehearse arguments that might be put to the Sultan to spare the life of the boy. The teacher can move about the groups and challenge student ideas through questioning.

6. The teacher, as the Advisor, narrates the presentation of the arguments to the Sultan, using examples from the arguments.[4] The Advisor suggests that the Sultan responded positively.

Activities explained

This sequence provides a complication and adds tension to the story. The role of the Chief Advisor (teacher-in-role) has to be performed with care. As the second in command (Morgan & Saxton 1987), the TiR as Advisor can defer decisions to the Sultan but also indicate support for the villagers. Participants are engaged in their own characters and the narrative and are keen to construct reasons and arguments to change the Sultan's mind. They are able to work at a language level they find comfortable as they construct and rehearse the arguments they will present to the Sultan. This episode allows every participant to speak.

Episode 6 (Focus – speaking and listening, considering alternative viewpoints).

1. Change of roles. It is the eve of the night that the Captain has been ordered to kill the boy. No one knows whether the Sultan has been persuaded to change his mind or not. Participants, in the groups that have prepared the arguments for the Sultan, again take up the collective role of the respective individual in a designated space in the room. Each of them is thinking of the arguments that they presented, and repeats an action that the character (see episodes 3.2 & 5.5) might perform, e.g. the captain sits and sharpens his sword, the first wife combs her long hair, the Sultan's son tosses a small ball repeatedly in the air, the Advisor writes down the events of the day, or other suggestions from the participants. These repeated movements establish a subdued rhythm.

---

4   The drama takes a time jump at this point.

2. The teacher asks the participants to lie down for a few moments of sleep.
3. Teacher narration: *It was the quietest of nights. No breeze stirred the palm leaves. The night birds were silent and the frogs had ceased croaking. It seemed as if the whole world was holding its breath, hoping that dawn would not come. In the dark of this night the Sultan's men went to the boy's home and began to stab him. His mattress filled with blood which kept on flowing and flowing. Even after the child was dead, the flow of blood did not stop, but spread down the hill, until finally it began to sink into the ground. The soil is still red today, and that is why we call the hill, Bukit Merah (Red Hill).*
4. The group deroles and debriefs.

Activities explained

This sequence often shocks the participants but, importantly holds to the original story since the story is familiar and the ending is well known. It leads to much discussion about the "why" the Sultan may have made the decision he did, and the impact on the community of villagers, as well as the characters who were close to the Sultan e.g. his family and close friends. It also leads to considerations of how difficult it can be to influence powerful individuals.

Episode 7 (Focus – speaking and listening, reading and writing, reflecting on the narrative).

1. The local museum wants to commemorate the legend of Bukit Merah by creating an interactive display that tells the story, using multiple voices. As a large group, participants discuss the characters and events that they believe are important to include in the museum display, list these and add details about how each section of the display might be presented.
2. In small groups, participants prepare a segment for the interactive display. The segments may take many forms e.g. rehearsed performances of events from the story; "talking heads" as individual characters share phrases or monologues; projections of digitally recorded images; soundscapes/wordscapes; or documentary-style narrations.
3. The exhibition is set up.
4. The group reflects on the drama and the learning it produced.

Activities explained

This sequence brings the story into the present and allows for the participants to have the power and agency to share their own perspectives on the traditional tale and the issues to be considered in the present day. Participants assume a playwright role to construct a new and insightful interpretation of the story to express and communicate ideas relevant to a contemporary audience.

Conclusion

The drama described above offers a rich opportunity to explore issues of hope, power, identity, and language. In practice, there is much more reflection on the drama process and the language generated and demanded within each activity, due to space constraints I cannot explore these moments in more detail in this chapter. I hope this discussion of my own practice is seen as an offering that honours and respects the enormous contribution that Manfred Schewe has made, and continues to make, to our important and developing field of endeavour and to a vibrant international community of performative practice.

References

Bowell, Pamela & Heap, Brian S. (2001): *Planning Process Drama*. London: David Fulton.

Dunn, Julie & Stinson, Madonna (2011): Not without the art!! The importance of teacher artistry when applying drama as pedagogy for additional language learning. In *Research in Drama Education: The Journal of Applied Theatre and Performance* 16/4, 617-633.

Erikson, Martin (2007): The meaning of the future: Toward a more specific definition of possible selves. In *Review of General Psychology* 11/4, 348-358.

Freire, Paulo (1992): *Pedagogy of Hope*. London: Continuum.

Haseman, Bradley C. (1991): Improvisation, process drama and dramatic art. In *London Drama* July, 19-21.

Haseman, Bradley C. & O'Toole, John (1990): *Communicate Live*. Melbourne: Heinemann Educational.

Haseman, Bradley C. & O'Toole, John (2017): *Dramawise Reimagined*. Sydney: Currency Press.

Kao, Shin-Mei & O'Neill, Cecily (1998): *Words into Worlds: Learning a Second Language through Process Drama*. Stamford: Ablex Publishing.

Krashen, Stephen (1981): *Second Language Acquisition and Second Language Learning*. New York: Pergamon Press.

Morgan, Norah & Saxton, Juliana (1987): *Teaching drama: A mind of many wonders*. Cheltenham: Hutchinson Education.

O'Neill, Cecily (1995): *Drama Worlds: A Framework for Process Drama*. Portsmouth, NH: Heinemann.

O'Toole, John (1992): *The Process of Drama: Negotiating Art and Meaning*. London: Routledge.

Pinar, William F. (ed.) (1998): *The Passionate Mind of Maxine Greene, 'I am ... not yet'.* London: Falmer Press.

Stinson, Madonna (2008): Drama, process drama and TESOL. In Michael Anderson, John Hughes & Jacqueline Manuel (eds.): *Drama in English Teaching: Imagination, Action and Engagement.* Oxford: Oxford University Press, 193-212.

Stinson, Madonna (2012): Accessing traditional tales: the legend of Bukit Merah. In John Winston (ed.): *Drama and Second Language Learning.* London/New York: Routledge, 69-80.

Stinson, Madonna & Freebody, Kelly (2006): The DOL project: An investigation into the contribution of process drama to improved results in English oral communication. In *Youth Theatre Journal* 20, 27-41.

Stinson, Madonna & Freebody, Kelly (2009): The contribution of process drama to improved results in English oral communication. In Rita Elaine Silver, Christine C. M. Goh & Lubna Alsagoff (eds.): *Acquisition and Development in New English Contexts: Evidence from Singapore.* London: Continuum, 147-165.

Mit Helden reisen

Oder wie viel Ästhetik verträgt der Fremdsprachenunterricht?[1]

Maik Walter

> *und scheiß auf die helden*
> *weil sowieso niemand so ist*
> *wie das alle erzählen*
>
> Spaceman Spiff: Han Solo

Einleitung

Ästhetisches Lernen kann sich in Freiräumen des Fremdsprachenunterrichts vollziehen (vgl. bspw. Walter 2012, die Beiträge in Bernstein & Lerchner 2014 sowie in Küppers et al. 2011). In Zeiten einer verordneten Bildungseffizienz, einer immer weiter um sich greifenden, zertifizierenden Prüfungssucht und nicht zuletzt eines falsch verstandenen GER-Schubladendenkens stehen die Chancen für ästhetisches Lernen zunächst einmal schlecht, vor allem auch im institutionalisierten Lernkontext. Anhand eines Theaterprojekts wird demonstriert, wie ästhetisches Lernen mit einer modernen kompetenzorientierten Sprachvermittlung verschränkt werden kann.

---

1 Dieser Beitrag ist nur durch die tatkräftige Hilfe des Auswärtigen Amts der Bundesrepublik Deutschland und der DHPS Windhoek ermöglicht worden, die das Theaterprojekt finanzierten und das Projekt unterstützten, wo es ihnen möglich war. Besonderer Dank gilt Marion Kross, die die Idee nach Namibia trug und dort zum Blühen brachte, sowie Jana Wall und Kristin Eichholz, die von der Idee schnell überzeugt wurden. Nicht zu vergessen sind die 25 Schüler*innen aus Namibia und ihre Lehrer*innen Andreas Robisch und Antje Stein, von denen ich viel lernen konnte. Ohne sie wäre diese Reise nie zu Stande gekommen. Den Zuhörer*innen auf der FaDaF-Jahrestagung 2016 in Essen sowie meinen Studierenden an den Universitäten in Wien, Tübingen und Paderborn danke ich für hilfreiche Kommentare zu diesem Beitrag.

Vom Geschichtenerzählen

Eine Geschichte kann auf unterschiedliche Weise erzählt werden. Die Kulturen der Menschheit kennen verschiedene Modelle, die im Laufe der Zeit weitergegeben, gefestigt und damit tradiert wurden. Ein weit verbreitetes Modell geht von fünf Ingredienzen aus, die in einer guten Geschichte vorhanden sein, bzw. geklärt werden müssen: *der Ort* und *die Situation, die Beziehung, das Problem, dessen Lösung* und *die Moral*. Diese narrativen Wegmarken können mit sprachlichen Mustern gestützt werden, um somit eine ‚Geschichte in fünf Sätzen‘ zu bauen. Im Storytelling und im Improvisationstheater wird diese Übung genutzt, um gemeinsam eine Geschichte zu erzählen (Vlcek 2003: 203). Dabei darf jeder Spieler nur einen Satz sagen, und gemeinsam entsteht eine Geschichte. Dieses kollaborative Erzählen erfordert intensives Zuhören, Reagieren auf die Impulse der Mitspieler*innen und mündet im besten Fall in einen sozialen Lernprozess. Ein solches Lernen kann auch für den Fremdsprachenunterricht ausgesprochen förderlich sein. Sprachlich ist bereits diese stark gesteuerte Aktivität durchaus komplex; hier werden u. a. nämlich lexikalische Strukturen aus verschiedenen Feldern, das Präteritum als Vergangenheitstempus, Pronomina und auch Konnektoren verwendet.

Noch komplexer wird es, wenn neben dem Helden andere Figuren hinzutreten, die Herausforderungen größer werden und der Held eine Reise antritt. Eine solche *Heldenreise*, ein weiteres narratives Konzept, kann als eine Ausdifferenzierung der Geschichte mit fünf Elementen verstanden werden. Sie besteht aus den Archetypen und typischen Stadien als den beiden Fundamenten einer gut gebauten Geschichte. Ein klassisches Beispiel wäre das Märchen vom Aschenputtel, das aus seiner Welt hinaustritt, mit Gegenspielern interagiert und am Ende sich verändert. Betrachten wir im nächsten Abschnitt dieses Konzept etwas genauer.

Das Konzept der Heldenreise

Die Heldenreise geht auf den amerikanischen Literaturwissenschaftler Joseph Campbell (1904-1987) zurück, der sich mit dem Mythos beschäftigte und in literarischen Werken Erzählstrukturen analysierte. Seine Überlegungen schrieb er 1949 in einem bis heute verlegten Klassiker nieder: *Der Heros in tausend Gestalten*. Die Heldenreise wurde auf unterschiedliche Kontexte übertragen, und so begaben sich in verschiedenen Professionen wie Psychologie, Literatur oder Pädagogik Helden auf die strukturierten Reisen.

Besonders einflussreich war der Leiter der Stoffentwicklungsabteilung von *Twentieth Century Fox* Christopher Vogler, der dieses Modell auf den Bereich des Films in seiner *Odyssee des Drehbuchschreibers* (*The Writer's Journey*) übertrug. Neben der Entwicklung von Drehbüchern (Vogler 2010: 385-462) profitiert vor allem das Improvisationstheater vom Modell der Heldenreise. Besonders in Langformaten wird häufig darauf zurückgegriffen (vgl. Lösel 2004). Auch in der Personalentwicklung/dem Management (vgl. Höcker 2011), wo Heldenreisen als Entwicklungswerkzeug in Trainings eingesetzt werden, in der Pädagogik (vgl. Mai o.J.) als Methode und in der Theaterpädagogik, beispielsweise als Mittel der Stückentwicklung (vgl. Batzel et al. 2013; Bryant 2012) sind Heldenreisen en vogue.

Das narrative Modell der Heldenreise stützt sich auf zwei Fundamente: Zum einen sind die sieben auf den Schweizer Psychiater Carl Gustav Jung (1875-1961) zurückgehenden *Archetypen* wichtig, zum anderen die typischen *Stadien* einer Heldenreise. Christopher Vogler führt neben dem *Helden*, den *Mentor*, den *Schwellenhüter*, den *Herold*, den *Gestaltwandler* sowie den *Schatten* und den *Trickster* an (Vogler 2010: 87-158). Diese Typen bilden das Grundpersonal einer *Heldenreise* und sind das „unverzichtbare Handwerkszeug des Geschichtenerzählers" (ibid. 84). Exemplarisch seien an dieser Stelle nur ausgewählte Eigenschaften des Helden mit den Worten Voglers erwähnt (vgl. ibid. 87-104):

- „Im tiefsten Sinne liegt dem Heros oder Helden damit der Begriff der Selbstaufopferung zugrunde. [...]
- er bietet dem Publikum einen Zugang zum Geschehen an. [...]
- Eine Geschichte lädt uns dazu ein, für einige Zeit einen Teil unserer eigenen Identität in den Helden zu investieren. [...] Auf gewisser Weise werden wir damit auf die Dauer der Geschichte selbst zum Helden. [...]
- Eine weitere wichtige Funktion des Helden in der Geschichte steht für Entwicklung und Lernprozesse [...], darin, die Handlung voranzutreiben. [...]
- Helden zeigen uns, wie man mit dem Tod umgeht."

Diese Eigenschaften konstituieren den archetypischen Helden. Es ist vielleicht das, was ein Großteil der Menschen in vielen Kulturen mit einem Helden verbindet oder, wie es im Lied von Spaceman Spiff (2014: Track 12) heißt, „wie das alle erzählen." Konstituiert wurde dieser Typus durch Religion, Mythen, Filme und Romane. In anderen Worten: Das Bild eines Helden prägt sich durch die Geschichten, die uns in unserem Leben erzählt werden. Ein Held ist in der Regel nicht allein, er trifft auf andere Typen wie auf den Mentor, den freundlichen Begleiter und Ermutiger oder auf den Schwellenhüter, der versucht, den Helden von seiner Reise abzuhalten bzw. ihn in der gewohnten Welt zu halten. Begibt sich ein Held auf die Reise, wird er verschiedene Phasen durchlaufen.

Die Stadien einer Heldenreise können mit einem klassischen Dreiakter beschrieben werden, im dem der Held aus der gewohnten Welt in eine andere tritt und am Ende verändert zurückkommt. Hier wird das Wesen einer solchen

Reise deutlich, das sich durch das Moment der Veränderung auszeichnet. Ein
Held wandelt sich durch Erfahrungen in einer anderen Welt, in der Fremde.
Zwar steckt bereits der Impuls zur Veränderung, mit anderen Worten die He-
rausforderung oder das Problem, in der gewohnten Welt. Ohne diesen Impuls
aber würde ein Held seine gewohnte Welt nie verlassen. Warum sollte er auch?
Denn der Alltag ist in der Regel vertraut, sicher und auch behaglich. Erst die
Herausforderungen setzen die Segel für den Helden. Die Lösung des Problems
liegt nicht in der gewohnten Routine, sondern in der Fremde. Hier erlebt der
Held seine Abenteuer, macht seine Erfahrungen und kommt am Ende gewandelt
zurück. Fehlt dieses Moment in einer Geschichte, so wird sie vom Zuhörer als
nicht als vollständig wahrgenommen. Die folgenden zwölf Stadien wurden von
Vogler als Teile der Reise postuliert (vgl. Vogler 2010: 159-384):

- Die gewohnte Welt
- Der Ruf des Abenteuers
- Die Weigerung
- Die Begegnung mit dem Mentor
- Das Überschreiten der ersten Schwelle
- Die Bewährungsproben, Das Treffen auf Verbündete und Feinde
- Das Vordringen zur tiefsten Höhle
- Die entscheidende Prüfung
- Die Belohnung
- Der Rückweg
- Die Auferstehung
- Die Rückkehr mit dem Elixier

Wie kann dieses Modell nun für den Fremdsprachenkontext adaptiert werden?
Der folgende Einblick in ein Theaterprojekt mit Jugendlichen soll darauf eine
Antwort geben. Begeben wir uns dazu in das südliche Afrika, nach Namibia.
Bevor wir die beiden bereits genannten Fundamente der Heldenreise als Orien-
tierungspunkte im fremdsprachlichen Spielprozess ausbuchstabieren, wird im
nächsten Abschnitt zunächst der Kontext des Projekts umrissen.

Helden in Namibia: Der Kontext des Theaterprojekts

Das Theaterprojekt fand im namibischen Windhoek statt. Namibia gilt als einer
der wirtschaftlichen Motoren auf dem afrikanischen Kontinent.

Das Land mit 2.402.858 Einwohner*innen (2014) zeichnet sich durch eine
große Sprachenvielfalt aus.[2] Deutsch spielt als ehemalige Kolonialsprache eine

---

2   www.bmz.de/de/laender_regionen/subsahara/namibia/index.html; eingesehen am 7.3.2016.

besondere Rolle, auch wenn es sich bei der Anzahl der L1-Sprecher*innen (N=11.200)[3] um eine Minderheitensprache handelt. Neben den anderen indogermanischen Sprachen Englisch, Afrikaans und Portugiesisch werden die Bantusprachen OshiWanbo, RuKavango, OtjiHerero. SiLozi und SeTswana sowie die Koisansprachen Khoekhoegowab und San gesprochen.

Das Projekt wurde auf Einladung an der Deutschen Höheren Privatschule[4], einer integrierten deutsch-namibischen Begegnungsschule, durchgeführt. Sie ist die einzige von der Bundesrepublik Deutschland geförderte Auslandsschule in Namibia, an der 1035 Schüler*innen der Klassen 1–12 von 92 Lehrkräften unterrichtet werden. Sie führt in der Hauptunterrichtssprache Deutsch vom Kindergarten bis zur 12. Klasse. Es können sowohl das namibische NSSC (Namibian Senior Secondary Certificate) und das Deutsche Internationale Abitur (DIAP) abgelegt werden. Ein deutscher Zweig führt zum Abitur-, Haupt- oder Realabschluss, ein englischer Zweig (345 Schüler*innen) zum NSSC, wobei zusätzlich das deutsche Sprachdiplom (DSD II) erworben werden kann. Die Erstsprachen (L1) der Schüler*innen sind Deutsch, Englisch, Französisch, Afrikaans, Oshivambo, Nama, Damara und Otjihero.

Das Heldenprojekt

Im Frühjahr 2015 erarbeiteten 25 Schüler*innen aus 2 weiteren Schulen (DHPS, Delta Secondary School Windhoek [DOSW] und St. Paul's College) aus den Klassen 8-11 eine Woche lang eine Collage zum Thema *Helden?* mit eigenen Texten in der Fremdsprache Deutsch. Geplant war eine Aufführung auf einer professionellen, gut ausgestatteten Bühne. Die fünf Probentage waren gleich strukturiert: 4 Blöcke mit 90 Minuten Theaterarbeit und einem integrierten Intensivunterricht in deutscher Sprache. Als ästhetischer Ansatz wurde das Postdramatischen Theater (Lehmann 2008) ausgewählt. In der geplanten Stückentwicklung wurde insbesondere auf Elemente des Erzähltheaters zurückgegriffen (Jahnke 2004, Streisand & Walter 2003, Wardetzky 2003, 2007, 2008). Als ästhetische Mittel wurden (chorische) Bewegungen (Choreografien), Szenen auf der Basis von Improvisationen (biografisches Arbeiten), Standbilder und die bereits eingeführte Heldenreise verwendet. Die Theaterarbeit wurde eng mit der Sprachvermittlung verzahnt (vgl. Walter 2012), denn nur so konnten beide Projektziele umgesetzt werden, nämlich eine kritische Auseinandersetzung mit dem Heldenbegriff und ein Kompetenzzuwachs in der Fremdsprache Deutsch. Im Folgenden wird die konkrete Umsetzung der Heldenreise im Projekt nachgezeichnet

---

3   www.ethnologue.com/country/NA/languages, eingesehen am 6.5.2018.
4   www.dhps-windhoek.de/lang-de/schule, eingesehen am 7.3.2016.

Bilder eines Helden

Die erste Aufgabe nach einer Aufwärmphase bestand darin, sich in einer Klein-
gruppe bewusst zu machen, welche Helden wichtig sind (vgl. Arbeitsauftrag 1)
und was die Figur eines Helden auszeichnet. Sprachlich vorbereitet wurde diese
Aufgabe durch eine Zusammenstellung von Eigenschaften eines fiktiven Helden
(vgl. Arbeitsauftrag 2).

Arbeitsauftrag 1: Wer ist für euch ein Held? Schreibt eine Liste mit zehn
Helden (und begründet, warum dies Helden sind).

Erwartungsgemäß wurden Heldenfiguren aus der Kinder- und Jugendliteratur
wie *Harry Potter* genannt, aber auch der eigene Vater und die eigene Mutter
kamen auf die Ranglisten. Unerwartet für die Teenager*innen waren die häufige
Nennung von Politiker*innen wie *Sam Nujoma*, der Namibia im Jahre 1990 in die
Unabhängigkeit führte, der Präsident des Landes *Hage Gottfried Geingob* oder
aber auch die deutsche Bundeskanzlerin *Angela Merkel*. Als Rechercheaufgabe
sollten die Schüler*innen in ihren Familien nach Helden fragen. Leider gab es
hier auch in den folgenden Tagen keine Antworten. Der Weg in die Familien-
geschichte(n) blieb für das Projekt verschlossen. Über die Gründe dieser Sprach-
losigkeit kann nur spekuliert werden.

Arbeitsauftrag 2: Welche Eigenschaften hat ein Held? Findet mindestens
10 Eigenschaften. Schreibt ein Adjektiv auf eine Karte. Schreibt die Übersetzung auf die Rückseite der Karte. Legt am Ende die Karten in einen Kreis.

Die Sammlung der konkreten Beispiele von Helden und ihrer Eigenschaften-
sollte eine Diskussion in Gang setzen. Auf Anfängerniveau kann hier auch die
Muttersprache herangezogen werden. Aus didaktischen Gründen war es wichtig, dass am Ende die zweiseitigen Wortkarten als Arbeitsergebnis gesichert
werden. Dies erfolgte im Plenum: Die Kleingruppen legten die Karten in einen
Kreis und bündelten mehrfach genannte Begriffe. Ob zutreffende Wörter ausgewählt wurden, kann mit der Übersetzung von den Lerner*innen selbst (und
im zweiten Schritt auch von der Lehrperson) überprüft werden. Hier bietet sich
ein guter Reflexionsanlass, nämlich die Sprachbewusstmachung im Wortfeld
der Personencharakteristik (*mutig, schön, klug, freundlich,...*). Bei dieser werden
semantische Gruppen gebildet und es werden Unterschiede im Sprachgebrauch
diskutiert, bzw. von der Lehrperson erklärt. Auch ist in dieser Phase dies der
Raum, um „falsche Freunde" wie *brav/mutig* zu erkennen. In einer anschließen-

den inhaltlichen Reflexion werden die Eigenschaften systematisiert. Wenn möglich, vollzieht sich die Begründung in der Fremdsprache (vgl. Arbeitsauftrag 3).

Arbeitsauftrag 3: Baut einen Helden! Was ist besonders wichtig? Welche Eigenschaften sind im Kopf, im Bauch, ...?

Nachdem im Plenum mit den Adjektivkarten gemeinsam ein Held entworfen wurde, erhielt diese Mosaikfigur auf dem Boden noch einen Namen. Am Ende stellten die Lernenden in Partnerarbeit den Helden mit seinen Eigenschaften vor und übten auf diese Weise die zuvor gesicherten Adjektive.

Abbildung 1: Das Bild eines Helden mit seinen Eigenschaften (Foto: Maik Walter)

Mit dem folgenden Schritt vollzog sich der Wechsel zur körperlich-ästhetischen Ebene: Die Lernenden bauten in Kleingruppen Standbilder eines Helden (vgl.

Arbeitsauftrag 4)⁵ und gestalteten zunächst im geschützten Raum der Gruppe eine menschliche Skulptur. Hierzu müssen die Jugendlichen einen abstrakten Begriff in ein Bild transformieren.

Arbeitsauftrag 4: Entwerft das Standbild eines Helden! Was ist für euch besonders wichtig?

Die Standbilder der Helden wurden im Plenum ausgewertet (vgl. Abbildung 2), wobei die Zuschauer zunächst beschrieben, was sie sahen, und im Anschluss das Dargestellte interpretierten.

Impulsfragen des Lehrers: Was seht ihr? Was könnte es darstellen/sein?

Abbildung 2: Ein prototypischer Held (Anwendung der Standbildtechnik) (Foto: Maik Walter)

---

5   Wurde die Inszenierungstechnik des Standbilds (vgl. Schewe 1995, Schewe & Woodhouse 2018, Walter 2016) noch nicht eingeführt, sollte dies zunächst an anderen Beispielen geübt werden.

Die Standbilder lieferten einen guten Sprechanlass, um stereotype Heldenbilder zu thematisieren, gerade auch um Geschlechterstereotype zu hinterfragen: Warum zum Beispiel werden primär Männer als Vorbilder für Helden genannt und weshalb sind die mit ihnen verbundenen Stereotype wie Mut und Durchsetzungskraft so präsent? Im weiteren Verlauf gab es eine szenische Aufgabe, in der sich mit den eigenen idealen Vorstellungen eines Helden auseinandergesetzt wurde. Viele Menschen haben in ihrem Leben kleine oder auch größere Heldentaten vollbracht. Darüber zu reden fällt gerade *wahren Helden* häufig schwer. Deshalb wurde eine andere Perspektive gewählt: Es sollten Situationen erzählt werden, in denen man sich gewünscht hätte, auf einen Helden zu treffen.

Arbeitsauftrag 5: Wann hast du einen Helden gebraucht? Sammelt Situationen in der Gruppe und wählt am Ende eine Situation aus, die ihr in ca. 2-3 Minuten den anderen vorspielt. Gebt der Szene einen Titel.

Abbildung 3: Eine Situation mit einem Helden (Improvisation auf der Basis eines biographischen Impulses) (Foto: Maik Walter)

Am Ende dieser Einheit hatten die Lernenden über eigene Heldenbilder nachgedacht und diese einer kritischen Betrachtung unterzogen. Außerdem wurden sprachlich die Persönlichkeitscharakteristika geübt und ggf. das Wortfeld durch die Lehrperson erweitert.

Bereits an dieser Stelle war eine Menge an Spielmaterial gesammelt worden, das später in die Inszenierung einfließen konnte.

Schritt für Schritt: Die Phasen der Reise

Die Heldenreise gibt mit ihren Schritten eine bewährte Struktur einer Geschichte vor. Diese Schritte wurden den Lernern in reduzierter Form erklärt, wobei jeweils ein Satz auf ein Blatt geschrieben und präsentiert wurde:

- Wie ist der Alltag?
- Es gibt ein Problem.
- Der Held geht auf die Reise.
- Jemand versucht, den Helden aufzuhalten.
- Der Held geht wirklich auf die Reise.
- Der Held trifft auf den Antihelden.
- Der Held bewährt sich. (Es gibt einen Kampf.)
- Der Held ist fast am Ziel.
- Es gibt noch ein Problem.
- Der Held löst das Problem.
- Der Held kehrt zurück nach Hause.

Mit diesen Sätzen ist es möglich, eine einfache Geschichte im Kreis zu erzählen. Nach der Demonstration eines Beispiels, bei dem der Held einer Geschichte mit Namen, Beruf, Alter, Geschlecht etc. ausgestattet wurde, erhielten die Lernenden jeweils eine Karte mit einem der oben genannten Sätze. Die Aufgabe bestand darin, einen Satz in der Fremdsprache zu äußern. Heißt der Held der Geschichte beispielsweise Manfred, der 65 Jahre alt ist und als Dramapädagoge arbeitet, kann nun gefragt werden „Wie ist der Alltag von Manfred?" Eine mögliche Antwort wäre: „Manfred geht jeden Tag in sein Büro, liest die vielen Mails aus aller Welt und überlegt sich, wie er seine ihm anvertrauten Menschen verzaubern und sie dabei in der Fremdsprache ein Stück weiter nach vorn bringen kann." Und nun entspinnt sich Erzähler für Erzählerin – Schritt für Schritt – im gemeinsamen Erzählen eine Geschichte. Diese Technik kann wie die anfangs skizzierte Impro-Übung auf einen Satz limitiert werden. Diese Begrenzung hat sich in der Fremdsprache bewährt.[6] Man kann die einzelnen Phasen aber auch in kleineren Sequenzen präsentieren und die Gruppe entscheidet, ob sie diesen Weg weitergehen will oder noch nach einer Alternative sucht (vgl. zu einem ähnlichen Vor-

---

6   Interessanterweise treffen sich in der Begrenzung die Kunstpädagogik und die Fremdsprachendidaktik. Während die Begrenzung in der Kunst ästhetische Räume öffnet, gibt sie in der Fremdsprachendidaktik den Lerner*innen Sicherheit und setzt in der Regel das methodisch-didaktische Prinzip der Erfolgsorientierung um.

gehen Hippe & Hippe 2011). Auch ein schriftliches Arbeiten ist möglich. Hierbei bietet sich an, am Ende das Ergebnis auf diese Weise zu fixieren.

Im hier beschriebenen Schulprojekt in Namibia erzählten die Lernenden ebenfalls zunächst im Kreis eine Geschichte, und zwar gemeinsam auf Deutsch.

> Held dieser Geschichte ist der Schüler Paul, der besonders gut in Mathematik ist und dessen Freund das Schulgeld an der Privatschule nicht mehr zahlen kann. Paul hört von seinem Mathematiklehrer, dass es in Swakopmund einen Mathematikwettbewerb gibt, bei dem ein Preisgeld ausgezahlt wird. Obwohl die Eltern – die Schwellenhüter in persona – versuchen, ihn davon abzuhalten, nimmt er den Bus durch die Wüstenlandschaft ans Meer. Beim Wettbewerb angekommen, erfährt er, dass Schüler aus Windhoek nicht teilnehmen dürfen. Durch einen geschickten T-Shirt-Tausch gelingt die Teilnahme, Paul siegt beim Wettbewerb, und nach seiner Rückkehr darf der Freund auch auf der Schule bleiben. Mit der Prämie werden die Schulden beglichen.

Kooperativ entwickelten die Lernenden diese Geschichte: Nur wenn alle Beteiligten einverstanden waren, ging man zur nächsten Phase über. Dies hat den Vorteil, dass im späteren Verlauf die gesamte Gruppe die entwickelte Geschichte als ihre eigene Geschichte akzeptiert und durch den anstrengenden Probenprozess mitträgt (vgl. Abbildung 4).

Abbildung 4: Probenprozess auf der Bühne der DHPS in Windhoek (Foto: Maik Walter)

Anschließend wurden Sprachgruppen gebildet, die die gesamte Geschichte noch einmal in ihrer Erstsprache erzählten, beispielsweise auf Englisch, Afrikaans oder Otjihero. Hierbei wurde deutlich, dass es Sprachen gibt, in denen man schnell erzählen muss oder mehr Worte benötigt als in anderen Sprachen. Im Anschluss diskutierten die Lernenden diese Unterschiede zwischen dem Erzählen in den verschiedenen Sprachen. Die entwickelte Geschichte wurde in mehreren Durchläufen verfeinert, präzisiert und verdichtet, bevor die Schüler*innen in Kleingruppen zwei Sequenzen in ihrer Muttersprache für eine Präsentation vorbereiteten.

Für alle Sequenzen wurden Standbilder entworfen, die den Fortgang der Geschichte für die Zuschauer sicherten, die die jeweilige Sprache nicht beherrschten. Für die Aufführung wurde die Geschichte am Ende wieder zusammengefügt, wobei eine Erzählgruppe die Phasen performte (vgl. Abbildung 5), die anderen Mitspieler die Geschichte zeitgleich in Standbildern präsentierten. Diese Bilder boten den Spielimpuls für die Entwicklung von kurzen Spielszenen, die zunächst improvisiert und daraufhin bühnentauglich ausgearbeitet wurden.

Abbildung 5: Das kollektive Erzählen der entwickelten Heldenreise (Foto: Maik Walter)

Nach einer Woche intensiver Projektarbeit standen 25 Schüler*innen auf der großen Bühne der DHPS in Windhoek. Die hier beschriebene Heldenreise war ein Bestandteil der ca. 45-minütigen Abschlusspräsentation. Voller Stolz zeigten sie diese mit Bewegungschören, Bildern, Liedern und Spielszenen angereicherte Collage ihren Familien, den beteiligten Schulen, den Mitarbeiter*innen der Deutschen Botschaft und der Presse und damit ihre individuelle Sicht auf Helden. Die Aufführung war ein wichtiges motivierendes Element, man kehrte nach einer Woche an den Ausgangspunkt einer intensiven Reise zurück, bei der 25 Teenager*innen anfangs schüchtern ihren Platz auf der großen Bühne suchten. In Auseinandersetzung mit den eigenen Bildern und in Konflikten mit den Anderen begaben sie sich auf eine Suche ihren Helden und ihren Geschichten. Auf dieser Reise trafen sie neue Freunde, neue Wörter, neue Möglichkeiten sich auszudrücken, sei es im Tanz, in der Musik oder auch in der fremden Sprache Deutsch.

Kommen wir am Ende zur ästhetischen Ausgangsfrage des Beitrags zurück.

Wie viel Ästhetik verträgt der DaF-Unterricht? Ein kurzes Fazit

Bereits 1993 hat Manfred Schewe in seiner Dissertation auf die Vielfalt und den Nutzen ästhetischen Lernens im Fremdsprachenunterricht hingewiesen (vgl. Schewe 1993). 25 Jahre später, um viele Einsichten reicher, kann die Antwort auf diese Frage nur lauten: Der DaF-Unterricht verträgt sehr viel mehr an Ästhetik, als derzeit praktiziert wird. Dazu bedarf es der *Integration* von (Fremd-)Sprache, Ästhetik und Kultur. Sowohl die empirische Wirkungsforschung (Küppers & Walter 2012) als auch die aktuellen Erkenntnisse der Neurodidaktik (Sambanis 2013, Arndt & Sambanis 2017, Sambanis & Walter 2019) liefern wichtige Argumente, entsprechende Freiräume für den DaF-Unterricht zu schaffen. Das ästhetische Lernen setzt einen spielerischen und zugleich professionellen Rahmen für die Lernenden. Das Agieren in ästhetischen Räumen ermöglicht ihnen Erfahrungen, die weit über deren gewöhnlichen Handlungsraum im Fremdsprachenunterricht hinausgehen. Sobald eine Szene, ein Standbild oder eine Performance vor einem Publikum präsentiert werden, verstärkt sich in einer Lerngruppe der Anspruch auf professionelle Arbeitsergebnisse, die beispielsweise in einer präzisen Aussprache oder in einer klaren Körpersprache festgemacht werden können.

Die vorgeschlagene Didaktisierung wurde bereits in mehreren Ländern vorgestellt und ausprobiert, beispielsweise bei den 2017 stattgefundenen Studientagen der Deutschlehrer*innen im kroatischen Zagreb. Das positive Feedback aus den Klassenzimmern, in denen es anschließend umgesetzt wurde, bestätigt die einfachen Adaptionsmöglichkeiten des Modells. Und das kann ein guter Anfang sein, um mit seinen Lernenden Freiräume auszuloten, zu nutzen und sich mit ihnen auf eine Reise in die Fremde zu begeben. Es lohnt sich!

Literatur

Arndt, Petra A. & Sambanis, Michaela (Hg.) (2017): *Didaktik und Neurowissenschaften.*
Dialog zwischen Wissenschaft und Praxis. Tübingen: Narr Francke Attempto.

Batzel, Andrea; Bohl, Thorsten & Bryant, Doreen (2013): *Evaluation des Tübinger*
Theatercamps "Stadt der Kinder". Ein Ferienprojekt zur Förderung von Sprache und
sozialer Kompetenz. Baltmannsweiler: Schneider Verlag Hohengehren.

Bernstein, Nils & Lerchner, Charlotte (Hg.) (2014): *Ästhetisches Lernen im DaF-/*
DaZ-Unterricht. Literatur – Theater – Bildende Kunst – Musik – Film. Göttingen:
Universitätsverlag Göttingen.

Bryant, Doreen (2012): DaZ und Theater: Der dramapädagogische Ansatz zur Förderung der Bildungssprache. In *Scenario* VI/01, 28-58.

Campbell, Joseph (2011): *Der Heros in tausend Gestalten.* Frankfurt a. M.: Insel-Verlag.

Hippe, Eva & Hippe, Lorenz (2011): *Theater direkt – das Theater der Zuschauer. Ein*
Beitrag zur kollektiven Kreativität. Weinheim: Deutscher Theaterverlag.

Höcker, Angelika (2011): *Business Hero. Eine Heldenreise in 7 Etappen.* Offenbach:
GABAL Verlag.

Jahnke, Manfred (2004): Erzähltheater. Narrative Strukturen im Kinder- und Jugend-
theater als intermediales Experiment. In Hajo Kurzenberger & Annemarie Matzke
(Hg.): *Theorie, Theater, Praxis.* Berlin: Theater der Zeit (Theater der Zeit Recherchen
17), 298-315.

Küppers, Almut & Walter, Maik (2012): Theatermethoden auf dem Prüfstand der
Forschung. Einführung in die Themenausgabe. In *Scenario* VI/1, 1-9.

Küppers, Almut; Schmidt, Torben & Walter, Maik (Hg.) (2011): *Inszenierungen*
im Fremdsprachenunterricht. Grundlagen, Formen, Perspektiven. Braunschweig:
Schroedel/Diesterweg/Klinkhardt.

Kurtz, Jürgen (2008): Szenische Improvisationen: theoretische Grundlagen und unter-
richtliche Realisierungsmöglichkeiten. In Rüdiger Ahrens, Maria Eisenmann, Matthias Merkl (Hg.): *Moderne Dramendidaktik für den Englischunterricht.* Heidelberg:
Universitätsverlag Winter, 409-424.

Lehmann, Hans-Thies (2008): *Postdramatisches Theater.* 4. Aufl. Frankfurt a. M.: Verlag
der Autoren.

Lösel, Gunter (2004): *Theater ohne Absicht – Impulse zur Weiterentwicklung des Improvi-*
sationstheaters. Planegg: Impuls/Buschfunk.

Mai, Jesko (o. J.): Erzählung. In Kersten Reich (Hg.): *Methodenpool.* In http://methoden-
pool.uni-koeln.de, eingesehen am 5.3.2016.

Sambanis, Michaela (2013): *Fremdsprachenunterricht und Neurowissenschaften.*
Tübingen: Narr.

Sambanis, Michaela & Walter, Maik (2019): *In Motion – Theaterimpulse zum Sprachen-*
lernen. Von neuesten Befunden der Neurowissenschaft zu konkreten Unterrichts-
impulsen. Berlin: Cornelsen.

Schewe, Manfred (1993): *Fremdsprache inszenieren. Zur Fundierung einer dramapädago-*
gischen Lehr- und Lernpraxis. Oldenburg: Pädagogisches Zentrum.

Schewe, Manfred (1995): Zum methodischen Potential von Standbildern im DaF-Unterricht. In Armin Wolff & Winfried Welter (Hg.): *Mündliche Kommunikation. Unterrichts- und Übungsformen DaF. zielgruppenspezifische Auswahl von Unterrichtsmaterialien. Modelle für studien- und berufsbegleitenden Unterricht.* Regensburg: Fachverband Deutsch als Fremdsprache, 75-97.

Schewe, Manfred & Woodhouse, Fionn (2018): Performative Foreign Language Didactics in Progress: About Still Images and the Teacher as 'Formmeister' (Form Master). In *Scenario* XII/1, 53-69.

Spiff, Spaceman (2014): Han Solo. In *Endlich nichts.* CD. Hamburg: Grand Hotel van Cleef/Indigo.

Streisand, Marianne & Walter, Maik (Hg.) (2003): *Sprechtheater im DaF-Unterricht. Die Förderung der narrativen Kompetenz durch das szenische Spiel: Ein Dossier.* Berlin: Humboldt-Universität zu Berlin.

Vlcek, Radim (2003): *Workshop Improvisationstheater. Übungs- und Spielesammlung für Theaterarbeit, Ausdrucksfindung und Gruppenarbeit.* Donauwörth: Auer.

Vogler, Christopher (2010): *Die Odyssee des Drehbuchschreibers. Über die mythologischen Grundmuster des amerikanischen Erfolgskinos,* übersetzt von Frank Kuhnke. 6., akt. und erw. Aufl. Frankfurt a. M.: Zweitausendeins.

Walter, Maik (2012): Theater in der Fremdsprachenvermittlung. In Christoph Nix, Dietmar Sachser, Marianne Streisand (Hg.): *Theaterpädagogik.* Berlin: Theater der Zeit, 182-188.

Walter, Maik (2014): Mit Worten Räume bauen: Improvisationstheater und szenische Wortschatzvermittlung. In Nils Bernstein, Charlotte Lerchner (Hg.): *Ästhetisches Lernen im DaF-/ DaZ-Unterricht. Literatur – Theater – Bildende Kunst – Musik – Film.* Göttingen: Universitätsverlag Göttingen, 233-247.

Walter, Maik (2016): Theater im Deutschunterricht: Von der Sache mit den Tieren zu lebenden Bildern. In *Deutsch aktuell* 28, 30-33.

Wardetzky, Kristin (2003): Erzähltheater. In Gerd Koch, Marianne Streisand (Hg.): *Wörterbuch der Theaterpädagogik.* Berlin et al.: Schibri, 90-91.

Wardetzky, Kristin (2007): *Projekt Erzählen.* Baltmannsweiler: Schneider Verlag Hohengehren.

Wardetzky, Kristin & Weigel, Christiane (2008): *Sprachlos? Erzählen im interkulturellen Kontext. Erfahrungen aus einer Grundschule.* Baltmannsweiler: Schneider Verlag Hohengehren.

Empathy Matters

Oscillating between beer and baklava

Almut Küppers

Good morning dear audience! Welcome again to our special interest radio program "Innovation in Education". Language policy is an influential field in our societies which is usually controlled by states and implemented in top-down fashion by state institutions. However, schools are sometimes much faster than bureaucracies, administrations or academia when it comes to change and innovation. On the occasion of Manfred Schewe's 65th birthday today, we will broadcast a conversation between two scholars from the field of education who will talk about a successful grassroots project which emerged at the German school in Istanbul, Turkey. They will focus on empathy as a core concept and touch upon topics like institutional discrimination, language policy and ideology and heritage language teaching.

Introduction: In other people's shoes

Interviewer (Q): As a colleague in social science, you approached me a while ago with an uncommon request. You said you felt like "a barrel full of data" and that you were in need of someone who could help you unearth its content and make sense of it. I am delighted to assist you in this! Why a *barrel full of data*?
Interviewee (A): Well, I needed a catchy phrase, because I feel like a container full of experiences all revolving around language issues. We are a German-only speaking family. With my husband and our three children we have been living in Turkey for more than seven years now, and Istanbul is a very multilingual and diverse urban space, a city which has been called the New York of the 21st century. Our three girls attend the German school in the old city formerly called Pera, which is the lively tourist centre of Beyoğlu. All five of us learned Turkish very differently, so the barrel is filled with topics like language acquisition, language and migration, language policy, power and ideology, and at some point I started to think I would love to meet a person who would be interested in all this as data. When the invitation to contribute to Manfred Schewe's Festschrift came along, I suddenly realized how I could just as well explore some of this

myself as a piece of performative research. All of the above mentioned experiences account for "embodied knowledge" which is one of the key terms in Manfred's works on performative pedagogy and plays a major role in performative research, too. Manfred's recent publication *Performative Teaching, Learning, Research* (Even & Schewe 2016) confirmed the idea that I could just as well use a more creative way to explore this personal data as embodied knowledge.

Q: And why did you decide to employ autoethnography for this?
A: Autoethnography is a powerful research approach that seeks to describe and analyse personal experience in order to understand cultural and social processes. According to Carolyn Ellis, one of its protagonists, autoethnography developed out of the need in social science „to resist colonialist, sterile research impulses of authoritatively entering a culture, exploiting cultural members, and then recklessly leaving to write about the culture for monetary and /or professional gain, while disregarding relational ties to cultural members" (Ellis et al. 2011: xx). Hence, this particular interview situation I chose is both a process and a product; it will generate data during the writing process, and will develop into a narrative that generates insights from my participation in a grassroots project. I could not otherwise share this experience with the scholarly community as it has become embodied knowledge; not collected intentionally with a research project in mind.

Q: Tell us why you chose empathy as a core concept then.
A: Empathy has only recently emerged as a popular and highly regarded value in globalized societies, and some even argue that only empathetic societies are sustainable societies.[1] Yet if we look at theatre education, empathy has always been the bedrock of any dramatic process and any dramatization. Without empathy we could not effectively suspend our disbelief – empathy is seen as a precondition for taking up new perspectives. Manfred Schewe's ground-breaking works on performativity in foreign /second language education have helped to free the traditional notion of language as a two-dimensional text and promoted less tangible (and grade-able) but powerful dimensions of language such as body language, voice and emotions. In particular, Manfred (Schewe 2011: 24) has been arguing that while communication in expanding online worlds is increasingly disembodied, the whole human body needs to remain the core me-

---

1   There is even a kind of general belief that empathy is a force for goodness, compassion and helping others. By contrast, a number of strong voices have started to discuss the pitfalls of empathy e.g. Fritz Breithaupt in "Die dunklen Seiten der Empathie"(2017). In "Against Empathy" Paul Bloom (2016) even claims that in divided societies empathy, emotional empathy in particular, is apparently not the solution but the problem.

dium for communication and human understanding ("der Körper als zentrales menschliches Kommunikationsmedium und Erkenntnisinstrument"), hence the foundations of performative language pedagogy are built on holistic approaches of language and learning. Moreover, and for more than two decades now, empathy has been considered an important link between intercultural education and drama work in language teaching. Here again, Manfred – together with Susanne Even – has been one of the major voices who promoted intercultural dialogue in drama and theatre education with SCENARIO, an online journal and SCENARIO *Edition*, a book series, and, thus, inspired many colleagues, scholars and students in various disciplines around the world. Against this backdrop the underlying notion of language for my autoethnography includes pre-linguistic emotional mechanisms as well as relations of power and ideology. Joelle Aden argues that "empathy, as the basis of interaction, places language at the heart of human relationships without separating the linguistic aspects from all the neurophysiological and psychological sub-mechanisms that constitute the act of 'languaging'" (Aden 2017: 60). Thus, empathy as a social glue impacts all our human interactions but seems to have special implications in classroom situations. Eventually, empathy will also be the bridge into my interviewer's mind and I will try to look at my own experience through the eyes of a research colleague in order to lay open social dynamics that might otherwise remain hidden. This strategy ties in with empathy as a tool in performative research, at the heart of which we have empathetic movements between knowing and not-knowing (Gehm et al. 2007).

Learning and moving between beer and baklava

Q: Let's turn to the grassroots project then. What do we need to know about your professional background in order to understand what you have been doing in Turkey?
A: I am a professional foreign language teacher for English and German and have more than a decade of work experience as a teacher trainer at Frankfurt University under my belt. I wrote my PhD on emergent literacy in a foreign language and since my teacher training in the UK, where I first encountered the drama in education approach, I have focused on drama and intercultural learning and have employed drama for reflective teacher training. When we left for Turkey in 2010 I was able to explore aspects of diversity, multilingualism, and transnational education – in everyday life as a language learner and mother, but also conceptually and empirically through various projects at universities and other institutions. During the years 2013 and 2014 I carried out an ethnographic field study at an elementary school in Hannover, Germany. The school runs an

unusual bilingual German-Turkish language program and, thanks to a Mercator fellowship, I was able to document a very successful curriculum development process and researched its sociocultural impact.[2] Moreover, I have also been advising NGOs that work with refugee children on Turkish language education here in Turkey. Since 2015 – triggered by the so-called *refugee-crisis* – there has been a growing awareness in German academia for the so-called heritage languages. Hence, in the past two or three years I have been communicating a lot with colleagues in Germany and Turkey on the potential of the languages of migration in European societies.

Q: Given your experience revolving around language education, writing a piece of autoethnography sounds like a pretty straightforward idea. Was it as easy as it sounds?
A: Not at all! I had a lot of doubts initially, and felt inhibited and insecure. One reason is that I am so used to academic writing in which one always seems to be on top of everything. We write in a very factual manner, we follow strict rules, we employ a rational, academic style and jargon. Our "I" hardly ever surfaces in our writing. Instead we try to write from the perspective of the seemingly unbiased omniscient academic narrator. But I have often felt that the process of putting together arguments and the way we back them up with quotes and findings from studies is a creative act which very much resembles what artists do. We create a texture, a tapestry. The *performative turn* in the social sciences and the notion of *science as art and art as science* (Seitz 2012) which has meanwhile reached academic discourse on research methodology have eventually encouraged me to pursue this autoethnography. However, according to the performative paradigm it is far more important to be aware of one's biases and to lay them open as well as to reflect upon our hidden agendas instead of producing research which is seemingly reliable, objective and replicable. Instead, I acknowledge that my subjectivity and my emotions influence this process. I think you can see from my engagement with the German school that I do have an agenda and that has been *upgrading Turkish* and integrating it into the curriculum as a proper subject. The motives for this endeavour go beyond this strategic goal. Deep down my involvement has been powered by a struggle for equality, integration and equal opportunities, especially for the bilingual children who suffered most from the monolingual habitus of the German school. But there is a second reason why it took me so long to start writing, and that has been an ethical one. As a researcher I could never have entered the field in the

---

2   See https://uni-frankfurt.academia.edu/AlmutKüppers for the research report and papers
     on heritage language teaching and related issues.

way I did as an important stakeholder in a process of social change and school development. As a mother of three I was entitled to represent the parents, and for almost five years I was even the chairwoman of the parents' association at that school. I have been to countless formal and informal meetings and it would have been impossible to predict what would happen during those years, let alone devise a research agenda for something as unforeseeable as this. I also never looked at the process from a researcher's perspective, even though it was pretty obvious that I would be able to use much of my professional expertise as well as the insights I had gained from the Hannover study. But I always felt that I could not possibly share any of this experience since I had to protect other stakeholders in the field.

Q: This sounds very intriguing indeed. Tell us about how this process started and why you think you needed to protect some of the stakeholders.
A: When we arrived in Istanbul in 2010, we had no idea what to expect from the German School where we had registered our children. Somehow we had heard about its reputation as one of the best schools in Turkey, so we did not bother much. After the first year, when friends and family wanted to know about our Turkish experiences, I remember so well the sentences I always used: "The only real disappointment is the German school, everything else in Turkey is fascinating." Another one was: "I have been to many schools in Germany, but this is the most German school I have ever seen. In fact, it is a very, very German German school and somehow there is still a *Kaiserreich* atmosphere blowing through its corridors." The big disappointment had been the poor language program for the German classes in which more than two thirds of the children were actually bilingual with German and Turkish or other languages. However, a Turkish program was non-existent! There was no concept, no curriculum, no qualified Turkish foreign language teacher, no textbooks, no department. And what's more, at the same time in the Turkish part of the school, there was a modern bilingual German-Turkish program in existence, which provided German education with Abitur (leaving examination) to monolingual Turkish students from affluent families. In a way, the school's split character very much resembled some of the pressing issues within the German school system as if through a looking glass. Hans-Jürgen Krumm's term *Armuts- und Elitemehr- sprachigkeit* (2013), that translates into poverty- and elitist multilingualism, is very fitting. There is great public applause and praise when well-off monolin- gual children visit bilingual schools and start speaking a foreign language, but when disadvantaged bilingual children with a family history of migration come to school, they do not get praise for their skills in a second language. Instead, it is usually seen as a huge problem. The situation was exactly like this. Teachers

complained about the apparently deteriorating German skills of the bilingual students and their poor Turkish, and yet there was huge attention and floods of praise if a student from the elitist Turkish side of the school publicly produced a sentence in German.

There was another striking aspect. Just imagine an official Turkish school operating in Germany, run on a Turkish curriculum and not even teaching their students basic German. It would be an uproar close to a public scandal. But here in Istanbul, there was an official German institution – beholden to the German Foreign Ministry, by the way – which basically ignored the language needs of the children who lived here and did not know any Turkish. In case of an earthquake or a terror attack, many children would not have been able to express their needs in Turkish. This felt so wrong, so hypocritical. Germany, in comparison, requires all immigrants to learn German, in some cases even before entering the country. Thus, Germany is protected by a language barrier to prevent unwanted immigration. And in the rumbling public discourse, hardly anything is so yin and yang like *learning German* and *successful integration*. Of course, knowing the host country's language is considered paramount for integration. This used to be in stark contrast to the language policy in the German School in Istanbul: A German institution abroad ignores the necessity of speaking the host country's language? Not only did this feel like Western European arrogance to us; it was utterly irresponsible.

Q: This sounds quite outrageous indeed, especially in light of the fact that most of the 140 German schools abroad provide instruction in the host country's language. But you said you felt the need to protect the stakeholders. Can you elaborate on that?

A: Sure. I would say that what we encountered was a long tradition of how a German institution abroad put into practice its nation-state language ideology and in so doing – intentionally or not – subjected many school children to institutional discrimination. "This is a German school – only German is spoken here", was a typical phrase the children often heard. They were not allowed to use Turkish in the classrooms. Hence, I thought, I could not refer to those statements without presenting the stakeholders in a very questionable light. That's why I had doubts. Right from the beginning and together with other parents we started initiatives to include Turkish in the curriculum through the parents' association committee. But all of these attempts were rejected by the school management – usually by employing seemingly formal but in fact very flimsy arguments like "there is no room for Turkish in the overloaded schedule", "the German education authorities (KMK) would never subscribe to Turkish as a Foreign Language (TFL) in the curriculum" and, apparently, nobody would be interested in learning this language. "Why should we offer Turkish then – and, above all, this language is too hard to learn anyway." Moreover, "what's the point in learning Turkish?!" In the end, there was just one single occasion in which we, the parents, at least succeeded in discussing the topic based on content arguments. Those were:

- the integration argument – all children with no Turkish needed at least some basic language skills to connect to locals and to cope in emergency situations;
- the added-value argument – Turkish is a vivid language in Germany, it can be used and spoken at home (and some other countries);
- the language awareness argument – due to the unusual agglutinative structure of Turkish, it provides valuable language learning experience for learners;
- the identity argument – to enhance the potential of bilingual learners who could speak but often not yet write or read in Turkish; and finally,
- the resource argument – to use previous knowledge of Turkish for educational success.

That night the principal got so furious that already the next day at noon the chairman of the parents' association had received an email from the school management saying we would not be allowed to put Turkish as a topic on the agenda any more – at any time.

Q: In other words, the topic of Turkish had turned into a battlefield? Did you stick to the prohibition which was imposed?
A: It was ridiculous! And no, of course not. The school management had always tried to render our initiatives ineffective by either using seemingly formal arguments as knock-outs or by claiming that the parents should prove that the families were interested in Turkish classes. It was argued that there was an extra-curricular club for Turkish in the afternoon, but as nobody ever turned up to participate this was enough evidence that there was no interest in the host country's language. So, we decided to conduct an online survey to ask the families what they thought about Turkish lessons. Our numbers were solid and the result was crystal clear: Two thirds of all families wanted Turkish to be included in the curriculum. They would even accept slightly longer school days for their children because of additional lessons. And two thirds agreed that Turkish could be one of the school subjects tested in the leaving examinations. That was in summer 2013, which was Istanbul's Gezi summer. And in the upcoming academic year we used the survey results for a new initiative.

Towards a paradigm shift

Q: How did the situation develop from there?
A: After the Gezi summer, the news trickled through that the principal would leave the school. The paradigm shift really started when the new head teacher entered the school management in summer 2014. There had also been personnel changes on the board of governors. Whereas before communication and procedures had been highly problematic and non-transparent, the new principal started to consider parents as partners in the educational endeavours for their children – as one should. Consequently, I agreed to run the parents' association as chairwoman. I hoped to increase parental influence in curricular matters and to push the languages question.

Q: How far did you get and what was the next turning point?
A: The most important thing, in hindsight, was a coincidence! The right group of people got together. The new principal quickly took a number of important staffing decisions and did not prolong the contracts of three other members in the management team. Apparently, they had been advocates of the old ideology. Those posts were filled with new colleagues, the most important one being the head of the lower secondary department of the school. This post was given to a young teacher who himself was a Turkish-German bilingual with a family history of immigration to Germany. Soon it became clear that we acted in concert. While I had started to raise awareness of the potential of bilingualism and multilingualism amongst the families, he started to plough the field for Turkish from the administrative side. The principal's policy was pretty obvious. He wanted to free the school from its educational standstill by triggering a necessary school development process but was very open topic-wise. He opened doors and created room for anybody who wanted to get involved from within the school community. And that explicitly included parents. Turkish was powerfully pushed from two sides now but resistance within the staff room was still high. Within the first year, an evening event was organized on the topic "Multilingualism and its potential at the German school". All parents were invited, plus all teachers – also from the neighbouring elementary school. The French teacher presented the existing foreign language program and as a special guest the Turkish teacher from the German school in Izmir gave a talk on how Turkish was taught at his school.

Q: How was the event received and what was its effect?
A: The turnout was quite impressive. It became clear that there was space for Turkish in the schedule if French and English were to be downsized to the

standard 3 to 4 lessons per week (and not 5 as before) and one additional lesson added. Parents and teachers had come to the meeting, among them some teachers who had always been outspokenly critical about introducing Turkish. In the discussion following the presentations, the contrasting views clashed. Some teachers and parents argued that Turkish would take time away from seemingly more important subjects like Math, English, German, and French, and that Turkish would be a burden for the learners. The two moderators – also parents – offered additional points for discussion, such as the identity and especially resource argument – e.g. arguing that academic knowledge of Turkish would be an important additional qualification in the job market. In a way, the evening was evidence for the confrontation and huge resistance from parts of the school community. However, the most important side-effect was probably more subtle. The Turkish teacher from Izmir (with a teaching qualification from Germany) met the new principal who was generally very positive about implementing Turkish as a proper subject at the school, so after the summer holidays he was hired to teach Turkish at the German school in Istanbul!

Q: Congratulations! That seems like an impressive success. How did it go from there?
A: Let's put it this way, it was a victory but not yet a success. And the victory was a symbolic and very fragile one. It was like having a foot in the door. After cracking the school internal resistance in a top-down way, the real work began; namely, implementing a new subject. There was an officially qualified Turkish teacher now, but no concept, no curriculum, no resources, no teaching approaches. It was still a long way to go and many obstacles were waiting on the path to integrate Turkish. At the beginning, there was a two-year pilot phase which was evaluated and after which a proposal was submitted to the KMK on how to run Turkish as a 2nd or 3rd alternative foreign language at the school. The concept also included a curriculum, a teaching methodology and, probably the most valuable element, an overview of how to test and evaluate competences. In the final stage before submitting the concept, there was a very close cooperation with a high-ranking officer of the KMK who gave us feedback on our draft papers. In fact, the concept is a result of a very intense collaboration between the Turkish teachers (two other foreign language teachers, one for English, one for Turkish, had joined the crew), the director for lower secondary and me and in the run-up to submission it was monitored by the KMK. What had unwillingly emerged, was a very rare laboratory situation in which feedback from teaching practice could merged with administrative expertise and was developed with reference to professional subject knowledge. The laboratory's output was finally test-cased against the high standards of the KMK as well as KMK policies.

Eventually, the concept paper was acknowledged by the BLAschA[3] committee just before Easter 2018. Turkish is now officially an alternative 2nd or 3rd foreign language at the school, besides French.

Opening a new door – exploring new territory

Q: Finally, this sounds like a success story, doesn't it? And it sounds as if you have pushed open a new door. How and what did you find?

A: I guess, yes, it has been a success indeed – and yet admittedly, the ideal (concept) and reality (teaching practice) are still light years apart. However, the reason why the concept might also have transmissibility powers can be seen in its inclusiveness. In the past decade, inclusion has developed into one of the buzzwords in education in Europe, and this concept might be one attempt how to translate it into teaching practice. It might even be a blueprint for heritage language teaching in the German /European contexts in order to upgrade languages of migration like Turkish or Arabic and add them as fully-fledged foreign languages subjects to the menu of school languages. Currently, heritage language teaching is an inconvenient and neglected add-on in our education system and heritage languages are mostly just recognized in connection with German as a second language. Manfred Schewe, however, has addressed what I would call European language blindness. Together with John Crutchfield in the publication "Going Performative in Intercultural Education" (2017) the authors quite rightly point to the fact that despite the appraisal for multilingualism in Europe, in our education and training systems non-European languages are almost non-existent (Crutchfield & Schewe 2017: xxii with reference to Schröder 2016). To embrace the languages of migration by teaching them as inclusive 2nd or 3rd foreign language subjects – open to all who want to learn them – could mean unlocking a huge potential for learning and education, especially for the promotion of intercultural dialogue and social cohesion.

Q: Could you please elaborate on this and fill us in on the concrete features of the concept?

The rationale behind the inclusive approach stems from the realization that diversity in the Turkish lessons at the German school has been so high, that after the first piloting year the classical streaming approach, which had been applied, was dropped. As a result, the distinction between "foreign language learners" and "bilinguals" was dismissed. We have had and will always have

---

3   BLAschA = Bund-Länder Ausschuss für schulische Arbeit im Ausland, a committee subordinate to the KMK

groups of learners with different interests, abilities, competencies and learning needs. Diversity has been exploding in urban classrooms lately and will continue to do so. Hence, diversity in the Turkish concept has been acknowledged and will be used productively by turning differentiation and mediation into teaching principles and adding tandem learning. The inherent paradigm shift can be seen in changing from the traditional "I can shine better if your grades are bad" principle to the "as a group we are much better than we could ever be as individuals". This has been something really new for learners who are used to traditional grading and working in a competitive atmosphere. As a consequence of the paradigm shift, teaching Turkish takes place on two levels: individual learning and cooperative learning. Individual learning will be supported by digital learning, self-study materials, online tools like dictionaries, vocabulary and grammar learning applications as well as portfolios for assessment purposes. On the collaborative level doors have been opened for imagination and creativity, and teaching brings pupils with different competencies, talents and skills together. Here, learning can take place in "third spaces", understood in Manfred's sense as a social process which makes (embodied) learning with and from each other possible – either in small-scale forms (Schewe 2013) such as role plays, hot seating, press conferences, research tasks or small digital projects, or in larger forms such as shows or plays for an audience. In any case, cooperative phases appear perfectly suited to performative pedagogy.

Teaching and learning empathy

Q: You said mediation has been made a teaching principle and tandem learning was added. How does this look like in teaching practice and how does empathy feature in all this?

A: Teaching is by nature a profession that requires a lot of empathy – not just for planning lessons, formulating objectives or dealing with conflicts. Empathetic teachers understand how their students think and feel about what is going on around them and will more easily build strong, constructive relationships with them. There is evidence e.g. from the Hattie study (2009) that powerful relationships will have a positive impact on students' achievements. In the Turkish concept, classroom procedures are based on a set of special rules for teachers and learners. For instance, reflective use of classroom phrases is paramount for an inclusive approach as it helps weaker learners to tune in. Equally important are classroom rules on "How we can support each other?", which apply for general teaching procedures as well as tandem phases. The reciprocity principle (on which tandem learning is grounded; i.e. "I am not only responsible for my learning but also for improving *your* Turkish") increases the need for empathy in classroom interactions. While in a competitive system asking for help seems like a weakness, in a collaborative setting it is vital to realize that another person may be in need of help, which requires empathy, e.g., "You seem to struggle with your task, do you want me to support you?" or vice versa in "if you are done with your exercise, do you think you can help me with this?".

The concept aims to promote mediation which means mediating classroom situations, teacher instructions and, more generally, language and texts. Mediation, too, is a highly sophisticated skill which requires a lot of empathy as the mediator has to put him- or herself into the other person's shoes by asking "What does my partner really need to know?" In class, bilingual learners are often those who interpret situations and tasks for other learners in order to provide access to understanding. When it comes to mediating cultural concepts, small scale performative tasks are most powerful and again, empathy is in the limelight. Take, for instance, the taboo in Turkish cultures when it comes to cleaning and blowing one's nose in a public or semi-public space. Usually Turkish people leave the room and head for a quiet place when they feel this urge coming. Moreover, many Turks feel disgusted or even offended if they unwillingly have to witness such nose cleaning procedures – which are common amongst many Germans. In a grade 7 class, a critical incident based on this conflict was introduced by means of a roleplay which focused on a business meeting in which a German manager who took part in a meeting in Istanbul in winter, had a nasty flu and thus violated this social convention. Whereas teenagers who were raised in predominantely Turkish speaking families could immediately relate to the experience of disgust, learners from German speaking families were surprised as they could not even see a conflict at first. An authentic third space opened up and students learned about /from each other's underlying values. Alternative scenes were developed (in a theatre, the metro, a talk show, a romantic dinner), once in a German – once in a Turkish setting, acted out and differences discussed. The final task was to relate the incident to a friend who had come over for a holiday. Here again, it required empathy to imagine what the friend knows or does not know, what he might feel and what kind of socio-cultural background knowledge is required for a better understanding.

Outlook: Going digital and *going* performative

Q: Unfortunately, our time is up for this interview – but at the end, I can sense that you would probably like to briefly talk about conclusions you draw from the grassroots project in Istanbul.

A: Oh, definitely, thank you very much! There are many conclusions, one which is also confirmed by the Hannover study: No change is possible in schools without the school management – but the best change agents in our societies are learners who say "Turkish (or Arabic, or Russian, or Persian) is cool". In other words: While in Europe multilingualism has been celebrated for decades as a highly appreciated value and characteristic, English has developed into Europe's uncontested lingua franca. Almost all children in Europe learn English while fewer and fewer other languages are learned. In contrast, heritage languages with their high vitality in urban spaces as community languages seem to be untouched treasures. Taught as inclusive foreign language subjects based on approaches which reach out to the neighbourhood and tap into the potential for incidental learning, heritage language classes can turn into spaces for inter-cultural dialogue and embodied experience. Ten years ago the European Commission proposed the "adoptive language concept" which was hoped to result in breaking up the hierarchy amongst language subjects in European school systems (Reich 2016). Following the European aim of trilingualism, every European would learn the official (school) language of the country in which he or she lives, plus a lingua franca. The third language would be one of personal choice or special interest – e.g., a language spoken in the family or amongst friends. As a result, also non-European languages would appear in the field of vision as equally valuable sources for education. It seems likely that digitalization can help to organize school settings in which also smaller languages can be learned and used as qualifications for school success. However, while digitalization seems to get off the ground in education (and school doors are being opened for Microsoft, Apple and Google for conquering a hitherto untouched market), there is a growing need for teaching approaches which balance disembodied computer driven learning with focussing on learning as embodied collaborative experience. Thanks to Manfred and his unflagging dedication in the past three decades to learning through drama and theatre, we can draw on performative pedagogy as an established field in education which will help to develop such inclusive approaches. *Inşallah! Iyi ki doğdun Manfred, iyi ki varsın!*

References

Aden, Joëlle (2017): Developing empathy through theatre: a transcultural perspective in second language education. In John Crutchfield et al. (eds.), 59-81.

Bloom, Paul (2016): *Against Empathy. The Case for Rational Compassion.* London: Vintage.

Breithaupt, Fritz (2017): *Die dunklen Seiten der Empathie.* Berlin: Suhrkamp.

Crutchfield, John & Schewe, Manfred (eds.) (2017): *Going Performative in Intercultural Education: International Contexts – Theoretical Perspectives – Models of Practice.* Bristol: Multilingual Matters.

Ellis, Carolyn; Adams, Tony E. & Bochner, Arthur P. (2011): Autoethnography: An Overview. In *Forum: Qualitative Social Research* 12/1, Art. 10.

Even, Susanne & Schewe, Manfred (eds.) (2016): *Performatives Lehren, Lernen, Forschen. Performative Teaching, Learning, Research.* Berlin et al.: Schibri.

Gehm, Sabine; Husemann, Pirkko & von Wilcke, Katharina (eds.) (2007): *Wissen in Bewegung. Perspektiven der künsterlischen und wissenschaftlichen Forschung im Tanz.* Bielefeld: transcript.

Hattie, John (2009): *Visible Learning. A Synthesis of over 800 Meta-Analyses Relating to Achievement.* New York: Routledge.

Krumm, Hans-Jürgen (2013): *Elite- oder Armutsmehrsprachigkeit: Herausforderungen für das österreichische Bildungswesen.* Abschlussvortrag zur Tagung „Mehrsprachigkeit und Interkulturelles Lernen" an der Universität Wien vom 28.2. bis 1.3.2013, https://homepage.univie.ac.at/Hans-Juergen.Krumm, last accessed: 10/06/2016.

Reich, Hans H. (2016): Herkunftssprachen. In Eva Burwitz-Melzer, Grit Mehlhorn, Claudia Riemer, Karl-Richard Bausch & Hans-Jürgen Krumm (eds.): *Handbuch Fremdsprachenunterricht.* 6., v. ü. und erw. Aufl. Tübingen: A. Francke, 221-226.

Schewe, Manfred (2011): Die Welt auch im fremdsprachlichen Unterricht immer wieder neu verzaubern – Plädoyer für eine performative Lehr- und Lernkultur! In Almut Küppers, Torben Schmidt & Maik Walter (eds.): *Inszenierungen im Fremdsprachenunterricht. Grundlagen, Formen, Perspektiven.* Braunschweig: Schroedel/ Diesterweg/ Klinkhardt, 20-31.

Schewe, Manfred (2013): Taking stock and looking ahead: drama pedagogy as a gateway to a performative teaching and learning culture. In *Scenario* VII/1, 5-23.

Seitz, Hanne (2012): Performative Research. In *Kulturelle Bildung Online* https://www.kubi-online.de/artikel/performative-research, last accessed: 10/12/2017.

Theaterorte: Sprachliches, ästhetisches und kulturelles Lernen in textuellen, institutionellen und virtuellen Räumen

Carola Surkamp

Einleitung

Mit Theater als Ort wird im schulischen Kontext ganz häufig ein außerschulischer Lernort in Form eines konkreten Gebäudes assoziiert, in dem Theater gespielt wird und das man für den Besuch einer Aufführung betreten kann. Dass diese Betrachtung zu kurz greift, wird deutlich, wenn man sich weitere Raumkonzepte bzw. -praktiken vor Augen führt, die für den Fremdsprachenunterricht eine bedeutende Rolle spielen: das fremdsprachliche Klassenzimmer als physischer Raum und Begegnungszentrum, als Bühne, Textatelier und Fenster zur Welt sowie als Forschungs- und Lernwerkstatt (vgl. Legutke 2010a). All diese verschiedenen Raumdimensionen tragen auf unterschiedliche Weise zur Verfolgung fremdsprachendidaktischer Lernziele bei – und dies oftmals in Verbindung mit textuellen und/oder virtuellen Räumen. An sie ist beispielsweise die Förderung kommunikativer, interkultureller und performativer Kompetenzen geknüpft, da in ihnen bzw. durch sie Begegnungssituationen geschaffen werden können, die nah an der Lebenswelt der Lernenden sind. Sie können aber auch zur Recherche, Verarbeitung und Präsentation von Texten genutzt werden und dadurch rezeptive und produktive Kompetenzen schulen. Gemeinsamer Nenner der Einbindung unterschiedlicher Lernorte in den Fremdsprachenunterricht ist es, Schüler*innen die Teilnahme an möglichst authentischen Kommunikationssituationen zu ermöglichen und sie die Zielsprache als Instrument erfahren zu lassen, das sie zur Verfolgung eigener kommunikativer Absichten einsetzen können (vgl. ibid.).

Im Folgenden möchte ich aus literatur- und dramapädagogischer Perspektive erkunden, inwiefern das Theater in der skizzierten Bedeutungsvielfalt ein Lernort für den Fremdsprachenunterricht sein kann, welche Potentiale einzelne Theaterorte mit ihren Besonderheiten für das sprachliche, ästhetische und kulturelle Lernen bieten und wie sich die verschiedenen Theaterorte integrieren und methodisch in den fremdsprachlichen Unterricht einbinden lassen.

Raum als ästhetisch vermittelter Ort in dramatischen Texten

Raum ist in einem Fremdsprachenunterricht, in dem dramatische Texte zum Einsatz kommen, zunächst einmal als ästhetisch vermittelter Ort zu berücksichtigen. Nur in Einzelfällen erkunden Lernende fremdsprachige Räume und ihre Akteur*innen durch eigene Anschauung vor Ort, z.B. im Rahmen eines Schüler*innenaustausches. Wesentlich häufiger erfahren sie anderskulturelle Wirklichkeiten als textuell und medial vermittelt.

Dies bedeutet jedoch nicht, dass Räume in Texten als einfache Widerspiegelung der Realität angesehen werden sollten. Sie stehen vielmehr in einem engen dynamischen Wechselverhältnis zur außertextuellen Wirklichkeit, die sie symbolisch repräsentieren und auch kritisch inszenieren (vgl. Surkamp & Nünning 2016: 41f.). In Texten entworfene Räume sind nicht nur Schauplätze der Handlung, sondern immer auch kulturelle Bedeutungsträger, wie auch Hallet & Neumann (2009: 11) hervorheben:

> Kulturell vorherrschende Normen, Werthierarchien, kursierende Kollektivvorstellungen von Zentralität und Marginalität, von Eigenem und Fremdem sowie Verortungen des Individuums zwischen Vertrautem und Fremdem erfahren im Raum eine konkret anschauliche Manifestation."

Auf diese Weise werden gesellschaftliche Erfahrungen sowie kulturelles Wissen in literarischen Texten aufgegriffen und interpretierend verarbeitet.

Beispiele für Raumsemantisierungen in dramatischen Texten gibt es viele. So kann eine Figur implizit durch den Raum, in dem sie lebt, charakterisiert sein – auch kulturspezifisch. Positionierungen im Raum und räumliche Grenzüberschreitungen können Hinweise auf die interkulturellen Beziehungen zwischen Figuren sowie auf unterschiedliche Normen und Wertvorstellungen liefern. Dies lässt sich am Beispiel des Kurzdramas *Survival in the South* der kanadischen Schriftstellerin Minnie Aodla Freeman illustrieren, in dem eine junge Frau ihren Kulturkreis der Inuit in der kanadischen Arktis verlässt, um in einer Großstadt im Süden Kanadas als Übersetzerin ein neues Leben zu beginnen, und dabei auf allerlei Unbekanntes stößt (vgl. Surkamp & Nünning 2018: Kap. II.2). Interpretatorisch aufschlussreich sind in Theaterstücken zudem die Relationen innerhalb eines Schauplatzes, zwischen Schauplatz und *off stage* sowie zwischen mehreren Schauplätzen, wie z.B. zwischen Zivilisation und Natur in Shakespeares *A Midsummer Night's Dream* und *As You Like It* (vgl. Surkamp & Nünning 2016: 177). Räume in literarischen Texten sind daher häufig „Ergebnis von sozialen Relationen, von Praktiken und Machtverhältnissen, von Nutzung oder Aneignung" (Hauthal 2009: 372), und in dieser Funktion können sie auch veranschaulichen, wie Menschen sich in Begegnungssituationen präsentieren, wie zwischenmenschliches Zusammentreffen abläuft und wie soziale Interaktionen strukturiert sind (vgl. Hallet 2015: 65).

In didaktischen Überlegungen zu Lernorten finden ästhetische Rauminszenierungen und symbolische Raumrepräsentationen bislang jedoch keine Berücksichtigung. Dabei erlangen sie gerade dadurch eine besondere Bedeutung für den Fremdsprachenunterricht, dass zentrale Aspekte fremder Lebensräume sowie interkultureller Begegnungen insbesondere auch durch materielle Manifestationen (wie z.B. Darstellungen in Texten) beobachtbar und dadurch im Klassenzimmer überhaupt erst erfahrbar werden. Da solche Raumrepräsentationen die Vorstellungen der Lernenden von fremdsprachigen Kulturen und sozialen bzw. interkulturellen Positionierungen wesentlich prägen, kommt der Dekodierung von dramenspezifischen Darstellungsverfahren im Abgleich mit dem spezifischen historischen und kulturellen Kontext eines Textes ein zentraler Stellenwert zu. Aufgabe des fremdsprachlichen Dramenunterrichts ist daher auch die Förderung ästhetisch-kognitiver Kompetenzen. Auf der einen Seite gilt es, die Lernenden im Sinne des *close reading* zur Analyse verschiedener Techniken der Raumdarstellung – wie Hinweisen zu Bühnenbild und Requisiten im Nebentext bzw. Verwendung der sog. Wortkulisse als subjektiver Form der Raumdarstellung aus der Perspektive einer der Figuren – zu befähigen. Auf der anderen Seite sollten Schüler*innen über entsprechende Aufgaben und Zusatzmaterialien (wie Landkarten, Bilder, biografische Texte etc.) die kontextualisierende Erschließung (also das *wide reading*) der in einem Drama inszenierten Räume üben (vgl. Genetsch & Hallet 2010; zu Kontextualisierungsmöglichkeiten des oben erwähnten Kurzdramas vgl. Surkamp & Nünning 2018: Kap. II.2.2). Hallet (2015: 64) spricht in diesem Zusammenhang sogar von der Notwendigkeit des Erwerbs einer „raumsymbolischen *literacy*" als der Fähigkeit, sprachliche Beschreibungen und auch visuelle Darstellungen fremdsprachiger Räume zu verstehen, zu nutzen und über sie zu reflektieren.

Textinteraktionen im Klassenzimmer als physischem Raum

Für die Interaktion mit dramatischen Texten im Fremdsprachenunterricht können verschiedene didaktische Begegnungssituationen im Klassenzimmer konzeptualisiert werden. Die Lernenden und die Lehrenden befinden sich im Literaturunterricht in einer gemeinsamen Lehr/Lernsituation, in der der literarische Text als Kommunikationsanlass fungiert. Wie Bredella & Burwitz-Melzer (2004: 234) herausstellen, ist die schulische Beschäftigung mit Literatur über die individuelle Textrezeption hinaus ein sozialer Prozess, „in dem die Leser-TextBeziehung zu einer LeserLehrkraftTextBeziehung und im Idealfall auf eine LeserLeserLehrkraftTextBeziehung erweitert wird". Vor, während und nach dem

Rezeptionsprozess fungiert die Lehrperson als Vermittlerin und Impulsgeberin, und dies nicht nur zwischen dem einzelnen Leser bzw. der einzelnen Leserin und dem Text, sondern auch zwischen den Lernenden untereinander. Ziel ist es, in der Fremdsprache zu einem Austausch über individuelle Rezeptionserfahrungen und Lesarten sowie zu einem gemeinsamen Aushandeln von Bedeutung zu kommen.

Dieses Aushandeln von Bedeutungen kann im Klassenzimmer nicht nur analytisch-diskursiv, sondern auch szenisch-kreativ erfolgen. Die Lernenden schlüpfen in Rollen und erspielen den Text mittels verschiedener Methoden, z. B. durch das Experimentieren mit Sprechhaltungen, gestisch-mimischen Ausdrucksformen oder Positionierungen im Raum. Auch szenische Interpretationsverfahren wie der Standbildbau zur Visualisierung der Figurenkonstellation in einem Theaterstück, Stimmenskulpturen zur Darstellung der Innenwelt einer Figur oder Dialogspiele wie der sog. ‚Heiße Stuhl' können zum Einsatz kommen. Solche Zugangsformen zu dramatischen Texten erfordern ein spezifisches *classroom design* (z. B. keine Tisch- und Stuhlreihen und auch keine Gruppentische) und können damit das traditionelle Klassenzimmer im wörtlichen Sinne zur Bühne erweitern (vgl. Reisener 2005).

Spielerische Zugangsformen ermöglichen eine Erweiterung des sprachlichen Lernens im fremdsprachlichen Literaturunterricht. Durch die Umsetzung des Theatertextes ins Mimische und Gestische, durch den Einsatz stimmlicher Kommunikationsmittel wie Sprachmelodie oder Artikulationsweise sowie durch Bewegungen im Raum können die Lernenden die Fremdsprache mit allen Sinnen und dem ganzen Körper erfahren (vgl. Schewe 1993: 6 f.). Dass non- und paraverbalen Elementen eine besondere Bedeutung für das Sprachenlernen zukommt, wird in dramapädagogischen Arbeiten mit Bezug auf den Fremdsprachenunterricht immer wieder herausgestellt, insbesondere im Hinblick auf die Schaffung von möglichst authentischen Gesprächssituationen im Klassenzimmer und – damit einhergehend – die Sensibilisierung für die bedeutungsgebende Funktion des stimmlichen Ausdrucks bei der Kommunikation, z. B. zur Übermittlung einer bestimmten Stimmung oder kommunikativen Absicht (vgl. ibid.: 175). Körpersprache kann aber auch als Kompensationsstrategie beim Hörverstehen und beim Sprechen sowie im Kontext des interkulturellen Lernens eine wichtige Rolle spielen (vgl. zusammenfassend Surkamp 2014).

Ein wesentlicher Vorzug dramapädagogischer Verfahren besteht Manfred Schewe (1993: 5 f.) zufolge außerdem in der Wechselwirkung von Produktion und Rezeption. Bei zahlreichen dramapädagogischen Kleinformen (vgl. Schewe 2015) sind die Lernenden selbst sowohl Akteur*innen, Regisseur*innen als auch Zuschauer*innen (vgl. auch Schewe 2017: 50 f.). Da Agierende zugleich Betrachtende sind und umgekehrt, kann ein Austausch über intendierte und tatsächlich erzielte Wirkungsweisen von nonverbalem Verhalten beim Spiel erfolgen. Den jeweils zuschauenden Schüler*innen werden zu diesem Zweck spezielle Beobachtungsaufträge gegeben. Ihre Aufgabe ist es dann nicht allein, sich auf den gesprochenen Text zu konzentrieren, sondern auch das für die Gesamtwirkung entscheidende Zusammenspiel von verbalen und nonverbalen Zeichen zu beachten. Ein solches Vorgehen kann insbesondere im Hinblick auf die Reflexion von solchen nonverbalen Kommunikationsformen aufschlussreich sein, die in der Regel nicht bewusst eingesetzt werden, wie z.B. die Körperhaltung.

Auch ästhetisches Lernen kann durch handlungsorientierte Textinteraktionen erweitert werden. Das Augenmerk liegt nicht mehr alleine auf dem dramatischen Text als Lesetext, sondern durch stimmliche, körperliche und räumliche Umsetzungen wird auch dessen Aufführungsdimension mit einbezogen. Schüler*innen erfahren, dass es sich im Gegensatz zur Dramenlektüre bei einer Inszenierung um einen sehr viel komplexeren Kommunikationsprozess handelt. So trägt z.B. die Art und Weise, *wie* in einem Dialog gesprochen wird, welche Mimik und Gestik Dialogpartner*innen einsetzen und wie sie sich im Raum bewegen, wesentlich zur Bedeutung des Gesagten bei. Non- und paraverbale Elemente können Aufschluss über die Gefühle, Gedanken und Haltungen, aber auch die Persönlichkeit eines Sprechers bzw. einer Sprecherin geben. Außerdem visualisieren sie die sozialen Rollen von und die Beziehung zwischen Gesprächspartner*innen, und sie können den Gesprächsinhalt besonders akzentuieren, ergänzen oder auch in Frage stellen.

Arbeiten die Lernenden nicht nur mit einzelnen Szenen aus einem Text, sondern an der Produktion eines ganzen Stückes mit eventueller Aufführung auf der Schulbühne oder gar außerhalb des Schulgebäudes, dann erfahren sie darüber hinaus Theater als kollaborativen Prozess. Verschiedene Deutungen von Haupt- und Nebentext im Hinblick auf die Gestaltung der Kostüme, Requisiten und des Bühnenbildes müssen ebenso ausgehandelt werden wie die Besetzung der Rollen und der Einsatz von Musik, anderen Medien und Lichteffekten. Stritzelberger (2015) zeigt auf, dass für die Umsetzung einer dramapädagogischen Großform sensu Schewe (2015) in Form einer Aufführung mit theatralen und multimedialen Elementen wie Audiosequenzen oder Fotostrecken das Klassenzimmer durch die Einbeziehung anderer Institutionen noch weiter geöffnet werden kann: In ihrem Projekt wurde die szenische Texterarbeitung durch eine Theaterpädagogin und die Medienarbeit durch einen Mitarbeiter des Landesmedienzentrums Baden-Württemberg unterstützt. Dabei haben die durchgeführten theaterpädagogischen Workshops zur eigenen Körpererfahrung den Lernenden auch erlaubt, „ihre festgefahrenen Klassenzimmerrollen zu erkennen und zu überdenken" (Stritzelberger 2015: 274).

Theaterspielen im Klassenzimmer als sozialem Raum

Theaterspielen im Fremdsprachenunterricht hat daher nicht nur Auswirkungen auf das Klassenzimmer als physischen Raum, sondern auch auf das Klassenzimmer als sozialen Raum, also auf die interpersonale Dimension des Lernens. Das Klassenzimmer ist in der Regel ein hoch konventionalisierter Lernort, der nach bestimmten sozialen Regeln funktioniert. Nach Hallet (2015: 60) hat die Beschaffenheit dieses Raumes mit Blick auf den Fremdsprachenunterricht Einfluss darauf, was überhaupt Gegenstand der sprachlichen Interaktion sein kann. Hinzufügen lässt sich, dass auch die Beschaffenheit der Begegnungssituation selbst, die durch räumliche Gegebenheiten mit hervorgerufen wird, die Möglichkeiten sprachlicher Interaktion bestimmt: Wenn Dramentexte nicht nur gelesen und analysiert, sondern im gemeinsamen Spiel handlungsorientiert angeeignet werden, und wenn sich die Lehrperson dabei im Sinne der Dramapädagogik als gleichberechtigte Mitspielerin begreift, dann verändern sich auch die Beziehungen zwischen den Akteur*innen im Klassenzimmer. Dies kann dazu führen, dass traditionell gefestigte Hierarchien zwischen Lehrperson und Lernenden wenn nicht aufgehoben, so doch temporär aufgebrochen und umgedeutet werden, dass also soziale Neupositionierungen möglich werden:

> Eine Möglichkeit, die durch die Übernahme einer Rolle in einer 'als ob'-Situation geschaffen wird, ist ein bedeutsamer Wechsel in der Rollenbeziehung zwischen Lehrer und Schülern, besonders im Hinblick auf die Autorität und die Verantwortung, die in dieser Rollenbeziehung angelegt sind. (Byron 1990: 26)

Darüber hinaus können Neupositionierungen für Lernende dadurch erfolgen, dass sie beim Theaterspielen nicht als sie selbst agieren. Sie schlüpfen in andere Rollen, inszenieren verschiedene Begegnungssituationen und eröffnen sich in diesen Spielräumen neue Erfahrungsräume und Perspektiven. Inszenierungen erlauben es ihnen, in spezifischen Kontexten mit Rede- und Verhaltensweisen zu experimentieren, sich als Agierende und Reagierende auszuprobieren und auch unterschiedliche Handlungsoptionen mit ihren jeweiligen Konsequenzen auszuloten. Dies hat auch Manfred Schewe in vielen seiner Arbeiten als ein wesentliches Potential dramapädagogischer Verfahren im Fremdsprachenunterricht hervorgehoben: „Indem junge Menschen an die Kunstform Theater herangeführt werden, werden sie befähigt, performances of power bzw. auch die Theatralität des Alltags besser zu durchschauen sowie die Mittel der Kunstform zu nutzen, um im geschützten Raum der Fiktion alternative Handlungsmöglichkeiten zu erproben" (Schewe 2011: 23). Dabei können auch persönliche Erfahrungen, Interessen und eigene Ideen eingebracht werden, um fremdsprachige Interaktionssituationen zu initiieren und mitzugestalten. Mit Blick auf das interkulturelle Lernen gewinnt diese Erkundung verschiedener Wirkungsweisen von Interaktionen im Schonraum der Spiele-Realität ebenfalls eine besondere Bedeutung (vgl. Bonnet & Küppers 2011: 45).

Insgesamt wird durch das Theaterspielen die performative Kompetenz von Lernenden gefördert. Diese umfasst diejenigen Kenntnisse, Fähigkeiten und Bereitschaften, die Lernende in der Lebenswelt benötigen, um den Inszenierungscharakter auch von sozialen Interaktionssituationen jenseits des Theaters zu erkennen und an unterschiedlichen Interaktionsformen mitzuwirken, diese aber auch kritisch-reflektiert zu hinterfragen (vgl. Surkamp & Hallet 2015: 11). Zur performativen Kompetenz gehört zudem das Wissen über die räumliche Dimension jeder zwischenmenschlichen Interaktion. Hallet (2017) hebt hervor, dass es keinen performativen Akt, keine soziale oder kommunikative Interaktion gibt, die nicht an einen Raum gebunden ist, der diese Interaktion zugleich mitbestimmt. So können z. B. hierarchische Gefüge zwischen Gesprächspartner*innen durch räumliche Positionierungen angezeigt werden, und auch Mechanismen der Inklusion oder der Ausgrenzung erfolgen nicht nur sprachlich, sondern auch räumlich. Im Sinne des sozialen und interkulturellen Lernens sollten Lernende daher dazu befähigt werden, „eigene Positionierungen im Raum in Aushandlungen mit anderen Akteuren vorzunehmen und eigene Raumpraktiken [...] kritisch zu reflektieren" (Hallet 2015: 66). Diese sowohl produktiven als auch rezeptiven Fähigkeiten lassen sich durch die Beschäftigung mit dramatischen Texten und dramapädagogischen Verfahren fördern, da Schüler*innen in einem solchen Unterricht erfahren, dass Orte und Raumkonstellationen mit Bedeutungen aufgeladen sind, dass diese Bedeutungen entschlüsselt werden können und dass das Wissen über räumliche Bedeutungsebenen für eigene soziale Interaktionen und Positionierungen genutzt werden kann (vgl. auch Hallet 2017).

Theater als außerschulischer Lernort

Auch das Theater als außerschulischer Lernort stellt einen komplexen Erfahrungsraum dar, der im Fremdsprachenunterricht sprachliches, ästhetisches und kulturelles Lernen ermöglicht. Im Rahmen einer Studienfahrt, aber auch in vielen Stadttheatern mit fremdsprachigen Inszenierungen vor Ort können Lernende Theatertexte mit verschiedenen Sinnen erfassen, die besondere Atmosphäre eines Theaterbesuchs erleben und sich mit anderen über ihre Rezepftionseindrücke und Interpretationen austauschen. Gehring (2010: 10) zufolge eröffnen Lernorte außerhalb der Schule „Zugänge zu realen, authentischen Umgebungen und Räumen, an denen man sich Wissen aneignen, das vorhandene Wissen vertiefen und anwenden kann". In Bezug auf den außerschulischen Lernort Theater bedeutet dies insbesondere, Theater in seiner spezifischen Ästhetik als Medium und Ort zugleich zu erschließen. Denn anders als beim dramatischen Lesetext handelt es sich beim aufgeführten Drama sensu Pfister (1994: 24) um eine ‚plurimediale Darstellungsform', welche sich nicht nur verbaler, sondern auch nonverbaler Kommunikationsmittel bedient und sowohl den akustischen (durch Stimmen, Geräusche und Musik) als auch den optischen Wahrnehmungskanal (durch Bühnenbild, Requisiten, Aussehen der Schauspieler, Gestik, Mimik, Bewegung und Lichteffekte) beansprucht. Zur Raumerfahrung hinzu kommt neben dem textuellen Raum als fiktivem Schauplatz der Handlung und dem im Nebentext entworfenen bzw. durch das Bühnenbild umgesetzten szenischen Raum außerdem noch der theatrale Raum, d. h. die Architektur des Theaters und die individuelle Bühnenform des Aufführungsortes (vgl. Hauthal 2009).

All diese akustischen, visuellen, darsteller- und raumbezogenen Zeichen haben in der besonderen Kommunikationssituation im Theater ein spezifisches Bedeutungspotential inne und sind in der Regel anders zu lesen als ähnliche Zeichen in der Alltagswelt der Lernenden (vgl. Steiner 2010: 96). Durch die Einbindung des außerschulischen Lernorts Theater in den Unterricht und entsprechende, auf den Theaterbesuch vorbereitende Aktivitäten können Lernende auf die ästhetische Deutung dieser Zeichen vorbereitet und somit zur kompetenten Rezeption von Theatertexten befähigt werden (vgl. Surkamp & Feuchert 2010). Über literar-ästhetische Bildung hinaus ermöglicht dies kulturelle Teilhabe, da nicht davon ausgegangen werden kann, dass alle Lernenden mit der Institution Theater vertraut sind:

> Die Theateraufführung bekommt als Ereignis selbst einen Wert. Sie ist singuläres Ereignis. Das Zusammenkommen von Menschen, Schauspielern und Zuschauern in einem Raum kann als besonders und unwiederholbar einmalig erlebt werden (Hentschel 2009: 115).

Die Lernenden erfahren Theater zudem nicht nur als Institution, sondern auch als sozialen und kulturellen Handlungsraum, in dem Theaterschaffende (Regisseur*innen, Bühnenbildner*innen, Kostümdesigner*innen, Darstellende etc.) und Theaterrezipierende kollaborativ agieren und dadurch zur Komplexität der Kommunikationssituation beitragen (z. B. wird die eigene Rezeptionserfahrung auch durch die Reaktionen der anderen Zuschauer*innen beeinflusst).

Die durch einen Theaterbesuch entstehenden neuen Begegnungs- und Kommunikationssituationen tragen auch zur Förderung sprachlicher Kompetenzen bei. Als eine Schlüsselkompetenz des Fremdsprachenlernens heute wird die fremdsprachliche Diskursfähigkeit angesehen (vgl. Hallet 2008). Damit wird die Fähigkeit von Lernenden bezeichnet, „an mehrsprachigen und komplexen gesellschaftlichen Prozessen und Diskursen teilhaben, sie mitbestimmen und mitgestalten zu können" (Legutke 2010b: 73). Der außerschulische Lernort Theater bietet sich in mehrfacher Hinsicht als „Interaktionsraum für fremdsprachliche Diskurse" (Gehring 2010: 14) an, da kommunikative Akte auf unterschiedlichen Ebenen ablaufen (vgl. Delius & Surkamp 2015). Auf der Ebene der Rezeption geht es darum, dass Schüler*innen lernen, einen aufgeführten dramatischen Text in der Fremdsprache unter Rückgriff auf ihr schon vorhandenes sprachliches Wissen und unter Einbeziehung der verschiedenen vermittelten auditiven und visuellen Zeichen zu verstehen. Zur Ebene der sprachlichen Produktion gehört die Fähigkeit, mit anderen in der Fremdsprache in einen Austausch über individuelle Reaktionen zum dramatischen Text und zu seiner Inszenierung auf der Bühne zu treten. Einige Theater bieten für Schulen sogar Gespräche mit den Theaterschaffenden, also mit Regisseur oder Schauspielenden im Nachgang einer Aufführung an, so dass durch die Begegnung mit neuen Akteur*innen neue Kommunikationsgelegenheiten für das fremdsprachliche Lernen geschaffen werden. Ebenso sollten die Lernenden dazu befähigt werden, eigene argumentative und auch kreative Texte zu einem Theaterstück in der Fremdsprache zu produzieren. Hierfür bieten sich insbesondere Genres an, die aus dem Theater als kulturellem Handlungsfeld stammen, z.B. das Schreiben einer Theaterkritik für die Schüler*innenzeitung oder die eigene Inszenierung einer zusätzlichen Szene zum Stück.

Theater im virtuellen Raum

Durch digitale Medien können Lernorte virtuell erweitert werden und so für Lernende „neue Formen der vermittelten und direkten interkulturellen Begegnung" (Grau & Legutke 2013: 4) bereitstellen. Für die Beschäftigung mit dramatischen Texten im Fremdsprachenunterricht ist dies in dreierlei Hinsicht interessant, da durch die Einbeziehung beispielsweise des Internets neue Texte und Inhalte, aber auch neue Interaktionsformen genutzt werden können und zudem eigene kreative Inszenierungen möglich werden (vgl. auch Baier et al. 2015).

Als Ressource für Texte und Inhalte bietet das Internet zunächst die Möglichkeit, die Aufführung eines Dramas online anzuschauen, da von vielen Stücken, die auch im Englischunterricht häufig behandelt werden, Inszenierungen aufgezeichnet zur Verfügung gestellt werden (z.B. unter https://www.digitaltheatreplus.com). Gerade wenn vor Ort keine fremdsprachigen Inszenierungen im Theater stattfinden, können Lernende auf diese Weise die Aufführungsdimension eines dramatischen Textes dennoch erfahren und den fremdsprachigen Text mit mehreren Sinnen aufnehmen (was wiederum auch die Rezeption unterstützen kann). Darüber hinaus liefert das Internet viele Zusatztexte zu Theaterstücken wie Interviews (mit Regisseur*innen, Schauspielenden oder Autor*innen), Kritiken oder wissenschaftliche Texte aus Literaturtheorie und

Theaterwissenschaft. Bild- und Filmmaterialien geben Lernenden zudem Einbli-
cke in reale Theater, auch hinter die Kulissen (z. B. rund um das Globe-Theatre
unter www.shakespearesglobe.com/education) – Wissen, das für die Erschließung von Kontexten ebenso verwendet werden kann wie für die Vorbereitung
einer Studienfahrt.

Das Internet kann im Fremdsprachenunterricht aber auch als kommunikati-
ves Instrument genutzt werden. Mithilfe digitaler Technologie kann die Textrezeption z. B. in unterschiedlichen Sozialformen stattfinden (vgl. Walker & White
2013: 51). Lesergemeinschaften auf Internetplattformen (z. B. *online book groups*)
ermöglichen es Schüler*innen, ihren Leseprozess mit anderen zu teilen und
die Entwicklung rezeptiver Kompetenzen dadurch ganz lernerorientiert zum
kollaborativen Prozess werden zu lassen. Lernende können das Internet aber
auch produktiv nutzen, wenn sie kreative Antworten zu dramatischen Texten
schreiben, also alternative Enden oder zusätzliche Szenen verfassen, und diese
online veröffentlichen (z. B. auf *fan fiction*-Seiten wie www.fanfiction.net oder
https://archiveofourown.org, auf denen es eigene Sektionen zu ‚plays‘ gibt). Ihre
Beiträge können dann wiederum von anderen Rezipient*innen kommentiert
werden, so dass durch mediale Vernetzungen neue Kommunikationswege in
der Fremdsprache entstehen (vgl. Lazar 2008: 159).

Des Weiteren können über das Internet kreative Schaffensprozesse auch
im Hinblick auf eigene Inszenierungen angestoßen werden. Wie Kist (2011)
am Beispiel eines *virtual role playing* aufzeigt, können internetgestützte In-
szenierungsprojekte ähnlich wie interaktive Theatersoftware (vgl. Baier 2008)
zurückhaltenden Lernenden, die nicht gerne am Theaterspiel in oder vor der
Klasse teilnehmen, helfen, dennoch in eine andere Rolle zu schlüpfen und aus
dieser heraus fremdsprachlich zu agieren. In Kists Projekt haben Schüler*innen
gemeinsam an einem Blog geschrieben – allerdings nicht aus ihrer eigenen
Perspektive, sondern aus der der Figuren aus einem Theaterstück, das zuvor
in der Lerngruppe behandelt worden war. Die Mitschüler*innen waren zudem
aufgefordert, die Beiträge der anderen Lernenden zu kommentieren. In einem
anderen englischdidaktischen Projekt (vgl. Schmidt 2011) haben Schüler*innen
auf der Basis eines Theaterstücks ihre Rezeptionseindrücke in Kurzfilmen verarbeitet (u. a. in Form von Interviews mit den Figuren des Stücks und fiktiven
Nachrichtensendungen über dessen Inhalt). Diese wurden auf YouTube veröf-
fentlicht und mit einer Klasse von einer anderen Schule, die sich ebenfalls mit
dem Theaterstück beschäftigt hatte, online diskutiert.

Solche Inszenierungsformen erfordern allerdings auch die Entwicklung von
Medienkompetenzen zum Umgang mit verschiedenen medialen Darstellungs-
formaten und elektronischen Rezeptions- und Distributionskontexten (vgl. Surkamp & Hallet 2015: 10). Ein zusätzliches Potential der Nutzung von Theater

als virtuellem Raum besteht darin, dass Schüler*innen lernen, im Sinne der Entwicklung ihrer performativen Kompetenzen auch mit eigenen medialen (Selbst-)Inszenierungen reflektiert umzugehen (vgl. ibid.). Auf diese Weise können literar-ästhetisches und kulturelles Lernen erneut miteinander verbunden werden.

Fazit

Wird Theater als Lernort mittels der hier skizzierten Raumdimensionen und -praktiken umfassend verstanden, so ermöglicht dies vielfältige sprachliche und kulturelle Begegnungen der Lernenden mit Texten, Inszenierungen und Personen. Es werden Partizipationsmöglichkeiten eröffnet, die weit über einen auf die Textrezeption ausgerichteten Dramenunterricht hinausgehen. Außerdem kann fremdsprachliche Diskursfähigkeit im ästhetisch-kulturellen Bereich gefördert werden, und es werden soziale, personale, interkulturelle und performative Kompetenzen entwickelt.

Jüngste Entwicklungen innerhalb der Dramapädagogik, zu denen Manfred Schewe maßgeblich beigetragen hat, betonen insbesondere das Potenzial dramapädagogischer Verfahren für die Förderung performativer Kompetenz (vgl. Schewe 2015, 2017). Gerade durch die Berücksichtigung des Lernorts Theater und den damit einhergehenden Einsatz dramapädagogischer Verfahren im Fremdsprachenunterricht kann auch das Handeln der Lernenden im lebensweltlichen Kontext in den Blick genommen werden. Als besonders motivierend gilt es, wenn dabei unterschiedliche Medien und weitere, z. B. digitale Inszenierungsformen jenseits von Bühne und Klassenzimmer einbezogen werden.

Literatur

Baier, Jochen (2008): Teaching literature by means of the computer: Examining the American dream by using Edwina Dakins' interactive drama *My Baby's Bracelet* in the foreign language classroom. In Jürgen Donnerstag & Laurenz Volkmann (Hg.): *Media and American Studies in the EFL-Classroom*. Heidelberg: Winter, 137-155.

Baier, Jochen; Bührle, Jasmin & Gecius, Melanie (2015): Szenisch-dramatische Verfahren und Aufführungen mit digitalen Medien und Internetformaten. In Wolfgang Hallet et al. (Hg.), 287-304.

Bonnet, Andreas & Küppers, Almut (2011): Wozu taugen kooperatives Lernen und Dramapädagogik? Vergleich zweier populärer Inszenierungsformen. In Almut Küppers, Torben Schmidt & Maik Walter (Hg.): *Inszenierungen im Fremdsprachenunterricht: Grundlagen, Formen, Perspektiven*. Braunschweig: Schroedel/Diesterweg/Klinkhardt, 32-52.

Bredella, Lothar & Burwitz-Melzer, Eva (2004): *Rezeptionsästhetische Literaturdidaktik mit Beispielen aus dem Fremdsprachenunterricht Englisch.* Tübingen: Narr.

Byron, Ken (1990): Drama und Sprache. In Manfred Schewe (Hg.): *Drama und Theater in der Schule und für die Schule: Beiträge zur Einführung in die britische Drama- und Theaterpädagogik.* Oldenburg: Pädagogisches Zentrum, 25-42.

Delius, Katharina & Surkamp, Carola (2015): Ästhetisches Erleben am außerschulischen Lernort Theater: Die Förderung fremdsprachlicher Diskursfähigkeit im Rahmen eines Theaterbesuchs. In Wolfgang Hallet et al. (Hg.), 117-142.

Gehring, Wolfgang (2010): Zur Einleitung: Lernort, Lernstandort, Lernumgebung. Warum ein Fremdsprachenunterricht auch außerhalb des Klassenzimmers ertragreich ist. In Wolfgang Gehring & Elisabeth Stinshoff (Hg.): *Außerschulische Lernorte des Fremdsprachenunterrichts.* Braunschweig: Schroedel/Diesterweg/Klinkhardt, 7-16.

Genetsch, Martin & Hallet, Wolfgang (2010): Kulturen repräsentieren, Texte kontextualisieren. In *Der fremdsprachliche Unterricht Englisch* 44, 10-11.

Grau, Maike & Legutke, Michael K. (2013): Vernetzte Lernorte: Englisch im Klassenzimmer und in der Lebenswelt lernen. In *Der fremdsprachliche Unterricht* 123, 4-7.

Hallet, Wolfgang (2008): Diskursfähigkeit heute. Der Diskursbegriff in Piephos Theorie der kommunikativen Kompetenz und seine zeitgemäße Weiterentwicklung für die Fremdsprachendidaktik. In Michael K. Legutke (Hg.): *Kommunikative Kompetenz als fremdsprachendidaktische Vision.* Tübingen: Narr, 76-96.

Hallet, Wolfgang (2015): Die Bedeutung der Orte: Topologien des Fremdsprachenlernens aus raumtheoretischer Perspektive. In Eva Burwitz-Melzer, Frank G. Königs & Claudia Riemer (Hg.): *Lernen an allen Orten? Die Rolle der Lernorte beim Lehren und Lernen von Fremdsprachen.* Tübingen: Narr, 60-69.

Hallet, Wolfgang (2017): The Performativity of Space and Performative Competence. Vortrag Cork/Irland, Performative Spaces in Language, Literature and Culture Education. 2nd International SCENARIO Forum Conference University College Cork, Ireland – 25.-28. Mai 2017.

Hallet, Wolfgang & Neumann, Birgit (2009): Raum und Bewegung in der Literatur: Zur Einführung. In Wolfgang Hallet & Birgit Neumann (Hg.): *Raum und Bewegung in der Literatur: Die Literaturwissenschaften und der Spatial Turn.* Bielefeld: Transcript, 11-32.

Hallet, Wolfgang & Surkamp, Carola (Hg.) (2015): *Dramendidaktik und Dramapädagogik im Fremdsprachenunterricht.* Trier: WVT.

Hauthal, Janine (2009): Von den Brettern, die die Welt bedeuten, zur ‚Bühne' des Textes. Inszenierungen des Raumes im Drama zwischen ‚mise en scène' und ‚mise en page'. In Wolfgan Hallet & Birgit Neumann (Hg.): *Raum und Bewegung in der Literatur: Die Literaturwissenschaften und der Spatial Turn.* Bielefeld: Transcript, 371-398.

Hentschel, Ingrid (2009): Ereignis und Erfahrung: Theaterpädagogik zwischen Vermittlung und künstlerischer Arbeit. In Wolfgang Schneider (Hg.): *Theater und Schule: Ein Handbuch zur kulturellen Bildung.* Bielefeld: Transcript, 105-128.

Kist, William (2011): Virtual Role-Playing. In Joanne Kilgour Dowdy & Sarah Kaplan (Hg.): *Teaching Drama in the Classroom. A Toolbox for Teachers.* Rotterdam et al.: SensePublishers, 37-40.

Lazar, Gilian (2008): Some Approaches to Literature, Language Teaching and the Internet. In *Fremdsprachen Lehren und Lernen* 37, 154-163.

Legutke, Michael K. (2010a): Merkmale des fremdsprachlichen Klassenzimmers. In Wolfgang Hallet & Frank G. Königs (Hg.): *Handbuch Fremdsprachendidaktik*. Seelze-Velber: Klett/Kallmeyer, 156-160.

Legutke, Michael K. (2010b): Kommunikative Kompetenz und Diskursfähigkeit. In Wolfgang Hallet & Frank G. Königs (Hg.): *Handbuch Fremdsprachendidaktik*. Seelze-Velber: Klett-Kallmeyer, 70-75.

Pfister, Manfred (1994): *Das Drama*. 8. Aufl. München: Fink.

Reisener, Helmut (2005): Das Klassenzimmer als Bühne. In *Der Fremdsprachliche Unterricht Englisch* 39/74, 20-27.

Schewe, Manfred (1993): Fremdsprache inszenieren: Zur Fundierung einer dramapädagogischen Lehr- und Lernpraxis. Oldenburg: Pädagogisches Zentrum.

Schewe, Manfred (2011): Die Welt auch im fremdsprachlichen Unterricht immer wieder neu verzaubern: Plädoyer für eine performative Lehr- und Lernkultur! In Almut Küppers, Torben Schmidt & Maik Walter (Hg.): *Inszenierungen im Fremdsprachenunterricht: Grundlagen, Formen, Perspektiven*. Braunschweig: Schroedel/Diesterweg/Klinkhardt, 20-31.

Schewe, Manfred (2015): Fokus Fachgeschichte: Die Dramapädagogik als Wegbereiterin einer performativen Fremdsprachendidaktik. In Wolfgang Hallet et al. (Hg.), 21-36.

Schewe, Manfred (2017): Dramapädagogik. In Carola Surkamp (Hg.). *Metzler Lexikon Fremdsprachendidaktik: Ansätze – Methoden – Grundbegriffe*. 2. erw. Aufl. Stuttgart: J. B. Metzler, 49-51.

Schmidt, Torben (2011): *Flippin' In*: Ein literaturbasiertes YouTube-Inszenierungsprojekt im Englischunterricht der Klasse 11. In Almut Küppers, Torben Schmidt & Maik Walter (Hg.): *Inszenierungen im Fremdsprachenunterricht: Grundlagen, Formen, Perspektiven*. Braunschweig: Schroedel/Diesterweg/Klinkhardt, 192-207.

Steiner, Anne (2010): ‚Kulturerlebnis Theater': Interkulturelle Lernchancen (nicht nur) für Zweitsprachlernende. In Wolfgang Gehring & Elisabeth Stinshoff (Hg.): *Außerschulische Lernorte des Fremdsprachenunterrichts*. Braunschweig: Schroedel/Diesterweg/Klinkhardt, 95-104.

Stritzelberger, Ingrid (2015): ‚Living and Loving': Medien und Theater als Unterrichtsprojekt. In Wolfgang Hallet et al. (Hg.), 269-286.

Surkamp, Carola (2014): Non-Verbal Communication: Why We Need It in Foreign Language Teaching and How We Can Foster It with Drama Activities. In *Scenario* VIII/2, 28-43.

Surkamp, Carola & Feuchert, Sascha (2010): Lernort Theater: Potentiale, Methoden und Anregungen für den fremdsprachlichen Dramenunterricht. In Wolfgang Gehring (Hg.): *Lernorte und Lernräume für den Fremdsprachenunterricht*. Braunschweig: Bildungshaus Schulbuchverlage, 78-94.

Surkamp, Carola & Hallet, Wolfgang (2015): Dramendidaktik und Dramapädagogik im Fremdsprachenunterricht: Zur Einleitung. In Wolfgang Hallet et al. (Hg.), 1-20.

Surkamp, Carola & Nünning, Ansgar (2016): *Englische Literatur unterrichten 1: Grundlagen und Methoden*. 4. Aufl. Seelze-Velber: Klett-Kallmeyer.

Surkamp, Carola & Nünning, Ansgar (2018): *Englische Literatur unterrichten 2: Unterrichtsmodelle und Materialien*. 3. Aufl. Seelze-Velber: Klett-Kallmeyer.

Walker, Aisha & White, Goodith (2013): *Technology Enhanced Language Learning: Connecting Theory and Practice*. Oxford: Oxford UP.

Theatraler Raum und performativer Lernprozess

Verwurzelung und Beweglichkeit

Florian Vaßen

Ohne Landschaften und Orte, vor allem aber ohne Räume gibt es kein Leben, keine Kunst, kurz: keine Menschen. Vor allem seit dem *spatial turn* (vgl. Dünne & Günzel 2016, Dünzel 2017) scheint der Raum von größerer Bedeutung als die Zeit, ja die Lokalität konkretisiert erst die Temporalität. Erinnerung macht sich oft fest an Orts- und Wegerfahrungen, d.h. an Gebundenheit und Sicherheit, man könnte auch von Heimat sprechen, und zugleich an Beweglichkeit und Offenheit, d.h. auch an der Fremde. Oskar Negt, der sich mit diesen Fragen in seiner Autobiographie *Überlebensglück* auseinandersetzt, betont, „dass bestimmte Orte, an denen Menschen gewohnt und gearbeitet haben, wie ein Wurzelgeflecht ihren Denkweisen zugrunde liegen." (Negt 2016: 51)

Diese Mischung aus Verwurzelung und Beweglichkeit verweist nicht nur auf Manfred Schewes Biographie – von Esterwegen, einer katholischen Gemeinde im Emsland, über die Universität in Oldenburg mit Studium und Promotion, England und die Schweiz bis zur Professur an der Universität in Cork, dem Haus in Crosshaven mit einem herrlichen Blick weit über die Irische See und der Metropole Berlin – sie bestimmt auch seine Forschung und Lehre, seine wissenschaftliche und performative Arbeit im Theater, in der Germanistik und Theaterwissenschaft sowie speziell im Bereich Deutsch als Fremdsprache (DaF).

Der Auftritt im Theater-Raum

Auch im Theater finden wir diese produktive Ambivalenz von *Gebundenheit* und *Beweglichkeit*, besonders ausgeprägt im Verhältnis von Szene/Bühne und Auftritt, der einen der wichtigsten Momente in einer Inszenierung/Theateraufführung, aber auch in einer experimentellen Theaterwerkstatt und sogar in theatralen Lernprozessen darstellt: Eine Schwelle wird überschritten, etwas Neues, oft Fremdes tritt auf die Bühne (vgl. Matzke et al. 2015). Bei dem Wechsel von Nicht-Präsenz zur Präsenz, vom *Off* zum *On*, finden entscheidende räumliche und personale Veränderungen statt, es konstituiert sich ein Theater-Raum.

Mit dem Auftreten einer Figur, d. h. der theatralen Figuration, entsteht zunächst Sichtbarkeit, gefolgt von Aufmerksamkeit (vgl. Glöde 2007), und es findet eine wichtige Trennung der theatral Handelnden von den Zuschauenden statt. Der Auftritt konstituiert demgemäß den Als-ob-Rahmen des Theaters.

Für Spiel- und Lernprozesse, ihre theatrale Intensität, ästhetische Qualität und inhaltliche Relevanz, ist der erste Schritt in den Raum, sozusagen auf die Bühne, ebenfalls sehr bedeutsam; für die Spielenden/Schauspieler*innen wie für die Zuschauenden, also für die gesamte Konstellation, finden in diesem Augenblick wichtige Veränderungen statt. Beim Auftreten entsteht eine Figur, wird ein Thema angesprochen und eine ‚Botschaft‘ überbracht, entwickelt sich eine kommunikative Situation und beginnt eine ästhetisch-theatrale Setzung. Mit der Figur tritt etwas Anderes, ja sogar Fremdes auf und ein, das die Zuschauenden anspricht und zugleich separiert. Die fremde Figur als das Neue macht neugierig oder verunsichert, wirkt anziehend oder abstoßend, verbreitet Freude oder Schrecken.

Auffällig ist, dass der Auftritt konstitutiv von größerer Bedeutung für die Aufführung ist als der Abgang. Mit dem Wort ‚-tritt‘ wird zudem das Überschreiten einer Linie und damit der Schwellencharakter des Vorgangs betont: Eine Person tritt plötzlich aus dem Off ins On und wird so sichtbar. Das Morphem -*gang* dagegen bezeichnet einen Vor*gang*, eine zeitlich sich ausdehnende Gehbewegung, das Weggehen akzentuiert den Prozesscharakter. Sicherlich nicht zufällig hat die analoge Bezeichnung „Abtritt" in der Bedeutung von einem „einfachen Abort" (Deutsches Universalwörterbuch) durch ihre Verbindung mit Fäkalien eine negative Konnotation.

Da es nicht den *einen* Auftritt gibt, sondern durch die Jahrhunderte eine große Vielfalt von unterschiedlichen Auftrittsarten und -formen im europäischen Theater, ist eine inhaltliche Definition schwierig und letztlich weniger nützlich als die Frage nach der Funktion und Stellung in der Theater-Konstellation. Oft ist es ein Fremder und damit das Fremde, das in die existierende Situation ‚einbricht‘, wie z. B. im naturalistischen Drama, etwa in Gerhart Hauptmanns *Vor Sonnenaufgang*. Aber auch so unterschiedliche Figuren wie Herrscher, Fürst oder König als höchste Repräsentanten der Gesellschaft oder der Wandergeselle, Kaufmann und Soldat, Vertriebene oder Flüchtende, der Schurke und Feind oder der Heimkehrer und Freund, ja sogar die Narrenfigur, deren Auftreten an sich – gemäß dem Harlekin-Prinzip – ihre Botschaft ist, geben mit ihrem Auftritt der Handlung eine entscheidende Wendung. Wichtige Gegenfigurationen wie der antike Chor oder der Erzähler, Kommentator und Sänger, z. B. im epischen Theater, befinden sich dagegen in der Regel dauerhaft auf der Bühne und stehen für Kontinuität und Präsenz.

Ein historischer Überblick über das europäische Theater ist in diesem Kontext aufschlussreich, denn er zeigt, dass der Ursprung des Auftritts in Dionysos' Ankunft bei den Festspielen der Dionysien zu finden und demzufolge von

großer Bedeutung ist. In der nachfolgenden griechischen Tragödie stehen sich
der quasi negative, weil verhinderte oder destruierte Auftritt wie in Aischylos'
Die Perser und *Agamemnon* und der gelungene wie die Heimkehr von Odys-
seus und Orest gegenüber. Im römischen Theater wird die Vertikalität des Auftritts als triumphale Handlung besonders deutlich, der aufrechte Gang und der
kontrollierte Schritt werden zu Topoi des Auftritts. Auf das sich vermutlich
daraus entwickelnde prunkvolle *entrée*, d. h. die erlernte Choreographie des
richtigen Eintretens als Zeremonie und Herrscherinszenierung, z. B. am Hofe
Ludwig XIV., und dem sich daran orientierenden Theater- und Opernauftritt,
folgt im 17. Jahrhundert bald eine neue Ästhetik des eintretenden Körpers mit
vielfältigen, zum Teil pantomimischen Bewegungsformen wie Beschleunigen
oder Verlangsamen, Springen oder Kriechen, Rennen, Gleiten oder Schweben,
Stocken, Stolpern und sogar Fallen. Damit beginnen moderne ,fehlerhafte' und
dekonstruierte Auftrittsformen mit ihrer Depotenzierung der jubilatorischen
Repräsentation, man denke nur an den hinkenden, stolpernden und fallenden
Richter Adam in Kleists *Der zerbrochene Krug*, an Peter Handkes *Kaspar*, der
vor dem Sprechen das Gehen lernen muss, oder an den stolpernd auftretenden,
verunsicherten Torquato Tasso in Peter Steins Inszenierung des gleichnamigen
„Schauspiels" (Theater Bremen 1969).

Der theatrale Auftritt ist nicht nur geprägt von Formen des gesellschaftlichen
Auftretens in der antiken, der höfischen oder bürgerlichen Gesellschaft, auch die
Theaterarchitektur, besonders die Guckkasten- versus Raumbühne und die daraus sich ergebende Raumordnung beeinflusst entscheidend sowohl die Grenzen
und Möglichkeiten des theatralen Auftritts als auch den mehr oder weniger inszenierten Auftritt der Zuschauer*innen; beim Betreten des Theaters verlassen
sie die Alltagswirklichkeit und damit ihren gewohnten ,Lebensraum'. Analog zu
den Spielenden hat nämlich auch das Publikum während der Aufführung seinen
Auftritt, je unterschiedlich als distanzierte Beobachtung, engagiertes Mitgehen,
Begeisterung, Empörung oder Unmut, spontane Teilhabe oder sogar geplantes
Mitspielen. Mit der Theatertechnik, insbesondere der elektrischen Beleuchtung
seit Ende des 19. Jahrhunderts, werden etwa mit *black* bzw. Lichtkegeln von
grellen Scheinwerfern spezifische Erscheinungsformen bis hin zu medialen oder
virtuellen Auftritten möglich.

Die Art und Weise, wie die theatrale Bewegungsästhetik des Auftritts abläuft,
initiiert demnach den weiteren Spielprozess: Selbstbewusstes Auftreten oder
verängstigtes Eintreten, Stolzieren oder Stolpern, gehetztes Rennen oder Erstar-
ren, zögerliches Warten oder Hereinfallen zeigen unterschiedliche Perspektiven
an, auch wenn sie sich im Verlauf des Spielprozesses verändern (können); zumeist vor dem ersten gesprochenen Satz gibt der auftretende Körper und seine
spezifischen Bewegungen eine bestimmte Richtung vor.

Stellt das ‚Misslingen' des Auftritts im modernen Theater etwa in Form des
Stolperns eine Reduktion dar, so wird der physische Auftritt einer Person in der
Defiguration des postdramatischen Theaters grundlegend in Frage gestellt. Schauspieler*innen, die keine psychologische Figur darstellen, sondern rezitieren, Zitat-
collagen vortragen und Sprachflächen (z.B. in der Art von Elfriede Jelinek) arti-
kulieren, benötigen keinen Figuren-Auftritt im eigentlichen Sinne. Zwar gab es
schon immer die Teichoskopie und das Sprechen aus dem Off, aber heute variiert
die Form des Auftritts als Schwellen-Überschreitung – von der glanzvollen Repräsentation bis zur minimalistischen Reduktion – und löst sich nicht nur immanent
auf oder wird dekonstruiert, sondern ist in vielen Theaterformaten auch struk-
turell nicht mehr notwendig und oft gar nicht mehr existent. Stattdessen findet
ein theatraler Prozess im Raum statt, häufig ohne jegliche Auftritte und Abgänge.

Möglichkeitsraum – eine Theaterwerkstatt mit Heiner Müllers
Bildbeschreibung

In mehreren Theater-Werkstätten zu Heiner Müllers *Bildbeschreibung* (1999)
habe ich mit verschiedenen Gruppen diese veränderte Raum-Konstellationen
experimentell erprobt (vgl. Vaßen 1995, Vaßen 1996, Vaßen 2012). Die Werkstät-
ten begannen mit einer Räumung, sprich der Etablierung eines leeren Raumes,
der uns so überhaupt erst die Möglichkeit bot, ihn in Besitz zu nehmen und zu
gestalten. Diese ‚Entleerung' war der erste Schritt, es folgte eine Reinigung des
Raumes, wie es bekanntlich auch Grotowski bei seinen Theater-Projekten praktiziert hat. Erst nach dieser gemeinsam vorgenommenen ‚rituellen Waschung',
wie man es pointiert nennen könnte, war dieser Raum unser Raum – und wurde
ein theatraler Raum (siehe Abb. 1).

Abbildung 1: Vorbereitung des theatralen Raums (Foto: Florian Vaßen)

Leerer Raum und Stuhlkreis bildeten den Ausgangspunkt für die ersten Schritte, bei denen szenische und spielerische Elemente zunächst vor allem in kommunikativer und gruppendynamischer Hinsicht von großer Bedeutung waren. Es folgte die schriftliche und bildnerische Auseinandersetzung mit Heiner Müllers Text, indem alle Teilnehmer*innen ein Bild zur *Bildbeschreibung* malten sowie eine Textstelle auswählten und auf ein Blatt Papier schrieben. Mit diesen Produkten aus Bild und Schrift ,dekorierten' wir die Wände des immer noch leeren Raums, und zwar wie in Müllers *Bildbeschreibung* als Montage von Reihung und Variation. Doch der Raum veränderte sich nicht nur durch diese ,Dekoration' in der Fläche; es entstand durch die Form von Raum-Bewegungen, d. h. durch das ,Wandern' der Teilnehmer*innen entlang der Wände von Text zu Text und von Bild zu Bild, durch das Betrachten und Wahrnehmen, durch die Fremd- und Selbst-Kommentare zu den Bildern, auch eine spezifische Kommunikation untereinander (siehe Abb. 2).

Abbildung 2: Schriftliche und bildnerische Auseinandersetzung der Teilnehmer*innen mit dem Text von Heiner Müller (Foto: Florian Vaßen)

Nach diesem ersten Schritt unserer Produktion wandten wir uns im Folgenden sprachlich dem Text *Bildbeschreibung* zu: Wir setzten uns im Kreis auf den Boden und lasen gemeinsam laut mehrmals den Text, zunächst jede/r eine Zeile, dann von Satzzeichen zu Satzzeichen, dann so lange, wie jede/r das Bedürfnis hatte zu lesen. Im vielfältig differenten Lesen und im Klang der Wörter und

Laute entstand ein Hörraum, der ein tiefer gehendes Verständnis des Textes, seiner Struktur, seines Rhythmus, seiner Lyrismen, seiner sprachlichen und thematischen Komplexität und Offenheit ermöglichte. Klanglich füllte der Text den Raum und zugleich, vermittelt über das Hören, den Körper der Teilnehmer*innen – es entstand ein organischer (Körper-)Klang im (Theater-)Raum

Nun galt es den Raum auch in körperlicher Bewegung zu ‚erobern‘ und einen Bewegungsraum zu schaffen: Wir gingen laut lesend durch den Raum, zunächst jede/r für sich – kreuz und quer oder nach bestimmten selbst gewählten Mustern. Wir lasen dabei weiter, variierten Lautstärke und Lesegeschwindigkeit, Intonation und Sprachgestus, wir experimentierten mit Stimmungen. Körperhaltungen und Bewegungsarten kamen hinzu und traten in ein Verhältnis zum Sprechen – korrespondierend oder kontrastierend. Es blieb nicht aus, dass die Gehenden sich begegneten, sich nicht mehr nur auf sich selbst, ihre Sprache und Bewegung sowie auf den Raum konzentrierten, sondern begannen, die anderen wahrzunehmen und zunächst vorsichtig miteinander zu kommunizieren. So entstanden erste Versuche eines dialogischen oder eines chorischen Sprechens, es bildeten sich Paare, kleine Gruppen, die in einem Resonanzraum miteinander kommunizierten, flüchtig, wechselnd oder kontinuierlich.

Der gesprochene Text wurde dabei zunehmend fokussierend und auswählend gelesen, die Aufmerksamkeit konzentrierte sich auf bestimmte Passagen, Sätze, einzelne Wörter, die wiederholt – monoton seriell oder akzentuierend variierend – und in Korrespondenz mit anderen Sprechern intensiviert wurden. So wurde der Text nach der vorbereitenden konzentrierten, überwiegend stummen Lektüre nun auch sprechend stimmlich und körperlich räumlich erarbeitet. Jetzt erst wurden sein Rhythmus, die Reihungen und Variationen, die Bruchstellen und Zuspitzungen, die monologischen, dialogischen und chorischen Elemente sinnlich *erfahrbar* (siehe Abb. 3).

Abbildung 3: Szenische Theaterarbeit (Foto: Florian Vaßen)

Zugleich wurde der Raum durch diese dynamische Konfiguration, durch den Medienwechsel (Schrift, Sprache, Körper), verändert und ‚besetzt', es entstanden neue Raumerfahrungen in dem Sinne, dass die Akteure wahrnahmen, dass sie mit ihrem Agieren den Raum nicht nur gestalten, sondern durch ihre performative Praxis als offene Konstruktion konstituieren:

> Ein Raum entsteht, wenn man Richtungsvektoren, Geschwindigkeitsgrößen und Variabilität der Zeit in Verbindung bringt. Der Raum ist ein Geflecht von beweglichen Elementen. Er ist gewissermaßen von der Gesamtheit der Bewegungen erfüllt, die sich in ihm entfalten. [...] Im Gegensatz zum Ort gibt es also weder eine Eindeutigkeit noch die Stabilität von etwas ‚Eigenem'. Insgesamt ist *der Raum ein Ort* mit dem man etwas macht. (de Certeau 1988: 218, Herv. i. O.)

Im weiteren Arbeitsprozess entwickelten kleine Gruppen aus den ausgewählten Textfragmenten (siehe Abb. 4) kurze Szenen, die spielerisch erarbeitet, theatral umgesetzt, geprobt, als Collage zusammengefügt und am Ende der Werkstatt der Gruppe selbst präsentiert wurden (siehe Abb. 5); die Trennung von Spieler*innen und Zuschauer*innen war dabei aufgehoben.

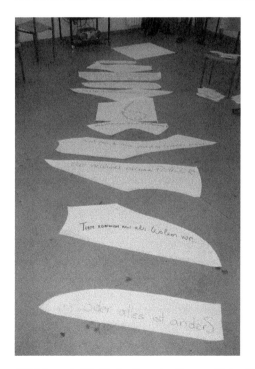

Abbildung 4: Die Textcollage der Gruppe (Foto: Florian Vaßen)

Zum Schluss konnte jede/r Teilnehmer*in ein neues Bild malen oder ihr/sein erstes übermalen, die selbst ausgewählte Text-Passage ‚weiterschreiben‘ oder eine neue Textstelle auswählen. Was war im Laufe des ästhetischen Prozesses geschehen? Was hatte sich verändert, was war gleichgeblieben, bei jeder/m Einzelnen, in der Gruppe? Diese Fragen wurden resümierend intensiv diskutiert.

Abbildung 5: Präsentation als Collage aus Texten, Bildern und szenischer Darstellung
(Foto: Florian Vaßen)

Nicht nur der Spiel-Raum mit den Bildern und Texten, Körpern und Stimmen, sondern auch der Außenraum war für uns von Bedeutung und zwar sowohl in den konkreten Verbindungsstellen und Öffnungen wie Fenstern und Türen, Vor- und Nebenräumen als auch in Bezug auf die angrenzenden Gebäude. Die ineinander verschachtelten Räume – Text-Raum, Körper-Raum, Spiel-Raum, Lehr- und Lern-Raum – bildeten eine multiperspektivische Struktur; sogar die weitere Umgebung in ihrer konkreten Situation und Zeit, der gesellschaftliche Außenbereich, spielte eine wichtige Rolle. Da alle Räume zur Szene gehörten, fanden keine Auftritte und Abgänge im eigentlichen Sinne statt, alles und alle waren immer anwesend.

Unser Spiel-Raum war zu einem offenen ‚Freiraum' geworden, einem anderen Raum, der mit seiner Differenz zum Alltäglichen, seiner Fremdheit eine neue Art von ästhetischer Erfahrung, vielleicht sogar Schwellenerfahrungen ermöglichte, aber auch zu Geselligkeit und Beisammensein führte. Dieser anderen Raum-Konzeption entsprach dabei eine deutlich veränderte Zeitstruktur als gewöhnlich in der Universität: Wir haben tagsüber mit nur kurzen Unterbrechungen nahezu vier Tage ‚durchgearbeitet'.

> Kunst ist in erster Linie dadurch politisch, dass sie ein raum-zeitliches Sensorium schafft, [...] dass sie einen bestimmten Raum und eine bestimmte Zeit aufteilt und dass die Gegenstände, mit denen sie diesen Raum bevölkert, und die Rhythmen, in die sie diese Zeit einteilt, eine spezifische Form der Erfahrung festlegen [...]. (Rancière 2016: 77)

Wir schufen unseren Möglichkeitsraum in einer Theater-Werkstatt, ein Begriff, weniger gebräuchlich als der aus dem Englischen entliehene Begriff *Workshop*, der aber schon semantisch die Betonung der Örtlichkeit enthält: Die Werkstatt ist ein Arbeitsraum, in dem etwas produziert wird, und ‚Statt' und ‚Stätte' bedeuten Ort, Platz, Stelle, oft als Schauplatz (*theatron*) wichtiger Ereignisse von besonderer Bedeutung. Es wäre vermutlich zu hoch gegriffen, von Heterotopie im Sinne Michel Foucaults zu sprechen, aber immerhin hatte eine „Entgegensetzung [...] zwischen dem kulturellen Raum und dem nützlichen Raum" (Foucault 1991: 67) stattgefunden. Foucault sieht in unserer Zeit eine „Epoche des Raumes" oder eine „Epoche des Simultanen" und konstatiert, „daß die heutige Unruhe grundlegend den Raum betrifft – jedenfalls viel mehr als die Zeit" (ibid. 66), wie man auch sowohl an der Globalisierung als auch an den Flüchtenden unschwer sehen kann, eine Situation, bei der sich Bewegung und erstarrte, scheinbare Sicherheit gegenüberstehen. Heiner Müllers *Bildbeschreibung* mit einer Ästhetik der Unterbrechung und Störung ist ein besonders prägnantes literarisches Beispiel für diese „Epoche des Raums" und deren Simultaneität, in denen sich die historische Dimension als Topographie entfaltet.

Körper und Raum im pädagogisch-theatralen Prozess

Auch in der pädagogischen Arbeit besitzt der Lern-Raum einen inszenatorischen Rahmen, es finden performative Prozesse statt, bei denen die Körperlichkeit der Lehrenden und Lernenden eine große Rolle spielt. Handlungs- und Wahrnehmungsaspekte sowie der Bereich der Sinne ergänzen dabei die kognitiven Prozesse, Interaktion und Kommunikation bestimmen letztlich die Lernsituation. Wie die Lehrenden sich den Lern-Raum ‚aneignen', wie sie etwa vor der Gruppe der Lernenden stehen, wie sie im Raum umhergehen, wie sie sich bewegen, wie sie sitzen oder den Kopf halten, vor allem wie sie die Lernenden ansehen und mit ihnen sprechen, kurz: mit welcher Körpersprache sie sich als Person im Raum präsentieren, ist nicht nur wichtig für die Kommunikation, sondern auch ein zentraler Aspekt des gesamten Lehr- und Lernprozesses. Da für den „Unterricht [...] seine soziale Ereignishaftigkeit, seine kulturelle Bedeutsamkeit und seine Performanzbezogenheit von elementarer Wichtigkeit" (Klepacki & Zirfas 2013: 190) sind, sollte sich auch die Ausbildung der Lehrenden viel stärker als bisher auf diese Bereiche konzentrieren.

In einem theaterpädagogisch oder dramapädagogisch fundierten Unterricht ist es von großer Bedeutung, in welcher Weise der Raum in den Lernprozess eingebunden wird – ist es das normale Klassenzimmer, wird es verändert, etwa indem Platz für Körperlichkeit und Bewegung geschaffen oder es zeichenhaft verwandelt wird, ist es ein Probenraum, eine Bühne, die Aula, oder wird mit den Gängen und dem Hof das gesamte Gebäude (der pädagogischen Institution) bespielt und darüber hinaus die Szene in das Umfeld, z. B. den Stadtteil, im Sinne des *site specific theatre* geöffnet?

Eine performative Didaktik ist demnach für die Lehrenden in allen pädagogischen Bereichen und Schularten notwendig, bei der es um die reale Substanz des Lehrens und Lernens im Sinne von Körperlichkeit, Inszenierung und Arrangement als kulturelle Praxis im Raum geht. Im Fach Deutsch und in den Fremdsprachen sowie in Geschichte und den Sozialwissenschaften und zum Teil sogar in den Naturwissenschaften werden heute in der Schule zunehmend über Rollenspiel und szenische Darstellung, Improvisation und Stehgreifspiel, Pantomime und Standbilder, szenisches Erarbeiten von Texten als literarisches Rollenspiel bzw. szenische Interpretation, szenisches Erkunden und Reflektieren, und Inszenierungen von Alltagssituationen – in Kombination mit anderen Techniken – Lerninhalte vermittelt (vgl. Even & Schewe 2016). Die offenen theatralen Lernformen ermöglichen mit ihrer Verbindung von Handeln und Reflektieren Lernsituationen, die über eine rein kognitive Herangehensweise hinausgehen und so durch die Einbeziehung raum-, körper-, sinnen-, und erfahrungsbezogener Elemente eine erweiterte Perspektive eröffnet (vgl. Brych et al. 2000).

Festzuhalten bleibt: Die zu vermittelnden Inhalte und die Art und Weise der Vermittlung sind nicht zu trennen von der Haltung der Lehrenden und Lernenden und deren Positionierung im Raum, erst ein Zusammenwirken dieser Aspekte ermöglicht eine besondere Qualität des Lehrens und Lernens.

‚Welttheater' und DaF-Praxis

Manfred Schewe hat über Jahre in vielfältiger Weise Theater und Theaterpädagogik/Dramapädagogik in den unterschiedlichsten theatralen Räumen und an den verschiedensten Orten nahezu auf allen Kontinenten gelehrt und praktiziert, von der begrenzten Theater-Praxis im Rahmen der Lernprozesse von Fremd- und Zweitsprachenerwerb (vgl. Schewe 1993) in einem Klassenraum bis zur Inszenierung von Thomas Hürlimanns *Das Einsiedler Welttheater* auf dem Campus der Universität in Cork (vgl. Boyd & Schewe 2011). Wenn Schewe mit Heathcote und Johnson/O'Neill die Relevanz „des Mediums Drama als Kunstform" (Schewe 1989: 20) betont und damit die „Erschütterung von Selbstverständlichkeiten" (ibid. 24) akzentuiert, dann verweist dieser Ansatz auf einen ästhetischen Prozess, in dem Differenzerfahrungen in einem theatralen Raum in besonderem Maße möglich sind.

Räume mit ihren Grenzen/Schwellen bilden den performativen Rahmen von Bildungs- und Lernprozessen. Entsprechend müssen beim Theater-Spielen in Schule und anderen Institutionen des Lehrens und Lernens die ästhetische Beschaffenheit der Räume bzw. ihre Auswahl besonders bedacht werden. Ob beim Theater spielen, in performativen Experimenten oder bei szenischen Übungen in der DaF-Arbeit: der Auftritt oder der Einstieg in die Szene und selbst noch der einfache Beginn des Spielens sind von besonderer Bedeutung für die gesamte Szene, für die Präsenz und Körperspannung der Agierenden und für die Aufmerksamkeit und Konzentration der Zuschauenden. Die ersten Momente der Szene, das Zusammentreffen von Figur/Person und Raum, geben sehr häufig Aufschluss über den weiteren Verlauf der Theaterarbeit, über eine Aufführung ebenso wie über Lernprozesse und Erfahrungen im pädagogischen Kontext und sollten dem entsprechend gut bedacht, genau geplant und präzise praktiziert werden.

Auch die pädagogische Arbeit in DaF bedarf eines dreidimensionalen sprachlich-körperlichen Spiel- und Kommunikationsprozesses im szenischen Raum. Manfred Schewe hat diese Art von DaF im deutschen Sprachraum initiiert, verbreitet, fruchtbar gemacht und zu einem umfassenden *Performativen Lehren, Lernen und Forschen* (vgl. Even & Schewe 2016; Crutchfield & Schewe 2017) weiterentwickelt.

Literatur

Boyd, Stephen & Schewe, Manfred (Hg.) (2011): *Welttheater übersetzen, adaptieren produzieren / World Theater. translation, adaption production.* Berlin et al.: Schibri.

Brych, Thomas; Schewe, Manfred & Schlemminger, Gerald (Hg.) (2000): *Deutsch als Fremdsprache. Pädagogische Konzepte für einen ganzheitlichen DaF-Unterricht.* Hannover: Cornelsen.

de Certeau, Michel (1988): *Die Kunst des Handelns.* Berlin: Merve.

Crutchfield, John & Schewe, Manfred (Hg.) (2017): *Going Performative in Intercultural Education. International Contexts, Theoretical Perspectives and Models of Practice.* Bristol: Multilingual Matters.

Dünne, Jörg & Günzel, Stephan (Hg.) (2006): *Raumtheorie. Grundlagentexte aus Philosophie und Kulturwissenschaften.* Frankfurt a. M.: Suhrkamp.

Even, Susanne & Schewe, Manfred (Hg.) (2016): *Performatives Lehren, Lernen, Forschen. Performative Teaching, Learning, Research.* Berlin et al.: Schibri.

Foucault, Michel (1991): Andere Räume. In Martin Wentz (Hg.): *Stadt-Räume.* Frankfurt am Main/New York: Campus, 65-72.

Glöde, Marc (2007): Zur Wahrnehmung zur Aufmerksamkeit. In Christian Lechtermann, Kirsten Wagner & Horst Wenzel (Hg.): *Möglichkeitsräume. Zur Performativität von sensorischer Wahrnehmung.* Berlin: Erich Schmidt, 31-42.

Günzel, Stephan (2017): *Raum. Eine kulturwissenschaftliche Einführung.* Bielefeld: Transcript.

Klepacki, Leopold & Zirfas, Jörg (2013): *Theatrale Didaktik. Ein pädagogischer Grundriss des schulischen Theaterunterrichts.* Weinheim: Beltz.

Matzke, Annemarie; Otto, Ulf & Roselt, Jens (Hg.) (2015): *Auftritte. Strategien des In-Erscheinung-Tretens in Künsten und Medien.* Bielefeld: Transcript.

Müller, Heiner (1999): Bildbeschreibung. In Frank Hörnigk (Hg.): *Heiner Müller: Werke. Bd. 2 Die Prosa.* Frankfurt a. M.: Suhrkamp, 112-119.

Negt, Oskar (2016): *Überlebensglück. Eine autobiographische Spurensuche.* Göttingen: Steidl.

Rancière, Jacques (2006): *Die Aufteilung des Sinnlichen. Die Politik der Kunst und ihre Paradoxien.* Berlin: b_books.

Schewe, Manfred (1989): Dramapädagogik – eine erziehungswissenschaftliche Teildisziplin? DRAMA – eine importwürdige Lehr-/Lernmethode? Oldenburg: Pädagogisches Zentrum.

Schewe, Manfred (1993): *Fremdsprache inszenieren. Zur Fundierung einer dramapädagogischen Lehr- und Lernpraxis.* Oldenburg: Pädagogisches Zentrum.

Schewe, Manfred & Shaw, Peter (Hg.) (1993): *Towards Drama as a Method in the Foreign Language Classroom.* Frankfurt a. M. et al.: Peter Lang.

Theater Bremen (1969): Johann Wolfgang von Goethe: Torquato Tasso (Bremer Bühnenfassung), Regie: Peter Stein. Bremen: Selbstverlag. [Programmheft]

Vaßen, Florian (1995): Images become text become images: Heiner Müller's „Bildbeschreibung" („Description of a Picture"). In Gerhard Fischer (Hg.): Heiner Müller. ConTEXTS and HISTORY. A Collection of Essays from the Sydney German Studies Symposium 1994 „Heiner Müller/Theatre-History-Performance". Tübingen: Stauffenburg, 165-187.

Vaßen, Florian (1996): Heiner Müller: „Bildbeschreibung". Experimenteller Text und Spiel-Modell. In *Korrespondenzen. Zeitschrift für Theaterpädagogik* 26, 49-54.

Vaßen, Florian (2012): RaumZeitRaum. Konstellationen von Schrift und Bild, Spiel und Raum. Werkstatt-Versuche mit Heiner Müllers „Bildbeschreibung" In Kristin Westphal (Hg.): *Räume der Unterbrechung. Theater Performance Pädagogik.* Oberhausen: Athena, 317-335.

The performativity of space and performative competence

The Performativity of social interaction and space

Wolfgang Hallet

There is no performative act, no performing, no social or communicative interaction whatsoever that does not happen in space. Surprisingly, it is quite a late discovery in the study of culture and also in pedagogy that, apart from time, space is an anthropological condition and constant of human existence and behaviour. No human interaction can occur outside space. It is one of the fundamental dimensions of every cultural and social life.

The core of this belated discovery is that space, rather than simply a physically given environment, is itself culturally produced and culturally productive, providing the ground, the territories, the platforms, buildings and rooms – the spaces – on and in which human interaction and social life take place. Whenever we perform, we need to set the scene and prepare the ground, there is a spatial environment that we inhabit or create and a 'somewhere' we go to, and there is a huge cultural network of routes, roads and paths that connect all of these places and spaces, itineraries and pathways that we take to move from A to B and that we define as points of departure and arrival. To generalise in Edward Soja's terms (1996: 46, orig. emphasis): "*There is no unspatialized social reality. There are no aspatial social processes*".

This is why, before anything else, we should refrain from looking at space as a metaphor. Rather, space is, in all its materiality and physicality, but also with its semiotic dimension of carrying and producing meaning, an existential dimension of cultural life and experience as well as of personal orientation and positioning. No action and no interaction can be performed in a vacuum, but interactions are not only always tied to spaces and places; reciprocally, spaces and their cultural meanings emerge from the social interactions and their specific character in terms of purpose, materials, architecture, the objects that are part of it, and human agents that use, move around and position themselves in these spaces.

Manfred Schewe, the Department of German and the other organisers did not simply take up and respond to this increased attention for the spatial dimension of cultural processes with their 2017 2nd International SCENARIO Forum Conference at University College Cork. Rather, they conceptualized and developed the notion of space further in three ways that are pertinent to this essay, as well: As the title of the conference, "Performative Spaces in Language, Literature and Culture Education", indicates,

- space is a dimension intrinsic to all performative acts, on the theatre and the social stage alike;
- space is itself 'performative', i.e. emerging and resulting from acts of social and cultural performance (an effect that could be termed 'spatial poiesis');
- education is a sociocultural domain that relies heavily on the spaces it offers, shapes and creates in all processes of teaching and learning.

This universal performativity of space, the creation of space in social interaction and constant acts of assigning meaning to it, this constant emergence of space when doing things in space, calls to mind, of course, William Shakespeare's most famous, often quoted lines from *As You Like It* in which he has condensed the performativity and theatricality of human life and of being in the world poetically:

> All the world's a stage,
> And all the men and women merely players;
> They have their exits and their entrances,
> And one man in his time plays many parts. (II, 7)

It is often forgotten that this 'stage' is a material entity and that this 'world' has a spatial dimension and encompasses all the places and spaces that we inhabit and produce, thereby turning every single place and space into a stage of everyday performance and becoming players in this spatial-material world ourselves. A 'stage', we must conclude, is not simply there; rather, we create it in the course of entering it and acting on it; and as much as any ground is transformed into a stage as soon as someone begins to use it or declare it as such, space in general is a product of social relations, actions and interactions (Lefebvre 1991); and so are the manifold stages on which we perform in everyday life.

Of course, there is a metaphysical dimension to Shakespeare's world-theatre metaphor. But in all of his plays the world as a stage materialises, and as in many of his plays staged events and the motif of a play-in-the-play are key scenes and a key dimension of his plays. This is why in a secularised world like ours, the metaphor also deserves some reconsideration, and particularly in an age of omnipresent media coverage, digital platforms and the cultural imperative of permanent visibility of the self.

In a short, seemingly marginal sequence from Franco Zefirelli's film version of Shakespeare's *Hamlet* (1990, with Mel Gibson as Hamlet) when the players' company arrives at Elsinor this world theatre metaphor is truly visualised. In a sense, it represents the transformation of the lifeworld – a castle and the court-yard – into an arena in which Hamlet takes centre stage . There are various dimensions of theatricality to this scene. For one, from medieval times the royal court has a long tradition of theatricality of its own, with all its rituals and cere-monies, as we are able to witness almost daily on TV and in globally circulated images of royal families. In the middle ages, all of these courtly performances theatricalised the sovereign's power and his people's role as subalterns and humble servants that hail and glorify his rule and God-given social, societal and political position. The theatre and the players entering and performing are therefore a common view in court-life, bringing entertainment, a taste of changing and swapping roles, at least fictionally, of masquerade and mockery into the middle of quite a static medieval world of predetermined social roles.

This short film sequence provides us with some of the core notions and concepts of theatricality and performativity: Hamlet is presented as a man who is able to turn the routine and the rather banal arrival of the players' company (that he has hired and instructed) into a social and entertaining event, dressing as one of the players himself, and starring on horseback in the play that he is staging. He is the only player playing so that his performance attracts everybody's attention. Also, Hamlet is so familiar with the spatial environment of the castle and the court-yard that he is able to transform them into a theatrical space, demonstrating for all who are witnessing his performance how easily the boundaries between the stage and the lifeworld can be blurred. Close-ups of other 'actors' and their responses show that they are well aware of this demonstrative character of Ham-let's performance. Thus, Zefirelli is able to condense the philosophical core of *Hamlet* in one of the shortest episodes of his film version of Shakespeare's play: the difficulty or even impossibility to distinguish between 'being' and 'seeming'.

This film scene also demonstrates that cultural spaces obviously have es-tablished meanings and histories so that those that inhabit them have a clear idea of the positions that they can occupy and the kind of activity that they are expected or allowed to perform. It is obvious that the Queen's distant, reflective vantage point 'from above' suggests an overall power position in contrast to the common people's and the groundlings' position at eye-level with the players. The structure and the semiotics of this court space predetermine the different ways in which various cultural actors inhabit and use it. In this scene, it is even difficult to decide whether the courtyard architecture lends itself easily to such theatrical events or whether it is Hamlet's art of performing in it, by

imitating, almost mocking the architecture of a theatre space, very much like
Shakespeare's Globe, with all the ranks, galleries and balconies, a centre stage
for the players in the play and the centre of this stage for Hamlet himself (see
Berensmeyer 2007: 79-80).

Hamlet is very well familiar with all the conventionalised cultural meanings
and implications of this space and the way people perform in it. He makes use
of the conventional meaning and purpose of the courtyard in order to turn the
players' – and his own – entrance into a theatrical event, thus transforming
the courtyard into an arena, a stage, producing an audience and creating a performative event that is recognized as such. Hamlet also makes use of the full
repertoire of theatricality in the literal sense, including entrance and exit rituals
of bowing and waving, and the fictionalisation of the event by putting on the
costume and the hat, and taking various positions in the arena. Thus, Hamlet
does not simply 'use' or reproduce this everyday space but he transforms and
redesigns it for his own purposes, making use of the transformative power of
performativity. By turning this royal world into a stage, he confronts his mother
Gertrud and step-father Claudius with the theatrical dimension of their false
lives and a veil of lies behind which the truth of old Hamlet's death is hidden.
Hamlet exhibits the theatrical dimension of the castle space and life at court,
demonstrating that lying is the core of the theatricality of the royal court.

The difference between 'being' and 'seeming' is not only performed and
brought to the stage through this play-in-the-play technique, but the difficulty
to distinguish between the two, even our inability to tell one from the other, is
explicitly addressed in the play. Hamlet's play with the ambiguity of both the
stage drama and the social drama of his father's death as well as his mother's
and his uncle's guilt is a leitmotif and plot-constituting type of action in this
play. As Hamlet says, addressing his mother's (true or pretended?) grief for old
Hamlet and his own signs of grief:

> Seems, madam! Nay, it is, I know not 'seems'.
> 'Tis not alone my inky cloak, good mother
> Nor customary suits of solemn black,
> Nor windy suspirations of forced breath
> No, nor the fruitful river in the eye,
> Nor the dejected haviour of the visage,
> Together with all forms, modes, shapes of grief,
> That can denote me truly. These indeed seem
> For they are actions that a man might play,
> But I have that within which passes show –
> These but the trappings and the suits of woe. (Hamlet I, ii. ll. 76-86)

Hamlet, in other words, has a clear idea of the performative character and the theatricality of everyday life and of how, pursuing his will to reveal the truth behind his father's death, can make use of it for his own purposes. In the end, reality is so theatrical that it can deceive the eye and conceal the truth, whereas the players' theatre play is the only way of unveiling and disclosing it, giving it visibility in the literal sense of the word: "Ultimately, the notion of performativity breaks down the traditional philosophical dualism of appearance and reality in pointing out how language [...] and cultural realities are interconnected." (Berensmeyer 2007: 78)

Based on this scene from a film version of *Hamlet,* a preliminary definition of performativity and the various shades of meaning that it always carries may read as follows: All discursive and social interaction constitutes (a new version of) the reality in which it takes place; social interaction produces this very situation, the social relations between those involved and the roles that they take or that are assigned (in Austin's speech act theory 1962: *How to do things with words*). Performativity also always constitutes the social spaces in which it occurs: It (re-) emerges in the act of doing something in this space. Prefigured meanings of a given space may thus be re-affirmed, transformed, but also challenged or critically questioned. Therefore, engaging in social interaction is performative work since a social interaction act creates the very social reality in which it unfolds.

The symbolic dimension of performance

The performativity of everyday life is the secular version of Shakespeare's world-theatre metaphor: We express and communicate grief by showing 'signs' of it; but when we show socially conventionalised signs that others can decode and understand (the 'trappings and the suits of woe'), how can we be sure that grief is not only performed? Can we grieve without performing grief, displaying a sad look, shedding tears? This semiotic dimension of performance, of the need to encode and decode all sorts of signs beyond the spoken or the written word, is always part of a whole cultural repertoire that we acquire and employ whenever we interact, and of the symbolic competence that we draw upon whenever we perform in social situations.

In the same vein, it is the symbolic form (of words, images, behaviour) that makes it possible for individuals to imagine themselves as selves (Kramsch 2009: 18-22). In the interactions and situations that are performed, individuals present and display their selves. They thus re-iteratively constitute, develop and transform these selves, but they are always constantly 'read' and interpreted by others. This is the performative dimension of selves and of the cultural patterns that they share with others, as described for the cultural formation of gender by Judith Butler (1988; see also McGrath 2004: 42).

This interdependence of showing and being, of displaying signs of who we (believe we) 'really' are, makes us aware of the symbolic quality of all actions and interactions: What we call reality always relies on signs; in terms of the philosophy of the symbolic form (Cassirer 1955), there is no symbolically un-mediated reality. The signs (the symbolic forms) that produce the reality which they denote (the various ways of worldmaking that Nelson Goodman describes; Goodman 1978: 20) are more or less conventionalised so that they can be decod-ed and shared. But since they are signs, they are also always ambiguous, open to interpretation and negotiation, and to redefinitions and redesigns. This sym-bolic dimension is the core of the theatricality of everyday life and, of course, of the theatre play.

As a matter of fact, in the present media age in which careers and personal-ities are actually presented and produced medially, this symbolic competence reaches far beyond the languages that we speak (as suggested in Kramsch 2009: 16-22 and 188-211). It encompasses all dimensions of signification, including the spaces that we inhabit, the clothes we wear and the ways we present our body to others. Symbolic competence in the broadest sense has therefore become a crucial dimension of people's performative competence. Being a TV celebrity or performing as a YouTuber in a video has blurred the boundary between being and showing, between theatricality and everyday life (see Fischer-Lichte 2002, 2004). If 'being a YouTuber' is real life, the performativity of everyday and medi-al life is a cultural, social and pedagogical core issue. Performative competence, therefore, is a bundle of interactional, discursive and symbolic abilities and com-petencies that we acquire in the social world, but also in and through education.

The performativity of space

The indissoluble interrelatedness of the real and the symbolically imagined applies to the constitution of spaces in which we act and interact, too: Be-having and simply 'being' in space is always a 'performative act of percep-tion'[1] (Doetsch 2004: 27): While we perceive and interpret the spatial signs, we simultaneously constitute that space according to our intentions, position or role in that space. We thus imagine this given space and our role in relation to the (symbolically prefigured and socially produced) conditions (Löw 2001) that equip any given space with meaning. Space is therefore always 'real-and-im-agined' (see Soja 1996), a 'real' (physical and sensual) experience as much as an

---

1   Original in German: "ein performativer Akt der Wahrnehmung."

imagination since, through its semiotic characteristics, it is always a symbolic and hence 'imaginable' form.

The challenge of performing in space is of a twofold, namely of an episte-mological and of a semiotic nature: The process of accessing and using space involves first and foremost the identification of objects, their material quality, their characteristic and relevant features and their 'meaning' in the given en-vironment. This apprehension of the elements of the spatial environment goes hand in hand with the development of a cognitive repertoire and a language or some other symbolic form that structure the perceived spatial world and the infinite number of material objects, elements and inhabitants of which it con-sists. This semiotisation of space is a process of signification in which perceiving the world, assigning meaning to these perceptions and finding a language for them are inextricably intertwined (see Hallet 2014). Even the minutest details, the materials, the ways in which objects and agents are arranged and take their positions, are all elements that contribute to the construction of the social space in which we interact and perform (the 'relational space', Löw 2004).

The various ways in which spaces, places and rooms are perceived and expe-rienced are quite challenging: Continuously presented with an infinite number of different and discontinuous sensual perceptions and based on the material quality of the spatial environment, we must transform them into a coherent representation of space – a room, a location, a city square, a landscape. 'Space' in itself does not exist unless it is signified and configured in symbolic form, both culturally and individually.

As cultural, everyday phenomena, such acts of spatial signification can be completely unproblematic since they are normally automatised and naturalised: The essentialisation and naturalisation of space are the result of the necessity to refer and relate to space constantly. Without the cognitive schematisation and automatised, culturally prefigured semiotisation of space as an everyday practice, spatial orientation and social interaction would be impossible. How-ever, as much as we need to reflect upon social interactions and performance in advanced stages of 'doing culture', we have to systematise and reflect upon spatial meanings and practices, and in the context of working with concepts of performativity and drama in particular: The stage is basically a spatial design, the creation of a space for social positions, configurations, and interactions. This is why the social drama and the stage drama are so closely interrelated, as Victor Turner contends (1982, 1988): They both rely on the same signifying and performative practices.

This ability to read and understand spaces, to assign meaning to material spatial constellations is a competence that is required in every act of social interaction, and it is always part of our performances. Understanding, making use of, designing and redesigning the specific quality of the spatial conditions of interaction makes it possible to act and interact, and to understand what kind of stage we are actually entering or the way we would like to design or redesign it. Therefore, stage design is not only relevant with respect to the theatre stage, but is also crucial to the social stage in everyday life.

This spatial reflexivity in the context of drama work is all the more important because even in everyday life it may be quite natural to experience material confusion, alienation and disorientation in a given space. These are moments in which those inhabiting or moving through spaces question, reconstruct or modify any given, prefigured meanings of space, an experience Frederic Jameson (1991: 44) refers to as the postmodern "spatial mutation".

According to Jameson, such spatial perturbation presents itself as a profound disturbance to the individual, as a loss of not only spatial, but also cultural orientation, of hitherto familiar spatio-cultural coordinates: "This latest mutation in space [...] has finally succeeded in transcending the capacities of the individual human body to locate itself, to organise its immediate surroundings perceptually, and cognitively to map its position in a mappable external world" (ibid.).

Since such disturbances and the conscious search for orientation, the need 'to organise the immediate surroundings perceptually', occur in intercultural and new cultural encounters in places and spaces hitherto unseen, spatial orientation is of particular interest to the context of foreign language and cultural learning: Making meaning of unknown and foreign spaces is something that must be learned and practiced. Drama work does exactly this: It trains us to assign meanings to all spatial perceptions, to organise our movements and behaviour according to our 'reading' of a space and also to re-define its meaning and purpose. This transformative force of signifying space is brought to life whenever we set the scene – on stage and in everyday life alike.

Therefore, spaces are themselves performative in two ways: For one, they are re-iteratively made, refigured and modified in acts of use and interaction. Space is not a physical container that is simply there to be used or that must be 'filled' somehow, but it emerges from acts of appropriation and negotiation and is the result of more or less active social construction or production. Secondly, every social performance has a spatial dimension, a space in which it unfolds, a setting that is designed for this specific kind of interaction or that may be redesigned for a non-conventional purpose.

As 'spacing' is a semiotic act of understanding and of making meaning, the symbolic dimension of space also requires us to learn the 'language of and for space' in cultural and social education in general, and a 'language for space' in language learning and in the foreign language classroom, in particular. It is quite a challenge in language pedagogy to understand and teach all of these implications for 'performing space' and for 'performing in space' (spatial 'theatricality' sensu Fischer-Lichte 2004) in language learning, and the role of discourse competence for the acquisition of performative competence in terms of symbolizing, negotiating and (re-)defining spatial meanings.

The performative dimension of the Language Classroom

What has been said about space and spacing in general also applies to the classroom all the more since the classroom is an institutional, quite strictly coded and highly regulated space that is defined by institutional hierarchies and also by those who interact in it. The performative dimension of education is the result of a social contract stipulating that the social, performative and discourse rules of 'serious, real social interaction' to some extent do not apply; they are suspended and have to be substituted by domain-specific, temporarily valid regulations of (classroom) interaction. Part of this 'pedagogical contract' which, to some degree, fictionalizes all behaviour and interactions in the classroom is a definition of a limited period of the day and of the spaces in which these rules apply.

However, alluding to the subtitle of Turner's book on cultural rituals (1982), it must be stated that there is an obvious 'seriousness to this play', since on the one hand educational spaces are institutionally separated from the lifeworld; learners are guided and supported, they are allowed to make mistakes, try out different behaviours and may even create fictional selves, and there are ample opportunities to engage in rather playful endeavours which, on the other hand, always bear traces of serious lifeworld contexts and experiences. On the other hand, the seriousness of the lifeworld provides the standards for the abilities and the knowledge that are trained and gradually acquired, and finally also tested and graded. These educational spaces are recreated and reconstituted in daily routines and interactions as long as those involved perform the roles that are assigned to them in the 'pedagogical contract', complying with the written or unwritten rules and laws of the educational time and space that are defined in societal, political and cultural negotiations.

The language classroom is yet another more specific space within the larger educational space of the school or educational institution. It is a space in which participants engage in theatrical interactions, if only because of the simple agreement that they 'are' speakers of another language and interact in (imaginary or simulated) other cultural contexts. Thus, for purposes of language learning, learners do not only adhere to the rules of the staged play and structured, conventionalised interactions of pedagogical plays, but in the language classroom they also frequently take over roles and navigate situations that are linguistically and culturally 'foreign' and hence imagined (as opposed to 'experienced). Furthermore, they are also exposed to dramatic or drama-like texts, whether these involve scenes from the lives of coursebook families or plays that they study and sometimes also enact in the literary classroom.

It becomes evident that educational spaces are quite a fragile construct precisely because of the seriousness of play and the playfulness of serious work in which learners and teachers engage. Drama work and all sorts of performative activities challenge the frames in which the learners have to position themselves. They are expected to bring their 'serious' lifeworld experiences and personalities to their performance; on the other hand, the serious rules of the lifeworld are suspended, in pedagogical spaces in general and in the language classroom in particular, and the institutional rules of classroom performance apply, including the fears and anxieties of failing.

Of course, as is the case for all cultural spaces, this fragility is precisely where the idea comes into play that like any other place and space, the classroom's spatial configuration and definition is not simply given once and for all. Instead, it is in constant need of readjustment, redesign and redefinition to reconcile the different types of seriousness and playfulness of the social and interactional frameworks that are simultaneously at work. In this sense, pre-defined meanings of educational spaces and prefigured spaces are constantly contested by all stakeholders, often also in a conflictual manner ('battles of space'; cf. Löw 2011: 47). Rules and conventions may be questioned and challenged, and pedagogical designs of the classroom as a whole may have to be re-negotiated by teachers and experts. Therefore, as Martina Löw (1999: 57) concludes, 'space' is, or needs to be established as a reflexive pedagogical category that is constantly negotiated by all agents in the realm of education, and among classroom actors in particular.

Performative Competence

What we have said about our ways of behaving, acting and interacting in social and cultural spaces and the various frameworks in which they belong may give us an idea of the complexity of what may be termed performative competence (see also Hallet 2015). It also emphasises that, before anything else, performative competence is gradually built up in daily interactions and social situations. As Victor Turner says:

> The basic stuff of social life is performance, 'the presentation of self in everyday life' (as Goffman entitled one of his books). Self is presented through the performance of roles, through performance that breaks rules, and through declaring to a given public

that one has undergone a transformation of state and status, been saved or damned, elevated or released. (Turner 1988: 80)

However, as teachers and representatives of pedagogical institutions we need to develop the learners' 'natural' competences further, systematise and train them, offer them opportunities to find their own performative styles, and to create spaces in which the seriousness of play can unfold. Summarizing and condensing everything that I have elaborated in the previous parts of this essay, I propose to define performative competence as a bundle of abilities and competencies that encompasses the ability to

- participate actively and respectfully in social interactions and negotiations, building on the assumption that the very situation in which they happen has to be identified and constituted (discourse as socially produced);
- identify and define one's own and other's positions and roles in social interaction;
- identify, define and constitute the time and space of intended interaction;
- structure interactional situations cognitively and discursively in terms of the underlying structures and the rhetoric of *social dramas*, with a positioning of the self vis-a-vis other participants, *role-taking*, turn-taking etc.;
- apprehend ('read'), define and actively re-design the social and interactional space, make use of one's symbolic repertoire and competence and to perform adequately in it, in terms of situational and spatial conditions and adequacy;
- reflect critically and self-critically upon one's own and others' performance and the presentation of the self and of others in face-to-face and in mediatised interaction;
- understand and reflect upon the stage drama, the literary scripts, the theatre play, the TV show or the feature film, all of which represent and model everyday social drama and performance in fictional form;
- engage in discourse on interactions and the performances of one's own, but also others', both in social life and in literature and drama.

As a matter of fact, such a reflexivity is a dimension that is inherent to every performative act; and at the same time, it is one of the prime goals of school education, of *Bildung*. That's why this reflexivity must be a standard dimension of all educational efforts because man is "a performing animal", as Turner states:

If man is [...] a performing animal, *Homo performans*, [...] his performances are, in a way, *reflexive*, in performing he reveals himself to himself. This can be in two ways: The actor may come to know himself better through acting or enactment; or one set of human beings may come to know themselves better through observing and/or participating in performances generated and presented by another set of human beings. (Turner 1986: 81, emphasis in orig.)

Performative competence, then, is the cognitive ability to perform according to one's own intentions and to interact with others according to the socio-cultural conditions that are, simultaneously, prefigured and refigured in such interactions.

References

Austin, John L. (1962): *How to Do Things with Words.* Cambridge: Harvard University Press.

Berensmeyer, Ingo (2007): *Shakespeare: Hamlet.* Stuttgart: Klett.

Butler, Judith (1988): Performative Acts and Gender Constitution. An Essay in Phenomenology and Feminist Theory. In Katie Conboy, Nadia Medina & Sarah Stanbury (eds.): *Writing on the body. Female embodiment and Feminist Theory.* New York: Columbia University Press, 401-417.

Cassirer, Ernst (1955) [1923]: *The Philosophy of Symbolic Forms.* Vol. 1. New Haven/London: Yale UP.

Doetsch, Hermann (2004): Intervall: Überlegungen zu einer Theorie von Räumlichkeit und Medialität. In Jörg Dünne, Hermann Doetsch & Roger Lüdeke (eds.). *Von Pilgerwegen, Schriftspuren und Blickpunkten. Raumpraktiken in medienhistorischer Perspektive.* Würzburg: Königshausen & Neumann, 23-56.

Fischer-Lichte, Erika (2002): Grenzgänge und Tauschhandel. Auf dem Wege zu einer performativen Kultur. In Uwe Wirth (ed.): *Performanz. Zwischen Sprachphilosophie und Kulturwissenschaften.* Frankfurt a. M.: Suhrkamp, 277-300.

Fischer-Lichte, Erika (2004): Einleitung: Theatralität als kulturelles Modell. In Erika Fischer-Lichte, Christian Horn, Sandra Umathum & Matthias Warstat (eds.). *Theatralität als Modell in den Kulturwissenschaften.* Tübingen/Basel: A. Francke, 7-26.

Goodman, Nelson (1978): *Ways of Worldmaking.* Indianapolis: Hackett.

Hallet, Wolfgang (2014): Fictions of space. A semiotic approach to perceiving, experiencing and signifying space in contemporary fiction. In Nora Berning, Christine Schwanecke & Philipp Schulte (eds.): *Experiencing Space – Spacing Experience: Concepts, Practices, and Materialities.* Trier: WVT, 39-56.

Hallet, Wolfgang (2015): Die Performativität und Theatralität des Alltagshandelns: Performative Kompetenz und kulturelles Lernen. In Wolfgang Hallet & Carola Surkamp (eds.): *Handbuch Dramendidaktik und Dramapädagogik.* Trier: WVT, 53-70.

Hamlet (1990): Dir. Franco Zeffirelli. Warner Bros.

Jameson, Fredric (1991): *Postmodernism, or, The Cultural Logic of Late Capitalism.* London/New York: Verso.

Kramsch, Claire (2009): *The Multilingual Subject.* Oxford: OUP.

Lefebvre, Henri (1991): *The Production of Space.* Oxford: Blackwell.

Löw, Martina (1999): Vom Raum zum Spacing. Neuformationen und deren Konsequenzen für Bildungsprozesse. In Eckart Liebau, Gisela Miller-Kipp & Christoph Wulf (eds.): *Metamorphosen des Raums. Erziehungswissenschaftliche Forschungen zur Chronotopologie.* Weinheim: Deutscher Studien Verlag, 48-59.

Löw, Martina (2001): *Raumsoziologie.* Frankfurt a. M.: Suhrkamp.

Löw, Martina (2011): Raum – Die topologischen Dimensionen der Kultur. In Friedrich Jaeger & Burkhard Liebsch (eds.): *Handbuch der Kulturwissenschaften. Grundlagen und Schlüsselbegriffe.* Vol. 1. Stuttgart & Weimar: Metzler, 46-59

McGrath, John (2004): *Loving Big Brother. Surveillance Culture and Performance Space.* London/New York: Routledge.

Soja, Edward W. (1996): *Thirdspace. Journeys to Los Angeles and Other Real-and-Imagined Places.* CambridgeOxford: Blackwell.

Turner, Victor (1982): *From Ritual to Theatre. The Human Seriousness of Play.* New York: PAJ.

Turner, Victor (1986): *The Anthropology of Performance.* New York: PAJ.

Drama for neoliberals

Barbara Schmenk

The aim of this book is to celebrate Manfred Schewe's countless contributions, his books, articles, chapters, presentations, lectures, personal communications and workshops, which have inspired educators across the globe. Acknowledging the many advantages and unique educational opportunities associated with drama pedagogy in the language classroom is a primary goal of all the authors in this *Festschrift*; the present chapter is no exception. Yet, it strikes me that while there is no better place to confirm and celebrate the unique richness of performative teaching approaches than the present volume; this may also be merely preaching to the choir, glossing over the challenges and caveats proponents of drama pedagogy are faced with today. One such challenge inadvertently arises in the current climate in educational institutions especially in the West (most obviously in member states of the OECD as I will explain below): They are dominated by neoliberal rhetoric.

At the heart of this chapter lies the deep divide we are currently witnessing: the divide between drama and neoliberalism. A dramatic divide in many ways, as it entails the clash of two worldviews and their respective educational philosophies. The present chapter seeks to shed light on the two, largely incommensurable worldviews and the educational dilemma to which their clash gives rise.

I first provide short introductions to the two worldviews related to drama-based language teaching (referred to simply as drama pedagogy) and to the discourse of neoliberalism respectively, outlining the ways in which these two differ. In order to do justice to the narrow perspective of neoliberal arguments in education, I will subsequently present an argument in favour of the use of drama-based language education that is tailored to neoliberals. Finally, I will turn towards non-neoliberal proponents of drama in the language classroom again, to conclude with a short debriefing section.

The drama/neoliberalism divide: Two worldviews

In a nutshell, the drama/neoliberalism divide involves two distinct worldviews that shall roughly be sketched first.

Worldview I is associated with proponents of drama pedagogy and conceives of drama as an art form, searching for ways to include performative and aesthetic dimensions into educational domains, to replace or at least complement (still widespread) traditional forms of language learning and teaching that are chiefly geared towards dry practice, blood- and mindless exchanges of (complete and correct) sentences which appear only on the surface as though they were somehow meaningful or appropriate or dialogical. Proponents of the first world-view seek to foster more complex (often called 'holistic') scenarios of language education, to integrate dramatic art forms, to include aesthetic dimensions of learning and language in general, to engage learners as people, who think and feel, who are embodied selves, who position and construct themselves and the world around them in and through language, and whose selves are constantly (re-)positioned and challenged through others' constructions. Worldview I, in other words, comes in the colours of the rainbow, and seeks to bring out and strengthen the multifaceted world of people learning, living, and playing with languages.

Worldview II, by contrast, is confined to a particular group of educators on a specific field. It is best described as a very widespread ideology that is based on a metaphor, the all-encompassing market-metaphor, buttressed by the belief that the market should guarantee free choice and allow for maximum growth. At its core lies the conviction that the world is a market, and everything that happens in the world (or that can or should or should not happen) can be ex-pressed in economic terms, because everything **is** a matter of market exchanges (Harvey 2005). According to Lakoff and Johnson's understanding of conceptual metaphor (2008), one can understand the market metaphor and its underlying worldview as based on the logic of an economic source domain (the market), which is transferred to different target domains such as, e.g., daily life, society in general, or education. Viewed through this lens, people are conceptualized as human capital, and depending on the extent and level of their participation in the grand market game, they may or may not succeed in maximizing profits and increasing growth. This worldview and its accompanying market-centred "master narrative" (Holborow 2015: 41) is so widespread that it seems necessary to point out that it is based on a metaphor. Indeed, most of its proponents take the market master narrative not as metaphorical but natural, stating the obvi-ous, a taken-for-granted description of things in our world. Source and target domains have become amalgamated in neoliberal discourses – and in many people's perception.

In short, the colour of worldview II is most likely a muddy shade of green, thanks to the dominance of the American dollar in the global market.

This description of the two worldviews remains brief and simplified, but it provides a first and general idea of what characterizes the two sides of the dra-ma/neoliberalism divide. In order to expand on this, the next section will explore the educational implications of the two worldviews more closely, before turning towards possible scenarios of encounters between the two.

Educational perspectives and ideals

Drama pedagogy
Proponents of drama pedagogy base their arguments on a number of observations and ideals surrounding the notion of performative pedagogy, highlighting the aesthetic dimension of language learning and language use. As Schewe (2013: 15) recalls, foreign language education

> was almost exclusively considered a scientific discipline. This emerges, for example, in Article 2 of the Statute of the *Deutsche Gesellschaft für Fremdsprachenforschung* (German Society for Foreign [and Second] Language Research), where, in the description of the purpose of Foreign Language Didactics, the word 'science' or 'scientific' is used thirteen times but the word 'art' or 'artistic' is not even mentioned once. It should be noted, however, that Foreign Language Didactics is increasingly opening itself up to include the aesthetic field, or rather the various arts (theatre, music, visual art, dance, film, performance art).

Meanwhile, Schewe continues, accepting that "dramatic art provides a platform for an intensive learning experience" (ibid. 16) has become more commonplace in the field of language education. He elaborates that performative language pedagogy intends

> to avail of the wealth of forms found in the arts for teaching and learning purposes. It is, above and beyond the disciplines usually associated with foreign language teaching and learning (e.g. general pedagogy, first language didactics, psychology, linguistics and literature), actively seeking dialogue and exchange with the arts, in particular with theatre arts and also school/university subjects related to the aesthetic field (including music, visual art, dance, literature, film). In this context, there are no clear-cut lines between science and art, theory and practice (ibid.).

Proponents of drama pedagogy consistently take issue with the simplistic and reductionist pedagogies that continue to dominate language classrooms, where students are mostly conceived of and addressed as bodiless minds whose learning and engagement is reduced to that of semi-cognizant sentence constructors and exchangers. Against the backdrop of bloodless dialogues and the persistence of language drills and more or less meaningless exchanges of sentences in pseudo-communicative language learning environments, proponents of drama pedagogy argue for more 'holistic' approaches to teaching and learning.

Students should be engaged as people in the Pestalozzian sense, engaging their minds, emotions, and bodies – a point Manfred Schewe made as early as in 1993 that has since been reiterated numerous times by many scholars in the field.

Such a "post-lingual" (Block 2014) framework allows for playful approaches to language learning and language use that entail the creation of an imaginary space of "as if", within which students and instructors alike can take over roles, try out the new language, create new selves and playfully tease out the options of their imagined personae in the context of the drama classroom (see also Cook 2000, Even 2003, 2011, Schewe 2007, 2011). As Bonnet and Küppers (2011) argue, it is the fictional space of "as if" that – paradoxically – provides a more authentic environment for language use. Setting up an environment that provides a multitude of experiences with the new language thus engages learners as thinking, feeling, and embodied selves. It affords a richer learning experience than traditional language classrooms (be they form-focused or communication-exercise-focused), which leave precious little to the imagination.

Furthermore, proponents of drama pedagogy have repeatedly pointed out the value of drama for the development of empathy and intercultural sensitivity (e.g., Bräuer 2002, Fleming 2006, Hallet 2010, Kessler 2008, Kessler & Küppers 2008, Weber 2017). The argument made by these scholars is that through drama it is possible to put oneself into somebody else's shoes; an important prerequisite for understanding others' feelings and intentions, and thus for the development of empathy. Trying to view the world through different lenses is also central to intercultural learning and transcultural reflection. Hence, many authors argue that drama may in principle be a most promising way to foster intercultural sensitivity, sometimes also highlighting that drama may have the potential to bring about critical thinking in students (Even in press, Kao & O'Neill 1998, Schmenk 2015, 2017). After all, the ability to distance oneself from one's habitual views and interpretations is critical to the ability to adopt different perspectives and to view something from more than one (namely, one's own) point of view. Once students are encouraged to explore alternative viewpoints of a given scenario or situation, and to embody other personae and their respective perspectives, they are inadvertently put into a position that requires them to compare different arguments and intentions, to take into consideration different lines of reasoning and their respective whereabouts, and to reflect on actual and possible worlds – in short, to think critically.

Neoliberal discourse

Central to the ideology of neoliberalism is the notion that the market captures a basic truth about human nature and social organization. It redefines the relationship between the individual and society with social behavior being guided, not by collective institutions and interaction, but by supply and demand, by entrepreneurs and consumer choice, by individual companies and individual people. Social activity and exchange becomes judged on their degree of conformity to market culture. (Holborow 2015: 34)

Readers are surely all too familiar with the rhetorical flavour of neoliberal educational agendas and their sole focus on economic values. Neoliberal epistemology lies behind widely familiar rhetorical makeovers: Education has been turned into an economic affair that needs to be marketized; universities are increasingly corporatized and required to compete in the global ranking business; students turned into income units or paying customers; teaching turned into a service or sellable product; research is viewed in light of the funding generated in order to conduct it (Schmenk et al. 2019). Pretty much all our activities need to be outcomes-based. As teachers and as researchers, we are constantly in need of selling ourselves and our product. In order to determine the value of what we do it has to be made (ac)countable, measurable, and competitive. In some parts of the world, teachers get fired when they do not reach their (or rather: their employer's) goals: e.g., when they fail to reach the target numbers because fewer of their students pass an exam, which in turn may lead to a cut in funding and leave the institution in financial turmoil... in many ways, the neoliberal makeover has turned the world of teaching and learning on its head.

It should also be pointed out that it was the Organization of *Economic* Cooperation and Development (OECD) that was instrumental in the global spread of neoliberal discourse in the world of education. With its mission to "promote policies that will improve the economic and social well-being of people around the world" (www.oecd.org/about/), the OECD has always had a focus on education as well. This chiefly involves a view of people in terms of their value:

In the global knowledge economy, people's skills, learning, talents and attributes – their human capital – have become key to both their ability to earn a living and to wider economic growth. Education systems can do much to help people realise their potential, but when they fail it can lead to lifelong social and economic problems. (http://www.oecd.org/insights/humancapital-thevalueofpeople.htm)

The kind of education the OECD envisages aims to maximize the "value of people" as outlined and is characterized by a number of catch phrases that occur frequently in OECD publications: Education needs to be geared towards maximizing human capital (*growth*), which includes the need to promote *lifelong learning*. This, in turn, requires a timely kind of flexible, adaptable compliance on the part of individuals who are to remain willing to learn/train and relearn/ retrain so as to be able to develop the *skills* needed to change careers swiftly and repeatedly in their lives. The OECD thus continues to fuel global competition of educational institutions (as manifest in, e.g., international rankings), through international testing and surveys (e.g., the PISA studies). The neoliberal agenda of the OECD is targeted towards setting up the fittest educational system; i.e., the system that best fits the needs identified in order to produce a maximum growth in human capital and economic well-being.

Due to the enormous influence of the OECD agenda in all its member states and their educational systems (and beyond), viewing education through the lens of the market metaphor has by now become the norm in many places across the globe. This is obvious at first sight; i.e., in the use of language: "Completely disregarding local traditions and cultures, the neoliberal language of the OECD cemented a highly centralized and cohesive neoliberal message. It made a unified linguistic neoliberalism a reality" (Holborow 2015: 106). The "unified linguistic neoliberalism" consists of a rather limited scope of high-frequency words in OECD publications which allow a global spread of neoliberal thinking in education, all centred around the market metaphor: In order to be successful, we educators are asked to play the grand market game and comply. We have to have a mission. We have to state our goal(s) and outcomes. We have to identify our strategies to reach our goals. We need to set students up for success in today's world; i.e. provide them with the skills necessary for success. If we fail, we take the blame. Just like in the real business world.

In the world of neoliberal educational thinking, the ultimate ideal is the persona of the entrepreneur (e.g., Block et al. 2012, Holborow 2015). The entrepreneurial self is an economic subject throughout: seeking profit, bearing risks, both innovator and coordinator (Bröckling 2016: 66 ff.), always ready, which includes the willingness to take responsibility for one's failure as well. Through the focus on individual responsibility, "promoting entrepreneurial thinking among students pinpoints individual talent as the primary explanation for securing better paid employment and thereby deflects the crisis in jobs away from social causes to individual ones" (Holborow 2015: 114).

The prominence of the entrepreneur in neoliberal educational discourse is widely visible. University College Cork, for instance, Manfred Schewe's academic habitat, bolsters its image on the internet using the tagline "Where entrepreneurship and innovation thrive" (https://www.ucc.ie/en/entrepreneurship/), maintaining that

[a]t University College Cork, we believe in creating an environment in which aca-demic excellence can be combined with opportunities for personal development. We also recognise UCC's role in job creation by nurturing entrepreneurship, supporting the acceleration of business start-ups and the turning of innovative ideas into inno-vative products and services. (https://www.ucc.ie/en/quercus/about/innovationentre-preneurship/)

Bearing in mind the neoliberal values of innovation, risk-taking, entrepreneur-ial thinking, maximizing profits and taking responsibility for one's own busi-ness, we will now return to the language classroom. What happens if neoliberal thinking and drama meet in the world of language education?

Drama meets neoliberalism

Clashes and divides

The educational philosophies associated with neoliberalism stand in sharp con-trast to those associated with drama. Most importantly, the economic outlook of people, life and learning is not a feature of pedagogical approaches that seek to foster empathy, dialogue, transcultural reflection, and critical thinking. Simi-larly, in light of the instrumentalism that characterizes neoliberal educational agendas, the aesthetic dimension of language learning and language use seems superfluous at best. Artist meets entrepreneur – a classic mismatch? Hopelessly incompatible? Destined to fail?

At this point, a few reflections are necessary. First, neoliberal thinking is so widespread and powerful that it is almost impossible to escape. Proponents of drama in language education are all too aware of the difficulties they are faced with when they wish to make a case for languages in general, and for drama pedagogy in particular. The values associated with drama appear so hopelessly out of sync with economic, entrepreneurial ideals! It is equally true that many proponents of drama will strongly object to neoliberal thinking and will try to continue their work despite the lack of recognition for themselves and their work. Yet others may pursue a different path, searching for ways to align neolib-eral thinking and drama pedagogy in language education. The question under-lying this approach: *Can drama somehow be integrated in neoliberal frameworks of education?* shall be explored in the following section.

Making things fit

How is it possible to link drama pedagogy in language education to neoliberal discourse? How can drama be promoted so as to appear appealing to neoliberals? In hindsight, this question involves another problem that needs to be re-solved, namely, the need to explain why languages matter and how that case can be made to convince neoliberals. Since they consider educational matters valuable only when they contribute to maximizing human capital, we have to argue in favour of languages as a profitable investment in this regard.

Our first task is to reframe language education so as to make it fit the neo-liberal worldview. This has been done before, so we do not have to reinvent the wheel. To begin with, we need to view language as a commodity. This is a popu-lar strategy, as has been pointed out by scholars who have critically investigated the neoliberal trend towards language commodification (e.g., Heller & Duchêne 2012). As a commodity, language – or the mastery of a language – morphs into a 'thing' (Block 2019). Its 'thinginess', in turn, allows us to conceptualize it as a *skill* and thus make it more accountable and marketable. Besides, the word 'skill' belongs to the neoliberal core lexicon. As a skill, languages can be added to people's *skill sets* and branded accordingly, which increases their value in the market and the overall human capital (see also Urciuoli 2009 on the role of skills in neoliberal educational rhetoric). Language education in this light needs to be promoted as skills training, aimed at maximizing knowledge mobilization and thus human capital and revenues; securing growth in economic and social well-being (for further details see also the contributions in Flubacher & Percio 2017). Once languages are seen in this light they become a currency in the global market.

Second, language education has to be reframed so as to fit the neoliberal mindset in vocabulary and in general outlook. Most importantly, this involves the formulation of a mission and a vision. As language educators, our mission and vision statements ought to include some thoughts about our dedication to the OECD mission:

> The mission of the Organisation for Economic Co-operation and Development (OECD) is to promote policies that will improve the economic and social well-being of people around the world. The OECD provides a forum in which governments can work to-gether to share experiences and seek solutions to common problems. We work with governments to understand what drives economic, social and environmental change [...]. We also look at issues that directly affect everyone's daily life [...]. We compare how different countries' school systems are readying their young people for modern life [...]. (https://www.oecd.org/about/)

"Readying young people" is a useful phrase for our neoliberal purposes as well. Our mission statement could include a note on our dedication to readying the young (and all others who are willing to be trained), pointing out that we are providing services that build essential skills for tomorrow (languages), for a better and more international world, i.e., granting access to global financial markets. Of course, we will deflect from the hardships of language learning and the pitfalls resulting from intercultural and transcultural complexity. We will also gloss over the messy and complex dimensions of emotions, attitudes and motivation in learning languages. Instead, we talk about learner investment (Norton Peirce 1995, Darvin & Norton 2015) and voice our commitment to and expectation of a high return value of investment in language training for learners and society at large, thus linking our case to the neoliberal resignification of the self. In sum, our mission and vision can be easily aligned with neoliberal thinking, as long as we stick to the notion of language as a commodity and the idea of skills training that is worth investing in.

Finally, when it comes to values and the idealized persona of the entrepreneur, we have another joker up our sleeves. After all, language education, more than any other field, has for decades touted the notion of learner autonomy. The autonomous learner, who takes charge of her/his learning; i.e., who successfully manages all the tasks and decisions involved in the learning process, and who is generally willing to take the blame if something goes wrong, is an entrepreneur *par excellence*. It is understood that we do not mention all the critical voices that have attempted to reject or refine this view to save the educational notion of autonomy from its economization (e.g., Benson 2013, Schmenk in press). If we want to sell our product to neoliberals, an undertheorized version of the phrase learner autonomy is one of our most valuable rhetorical assets.

Turning towards drama pedagogy now, we can make an argument (or rather: put together a strategic plan) in favour of drama-based language education. Several additional neoliberal buzzwords are at our disposal, most notably *innovation* and *excellence*; as well as any number of superlatives used in conjunction with these nouns (see Gramling 2019, for a critical analysis of the use of "innovation" in applied linguistics). Our teaching is excellent, our methods are innovative, we will ready people of all ages to be successful in the global market, thanks to their competitive edge resulting from their enhanced skill sets and their entrepreneurial spirits, as well as their willingness to reinvent themselves throughout their lifelong learning process. Our brand is drama, and we reinvent the business of language education to ensure people can deal with tomorrow's challenges successfully. Through drama-based language education, we contribute to better the life of people. Our mission is our dedication to innovation and excellence in language teaching. Our vision is a multilingual future that provides better economic and social opportunities for all. Through drama-based language teaching we uniquely contribute to readying people for the future in an ever more global world. Finally, in order to truly comply and produce an action plan, we will take a lot of time and break down our dramatic efforts into steps. Subsequently, we can allocate learning goals to each one of them (the CEFR provides a valuable resource for our endeavours). Having thus spelled out the expected outcomes of drama-based teaching units, we have surely satisfied a significant amount of neoliberal desires.

Conclusion: Irreconcilable differences and why they ought to be taken seriously

It may strike many readers that aligning drama pedagogy with neoliberal discourse is mainly a matter of getting our rhetoric right; and spelling out the outcomes of our teaching so as to satisfy the neoliberal educational accountants.

Viewing it this way, and complying with the accountability request, however, requires a substantial level of cynicism. This is what educational philosopher Roger Simon (2001) highlighted when he developed the notion of a "cynicism index" for universities:

> Such a measure might be extremely useful as a warning of the erosion of any sort of commitment to an idea of a university on the part of its participants, for indeed the erosion of commitment is the countercondition to thought, the countercondition of the university as a "place to think." One indication that a university has a low cynicism index would be evidence that its faculty were actually taking time to seriously argue over the character of thought in the university. (Simon 2001: 55, op. cit. Brenner 2006: 19)

In other words, our attempts to fulfill neoliberal desires and to reframe drama accordingly will inadvertently raise our rank on the cynicism scale, while at the same time decreasing our chances to think. Giving drama-based language education a neoliberal makeover thus involves more than just a change of rhetoric; rather, it amounts to complying at the expense of thinking, and of thinking about thought and education.

Many colleagues today do not (yet) think that the drama/neoliberalism divide poses much of a problem. Indeed, many have attempted to spell out drama pedagogy or specific projects in drama-based language teaching in terms of their outcomes and thus their immediate benefits that can be named and listed – and accounted for. Using the scales of the CEFR in order to describe learning outcomes of drama-based teaching and learning sequences, for example, is surely possible and has occasionally been done. However, let us be clear on what these attempts to reconcile drama and neoliberalism entail when we look at the bigger picture of the two worldviews roughly outlined above. It is precisely the openness, non-predictability of dramatic and all other art forms that render them artistic in the first place. Trying to make the arts and any creative endeavour accountable is an attempt at squaring the circle, and it is futile if one truly wants to foster artistic, aesthetic dimensions of education and language learning in particular. Similarly, complying with economic requests and trying to reframe drama pedagogy in language education as an activity that will ultimately enhance human capital and contribute to all sorts of capital and skills accumulation may look as though we have done our homework and completed our tasks in the grand neoliberal scheme. But we would do so at the expense of all thinking and questioning in and about the educational and political arenas within which languages are learnt, used, and taught.

Last but not least, Brenner (2006: 19) points out that Simon's proposal of a cynicism index is made with "'no small sense of irony.' For irony, as precisely that form which is poised between utopia and apocalypse, may be a most appropriate posture from which to reassess and resignify the place of pedagogy in the corporatized university". In this spirit, it is time to establish an irony imperative, in language education and beyond.

References

Benson, Phil (2013): Drifting in and out of view: autonomy and the social individual. In Phil Benson & Lucy Cooker (eds.): *The Applied Linguistic Individual. Sociocultural Approaches to Identity, Agency and Autonomy.* Sheffield/Bristol: equinox, 75-89.

Block, David (2014): Moving beyond 'lingualism.' Multilingual embodiment and multimodality in SLA. In Stephen May (ed.): *The multilingual turn. Implications for SLA, TESOL and Bilingual Education.* New York/London: Routledge, 54-77.

Block, David (2019): What on earth is language commodification? In Barbara Schmenk et al. (eds.), 121-141.

Block, David; Gray, John & Holborow, Marnie (2012): *Neoliberalism and Applied Linguistics.* Oxford/New York: Routledge.

Bonnet, Andreas & Küppers, Almut (2011): Wozu taugen kooperatives Lernen und Dramapädagogik? Vergleich zweier populärer Inszenierungsformen. In Almut Küppers, Torben Schmidt & Maik Walter (eds.): *Inszenierungen im Fremdsprachenunterricht. Grundlagen, Formen, Perspektiven.* Braunschweig: Schroedel/Diesterweg/Klinkhardt, 32-52.

Brenner, David (2006): Performative pedagogy. Resignifying teaching in the corporatized university. In *The Review of Education, Pedagogy, and Cultural Studies* 28, 3-24.

Bröckling, Ulrich (2016): *The entrepreneurial self. Fabricating a new type of subject.* London et al.: Sage.

Cook, Guy (2000): *Language Learning, Language Play.* Oxford: Oxford University Press.

Darvin, Ron & Norton, Bonnie (2015): Identity and a model of investment in applied linguistics. In *Annual Review of Applied Linguistics* 35, 36-56.

Even, Susanne (2003): *Drama Grammatik. Dramapädagogische Ansätze für den Grammatikunterricht Deutsch als Fremdsprache.* München: iudicium.

Even, Susanne (2011): Drama grammar: towards a performative postmethod pedagogy. In *Language Learning Journal* 39/3, 299-312.

Even, Susanne (in press): Critical thought, word, and deed: Drama pedagogy as a catalyst for critical empathic thinking. In Fred Devin & Julie B. Clark (eds.): *Criticality in Multilingual and Intercultural Education.* Charlotte: Information Age Publishing Inc.

Fleming, Ian (2006): Justifying the arts. Drama and intercultural education. In *Journal of Aesthetic Education* 40/1, 54-64.

Flubacher, Mi-Cha, & Percio, Alfonso Del (eds.) (2017): *Language, Education and Neoliberalism. Critical Studies in Sociolinguistics.* Bristol: Multilingual Matters.

Gramling, David (2019): We innovators. In Barbara Schmenk et al. (eds.), 19-41.

Hallet, Wolfgang (2010): Performative Kompetenz und Fremdsprachenunterricht. In *Scenario* IV/1, 5-18.

Harvey, David (2005): *A Brief History of Neoliberalism.* Oxford/New York: Oxford University Press.

Heller, Monica & Duchêne, Alexandra (eds.) (2012): *Language in Late Capitalism: Pride and Profit.* London/New York: Routledge.

Holborow, Marnie (2015): *Language and Neoliberalism.* London/New York: Routledge.

Kao, Shin-Mey & O'Neill, Cecily (1998): *Words into worlds: Learning a second language through process drama.* Stamford: Ablex.

Kessler, Benedikt (2008): *Interkulturelle Dramapädagogik. Dramatische Arbeit als Vehikel des interkulturellen Lernens im Fremdsprachenunterricht.* Frankfurt a.M. et al.: Peter Lang.

Kessler, Benedikt & Küppers, Almut (2008): A shared mission. Dramapädagogik, interkulturelle Kompetenz und holistisches Fremdsprachenlernen. In *Scenario* II/2, 3-24.

Kubota, Ryuko (2015): Neoliberal paradoxes in language learning. In *Journal of Multilingual and Multicultural Development* 37/5, 467-480.

Lakoff, George & Johnson, Mark (2008): *Metaphors We Live By* (updated ed.). Chicago/London: The University of Chicago Press.

Norton Peirce, Bonnie (1995): Social Identity, Investment, and Language Learning. In *TESOL Quarterly* 29/1, 9-31.

Schewe, Manfred (1993): *Fremdsprache inszenieren. Zur Fundierung einer dramapädagogischen Lehr- und Lernpraxis.* Oldenburg: Pädagogisches Zentrum.

Schewe, Manfred (2007): Drama und Theater in der Fremd- und Zweitsprachenlehre. Blick zurück nach vorn. In *Scenario* I/1, 129-141.

Schewe, Manfred (2011): Die Welt auch im fremdsprachlichen Unterricht immer wieder neu verzaubern – Plädoyer für eine performative Lehr- und Lernkultur! In Almut Küppers, Torben Schmidt & Maik Walter (eds.): *Inszenierungen im Fremdsprachenunterricht. Grundlagen, Formen, Perspektiven.* Braunschweig: Schroedel/Diesterweg/Klinkhardt, 20-31.

Schewe, Manfred (2013): Taking stock and looking ahead: Drama pedagogy as a gateway to a performative teaching and learning culture. In *Scenario* VII/1, 5-23.

Schmenk, Barbara (2015): Dramapädagogik im Spiegel von Bildungsstandards, GeRS und Kompetenzdiskussionen. In Wolfgang Hallet & Carola Surkamp (eds.): *Handbuch Dramendidaktik und Dramapädagogik im Fremdsprachenunterricht*. Trier: WVT, 37-50.

Schmenk, Barbara (2017): Drama in the classroom: Post-holistic considerations. In Lisa Parkes, Colleen Ryan & Stacey Katz Bourns (eds.): *Issues in language program direction: Integrating the arts: Creative thinking about FL curricula and language program direction*. Boston: Cengage Learning, 91-108.

Schmenk, Barbara (in press): Governmentality and the autonomous subject: Persistent contradictions in philosophies of (language) education. In Julia Lossau, Daniel Schmidt-Brücken & Ingo H. Warnke (eds.): *Spaces of Dissention. Towards a New Perspective on Contradiction*. Wiesbaden: Springer VS.

Schmenk, Barbara; Breidbach, Stephan & Küster, Lutz (2019): Sloganization in language education discourse: Introduction. In Barbara Schmenk et al. (eds.), 1-18.

Schmenk, Barbara; Breidbach, Stephan & Küster, Lutz (eds.) (2019): *Sloganization in Language Education Discourse. Conceptual Thinking in the Age of Academic Marketization*. Bristol: Multilingual Matters.

Simon, Roger I. (2001): The university: A place to think? In Henry A. Giroux & Kostas Myrsiades (eds.): *Beyond the Corporate University: Culture and Pedagogy in the New Millennium*. New York/Oxford: Roman & Littlefield, 45-56.

Urciuoli, Bonnie (2009): Neoliberal education. In Carol J. Greenhouse (ed.): *Ethnographies of Neoliberalis*. Philadelphia: University of Pennsylvania, 162-176.

Weber, Silja (2017): Drama pedagogy in intermediate German: Effects on anxiety. In *GFL Journal* 1, 1-21.

Publikationen

1984

The Hidden Journey. An Irish Theatre in Education Project for German Schools. In *Englisch-Amerikanische Studien* 4, 608-622, 635-641.

1987

Szenische Eindrücke aus dem Inselalltag. In Hans-Christian Oeser (Hg.): *Irland. Ein politisches Reisebuch.* Hamburg: vsa Verlag, 10-15.

1988

Fokus Lehrpraxis: Für einen integrierten, dramapädagogischen DaF-Unterricht für Fortgeschrittene. In *Info DaF* 4, 429-441.

1989

Dramapädagogik – eine erziehungswissenschaftliche Teildisziplin? Drama – eine importwürdige Lehr-/Lernmethode? Oldenburg: Pädagogisches Zentrum.

1990

Drama und Theater in der Schule und für die Schule. Beiträge zur Einführung in die britische Drama- und Theaterpädagogik. Oldenburg: Universität Oldenburg, Hg.

Dramapädagogik oder Unterricht als gestaltete Improvisation. In *Pädagogik* 42/7-8, 54-59.

Dramapädagogischer DaF-Unterricht: Skizze einer integrativen Lehr-/Lernmethode. In *PV-Aktuell* 9, 5-7.

Irish Experiences – Then and Now. Lehrbuch. München: Hueber, mit Hans Wrons-Passmann.

Irish Experiences – Then and Now. Lehrerhandbuch München: Hueber, mit Hans Wrons-Passmann.

Theater und Drama im Fremdsprachenunterricht. In *Jahrbuch der Aristoteles Universität Thessaloniki.* Thessaloniki: University of Thessaloniki, mit Joachim Neher-Louran und Hans-Simon Pelanda.

1991

Interkulturelles theaterpädagogisches Projekt für Schulen. In *Der Fremdsprach-liche Unterricht* 25/2.

1992

Wie kann das ‚dramatische Defizit‘ gängiger Übungsformen in Deutsch als Fremdsprache-Lehrwerken behoben werden? Argumente für eine bewußtere Inszenierung fremdsprachlicher Lernprozesse. In Armin Wolff (Hg.): *Deutsch als Fremdsprache im europäischen Binnenmarkt.* Regensburg: FaDaF, 219-251.

1993

An outside view of drama in education in Great Britain today. In *2D - Drama and Dance* 12/1, 22-24.

Fremdsprache inszenieren. Zur Fundierung einer dramapädagogischen Lehr- und Lernpraxis. Oldenburg: Pädagogisches Zentrum.

Lehren und Lernen mit Kopf, Herz, Hand und Fuß: Dramapädagogische Fremd-sprachenpraxis in multikulturellen DaF-Kursen. In *Fremdsprache Deutsch* 93/2, 44-52.

The theoretical architecture of a drama-based foreign language class: a structure founded on communication, and supported by action, interaction, real experien-ce and alternative methods. In Manfred Schewe & Peter Shaw (Hg.): *Towards Drama as a Method in Foreign Language Classroom.* Franfurt/Bern/New York: Peter Lang, 283-314.

Towards Drama as a Method in Foreign Language Classroom. Franfurt/Bern/New York: Peter Lang, Hg. mit Peter Shaw.

1994

Mit Kopf, Herz, Hand und Fuß. In *Abrapa Projekt-Revista dos professores de Alemão Brasil* 14, 6-9.

Video as a backstage to a (dramatic) teacher training course. In *Der Fremdsprach-liche Unterricht* 28/4, 28-31.

1995

Dramapädagogische Übungsformen. In Goethe Institut (Hg.): *Handbuch für Spracharbeit*. 3. Band. München: Goethe Institut, 1-9.

Research issues in the year abroad. In *Teangeolas* 35, 55-56.

Texte lesen, verstehen und inszenieren: Alfred Andersch – Sansibar oder der letzte Grund. München: Klett, mit Heinz Wilms.

Zum methodischen Potential von Standbildern im DaF-Unterricht In Armin Wolff & Wilfried Welter (Hg.): *Mündliche Kommunikation – Unterrichts- und Übungsformen DaF – Themen und zielgruppenspezifische Auswahl von Unterrichtsmaterialien – Modelle für studien- und berufsbegleitenden Unterricht: DaF im Ausland*. Regensburg: FaDaF, 75-97.

1997

DaF-LehrerInnen-Ausbildung: nicht nur als Wissenschaft, sondern ebenso als Kunst! In Armin Wolff, Gisela Tütken & Horst Liedtke (Hg.): *Gedächtnis und Sprachlernen: Prozeßorientiertes Fremdsprachenlernen. Deutschlehrerausbildung in West- und Osteuropa. Eine deutsche Literatur – AutorInnen nichtdeutscher Muttersprache*. Regensburg: FaDaF, 245-254.

Emotion und Kognition im Fremdsprachenunterricht – eine dramapädagogisch-ästhetische Perspektive. In Armin Wolff & Dietrich Eggers (Hg.): *Lern- und Studienstandort Deutschland. Emotion und Kognition. Lernen mit neuen Medien*. Regensburg: FaDaF, 162-178.

Seeing the dragons dancing together on the wind at sunset. An aesthetic approach to understanding another culture. In *FSU Zeitschrift für das Lehren und Lernen fremder Sprachen* 41/50, 418-422, mit Joachim Beug.

1998

Culture through literature through drama. In Michael Byram & Michael Fleming (Hg.): *Language Learning in Intercultural Perspective – Approaches through Drama and Ethnography*. Cambridge/New York: Cambridge University Press, 204-221.

Dramapädagogisch lehren und lernen – eine kurze Einführung in ein neueres didaktisch-methodisches Konzept für den fremdsprachlichen Deutschunterricht. In *Per Voi* 4, 3-8.

Dramapädagogisch lehren und lernen. In Udo O. H. Jung (Hg.): *Praktische Hand-reichung für Fremdsprachenlehrer.* Frankfurt/Bern/New York: Peter Lang, 334-340.

Interkulturelle Begegnung verstehen – ein dramapädagogischer Unterrichts-einstieg anhand eines literarischen Textes. Montreal: Articles.

Serie Fremdsprache inszenieren (1-2) – Teil 1: Einfühlungsfragen beantworten; Teil 2: Rollenmonolog. In *FSU Zeitschrift für das Lehren und Lernen fremder Sprachen* 42/51, 51-52.

Serie Fremdsprache inszenieren (3) – Teil 3: Standbild. In *FSU Zeitschrift für das Lehren und Lernen fremder Sprachen* 45/51, 206-207.

Serie Fremdsprache inszenieren (4-6) – Teil 4: Positionseinnahme; Teil 5: Selbst-vorstellung; Teil 6: Stimmencollage. In *FSU Zeitschrift für das Lehren und Lernen fremder Sprachen* 42/51, 363-364.

Serie Fremdsprache inszenieren (7-8) – Teil 7: Agierendes Erzählen; Teil 8: LiRo-Technik; Teil 9: LaRo-Technik. In *FSU Zeitschrift für das Lehren und Lernen fremder Sprachen* 42/51, 426-427.

1999

Learning and teaching culture from an aesthetic perspective. In Angela Cham-bers & Dónall P. Ó Baoill (Hg.): *Intercultural Communication and Language Learning.* Dublin: Royal Irish Academy/The Irish Association for Applied Lin-guistics, 119-134, mit Joachim Beug.

Neue Erfahrungen mit sich selbst machen: eine Voraussetzung für lebendiges Lehren! In *Fremdsprache Deutsch* I (Sondernummer), 50-56.

Theorie ist Nachdenken über die Praxis, um sie zu verändern. Ein besonderer Kollege, ein besonderer Lehrer: Heinz Wilms zum Gedenken. In *Erinnerungen an Heinz Wilms.* München: Langenscheidt, 10-11.

2000

DaF-Stunden dramapädagogisch gestalten – wie mache ich das? In Thomas Brysch, Manfred Lukas Schewe & Gerald Schlemminger (Hg.): *Pädagogische Kon-zepte für einen ganzheitlichen DaF-Unterricht.* Berlin: Cornelsen Verlag, 72-105.

Deutschunterricht und Germanistik-Studium in Irland. In Hans-Jürgen Krumm, Christian Fandrych, Britta Hufeisen & Claudia Riemer (Hg.): *Deutsch als Fremd-*

und Zweitsprache. Ein internationales Handbuch. Berlin/New York: De Gruyter, 1689-1692, mit Joachim Fischer.

Pädagogische Konzepte für einen ganzheitlichen DaF-Unterricht. Berlin: Cornelsen, Hg. mit Gerald Schlemminger und Thomas Brysch.

2001

La cultura a través de la literatura y a través del teatro. In Michael Byram & Mike Fleming (Hg.): *Perspectivas interculturales en el aprendizaje de idiomas. Enfoques a través del teatro y la etnografía.* Madrid: Cambridge University Press, 207-222.

Zukunftsgemäße Deutschlehrerausbildung – einige Assoziationen, Thesen, offene Fragen und Reformvorschläge. In *GFL* 2, 20-40.

2002

Literaturvermittlung auf dem Weg von gestern nach morgen – eine auslandsgermanistische Perspektive. In *GFL* 3, 25-47, mit Trina Scott.

Tapping the students' kinesthetic intelligence. In Gerd Bräuer (Hg.): *Body and Language: Intercultural Learning through Drama.* Westport et al.: Ablex Publishing, 73-94.

Theaterimpressionen in Deutschland im Jahre 2002 – ein (auch theaterpädagogischer) Blick von außen. In *Korrespondenzen* 17/41, 61-66.

2003

Literatur verstehen und inszenieren. Foreign language literature through drama. A research project. In *GFL* 3, 56-83, mit Trina Scott.

Literaturvermittlung auf dem Weg von gestern nach morgen – eine auslandsgermanistische Perspektive. In Armin Wolff & Ursula Renate Riedner (Hg.): *Grammatikvermittlung – Literaturreflexion – Wissenschaftspropädeutik – Qualifizierung für eine transnationale Kommunikation.* Regensburg: FaDaF, 33-55.

Teaching intelligently by tapping into the students' multiple intelligences. In *The Modern Problems of International Relations* 41/2, 298-302.

Theatre in Education. In Gerd Koch & Marianne Streisand (Hg.): *Wörterbuch der Theaterpädagogik.* Berlin: Schibri, 335.

2004

Einleitung: Dramapädagogik und fremdsprachlicher Deutschunterricht. In *GFL* 1, 1-6, mit Trina Scott.

Foreign Language Literature Through Drama: A Research Project. In Áine Hyland (Hg.): *University College Cork as a Learning Organisation.* Cork: UCC, 82-95, mit Trina Scott.

Himmlische Verhältnisse. Versuch einer szenischen Würdigung. In Hermann Rasche & Christiane Schönfeld (Hg.): *Denkbilder. Festschrift für Eoin Bourke.* Würzburg: Königshausen & Neumann, 479-487.

Literaturvermittlung in der Auslandsgermanistik. Einige Thesen und kritische Kommentare. In DAAD (Hg.): *Germanistentreffen. Tagungsbeiträge. Deutschland, Großbritannien. Irland.* Bonn: DAAD, 93-112.

Teaching intelligently by tapping into the students' multiple intelligences. In *Foreign Languages* 1, 53-55.

Theatre in Education. In Gerhard Koch, Sieglinde Roth, Florian Vaßen & Michael Wrentschur (Hg.): *Handbuch Theaterarbeit in sozialen Feldern/Handbook Theatre Work in Social Fields.* Frankfurt a. M.: Brandes & Apsel, 135-139.

2005

Ein Vollbad in Sprache, Text und Bildung. Bericht von einem Germanistentreffen. In Andreas Stuhlmann & Patrick Studer (Hg.): *Language – Text – Bildung. Sprache – Text – Bildung. Essays in Honour of Beate Dreike. Essays für Beate Dreike.* Frankfurt a. M.: Peter Lang, 333-344.

Impressions of Cork people and Cork life. In Joachim Fischer & Grace Neville (Hg.): *As Others Saw Us: Cork through European Eyes.* Cork: Collins Press, 308-319.

Theatre Work (in Social Fields). In Bernadette Cronin, Sieglinde Roth & Michael Wrentschur (Hg.): *Training Manual for Theatre Work in Social Fields.* Frankfurt a. M.: Brandes & Apsel, 14-20.

2006

Szenische Eindrücke aus dem Inselalltag: ein erster Update-Versuch. In Gisela Holfter & Hans-Walter Schmidt-Hannissa (Hg.): *German-Irish Encounters. Deutsch-irische Begegnungen.* Trier: WVT, 271-277.

2007

Über das Fremdwerden des Eigenen or 100 years of Switzerland, compressed into a collage of four scenes: Thomas Hürlimann's Das Lied der Heimat. In Patrick Studer & Sabine Eggers (Hg.): *From the Margins to the Centre. Irish Perspectives on Swiss Culture and Literature.* Frankfurt a. M.: Peter Lang, 93-118.

Drama und Theater in der Fremd- und Zweitsprachenlehre: Blick zurück nach vorn. In *Scenario* I/1, 127-139.

Research Bibliography Drama and Theatre in Foreign and Second Language Education, www.ucc.ie/en/scenario/scenarioforum/researchbibliography/, zuletzt eingesehen am 31.07.2018.

Zur Inszenierung von Fremd- und Zweitsprache – Von 1850 bis heute. In Margret Bülow-Schramm, Dietlinde Gipser & Doris Krohn (Hg.): *Bühne frei für Forschungstheater. Theatrale Inszenierungen als wissenschaftlicher Erkenntnisprozess.* Oldenburg: Paulo Freire Verlag, 113-124.

2008

Drama und Theater in der Fremd- und Zweitsprachenlehre. Ein historischer Abriss. In Ingrid Hentschel, Gerd Koch & Beatrix Wildt (Hg.): *Theater in der Lehre: Inszenierungsmuster und Methoden in Lehrveranstaltungen und Hochschulalltag.* Münster: LIT, 127-138.

TheaterPädagogikPolitik in Irland. In *Korrespondenzen* 24/53, 32-33.

2010

Community Theatre und Kulturtransfer. In Florian Vaßen (Hg.): *Korrespondenzen: Theater – Ästhetik – Pädagogik.* Berlin: Schibri, 173-195.

Deutsch in Irland. In Hans-Jürgen Krumm, Christian Fandrych, Britta Hufeisen & Claudia Riemer (Hg.): *Deutsch als Fremd- und Zweitsprache. Ein internationales Handbuch.* Berlin/New York: de Gruyter, 1689-1693, mit Joachim Fischer.

Drama- und Theaterpädagogik in Deutsch als Fremdsprache/Deutsch als Zweitsprache. In Hans-Jürgen Krumm et al. (Hg.): *Deutsch als Fremd- und Zweitsprache. Ein internationales Handbuch.* Berlin/New York: de Gruyter, 1589-1595.

Dramapädagogik. In Carola Surkamp (Hg.): *Metzler Lexikon Fremdsprachendidaktik.* Stuttgart/Weimar: Metzler, 38-41.

Szenisch-dramatische Formen. In Wolfgang Hallet & Frank G. Königs (Hg.): *Handbuch Fremdsprachendidaktik*. Seelze-Velber: Kallmeyer, 199-203.

2011

Cork's World Theatre: Ein Beispiel performativer Auslandsgermanistik. In Barbara Schmenk & Nikola Würffel (Hg.): *Drei Schritte vor und manchmal auch sechs zurück. Internationale Perspektive auf Entwicklungslinien im Bereich Deutsch als Fremdsprache. Festschrift für Dietmar Rösler zum 60. Geburtstag.* Tübingen: Narr, 203-215.

Die Welt auch im fremdsprachlichen Unterricht immer wieder neu verzaubern: Plädoyer für eine performative Lehr- und Lernkultur! In Almut Küppers, Torben Schmidt & Maik Walter (Hg.): *Inszenierungen im Fremdsprachenunterricht: Grundlagen, Formen, Perspektiven.* Braunschweig: Schroedel/Diesterweg/Klinkhardt, 20-31.

Die Zukunft der irischen Germanistik, oder: Trotz allem hartnäckig zuversichtlich? Plädoyer für eine stärkere Öffnung hin zu den (performativen) Künsten. In Joachim Fischer & Rolf Stehle (Hg.): *Contemporary German-Irish Cultural Relations in a European Perspective: Exploring Issues in Cultural Policy and Practice.* Trier: WVT, 243-252.

Learning with Head, Heart, Hands and Feet. In *Art Kitli* 2, 40-41.

2012

Weiter auf dem Wege zu einer performativen Fremd- und Zweitsprachendidaktik. In İnci Dirim, Hans-Jürgen Krumm, Paul Portmann-Tselikas & Sabine Schmölzer-Eibinger (Hg.): *Theorie und Praxis. Jahrbuch für Deutsch als Fremd- und Zweitsprache 1.* Graz: Präsens, 77-94.

Welttheater: übersetzen, adaptieren, inszenieren – World Theatre: Translation, Adaption, Production. Berlin: Schibri, Hg. mit Stephen Boyd.

2013

Skizze einer performativen Auslandsgermanistik. In Josefa Contreras, Ana Giménez & Maria Labarta (Hg.): *Performance in Deutsch als Fremd- und Fachsprache, Linguistik und Kulturwissenschaft.* Madrid: Federación de Asociacions de Germanistas en España.

Taking stock and looking ahead: Drama pedagogy as a gateway to a performative teaching and learning culture. In *Scenario* VII/1, 5-27.

2014

Einen Ort für das Ästhetische schaffen. Deutsch als Fremdsprache als Bauhaus – ein Vorentwurf. In Nils Bernstein & Charlotte Lerchner (Hg.): *Ästhetisches Lernen im DaF-/DaZ-Unterricht. Literatur – Theater – Bildende Kunst – Musik – Film.* Göttingen: Universitätsverlag, 167-177.

Paving the way towards a performative teaching and learning culture – the story of SCENARIO . In Carlo Nofri & Moreno Stracci (Hg.): *Performing Arts in Language Learning.* Rom: Edizioni Novacultur, 44-51.

2015

Fokus Fachgeschichte: Die Dramapädagogik als Wegbereiterin einer performativen Fremdsprachendidaktik. In Wolfgang Hallet & Carola Surkamp (Hg.): *Dramendidaktik und Dramapädagogik im Fremdsprachenunterricht.* Trier: WVT, 21-36.

2016

Drama in Foreign Language Classes – Theater im Fremdsprachenunterricht. MAGAZIN SPRACHE, www.goethe.de/en/spr/mag/20866409.html, eingesehen am 31.07.2018.

Dramapädagogische Ansätze. In Eva Burwitz-Melzer, Grit Mehlhorn, Claudia Riemer, Karl-Richard Bausch & Hans-Jürgen Krumm (Hg.): *Handbuch Fremdsprachenunterricht.* 6. vollst. überarb. u. erw. Auflage. Tübingen: Franke Verlag, 63-77.

Einige Gedanken zur Handlungsorientierung in der Dramapädagogik, ergänzt durch Vorschläge zum ‚begrifflichen Handeln'. In Anica Betz, Caroline Schuttkowski, Linda Stark & Anne-Kathrin Wilms (Hg.): *Sprache durch Dramapädagogik handelnd erfahren – Ansätze für den Sprachunterricht.* Baltmannsweiler: Schneider Verlag Hohengehren, 63-77.

Performative Teaching, Learning and Research – Performatives Lehren, Lernen und Forschen. Berlin: Schibri, Hg. mit Susanne Even.

Theater und Eigensinn. In *Korrespondenzen* 32/68, 53-54.

2017

Dramapädagogik. In Carola Surkamp (Hg.): *Metzler Lexikon Fremdsprachendidaktik. Ansätze – Methoden – Grundbegriffe.* 2. erw. Auflage. Stuttgart: J. B. Metzler, 49-51.

Going Performative in Intercultural Education – International Contexts, Theoretical Perspectives and Models of Practice. Clevedon: Multilingual Matters, Hg. mit John Crutchfield.

2018

Performative Foreign Language Didactics in Progress: About Still Images and the Teacher as 'Formmeister' (Form Master). In *Scenario* XII/1, 53-69, mit Fionn Woodhouse.

Performative Foreign Language Didactics in Progress: About Still Images and the Teacher as ‚Formmeister' (Form Master). In Olivier Mentz & Micha Fleiner (Hg.): *The Arts in Language Teaching. International Perspectives: Performative – Aesthetic – Transversal.* Münster: LIT Verlag, 21-41.

Im Druck

Drama- und Theaterpädagogik als Wegbereiter einer performativen Literaturdidaktik. In Christiane Lütge (Hg.): *Handbuch Literaturdidaktik.* Trier: WVT.

Dramapädagogische Methoden. In Wolfgang Hallet, Frank G. Königs & Hélène Martinez (Hg.): *Handbuch Methoden im Fremdsprachenunterricht.* Seelze-Velber: Kallmeyer.